Books
by Bob Thomas

Nonfiction
If I Knew Then (with Debbie Reynolds)
The Art of Animation
The Massie Case (with Peter Packer)
King Cohn
Thalberg
Selznick
The Secret Boss of California (with Arthur H. Samish)
The Heart of Hollywood
Winchell
Howard, The Amazing Mr. Hughes (with Noah Dietrich)

Fiction
The Flesh Merchants
Dead Ringer
Will Penny (with Tom Gries)
Star!
Weekend 33

For Children
Walt Disney: Magician of the Movies
Donna DeVarona, Gold Medal Winner

Anthology
Directors in Action

Marlon

Portrait of the Rebel as an Artist

Marlon
Portrait of the Rebel as an Artist

Bob Thomas

Random House
New York

To Anita and Sherman Hartman

Library of Congress Cataloging in Publication Data
Thomas, Bob, 1922-
Marlon, portrait of the rebel as an artist.
1 Brando, Marlon. I. Title.
PN2287.B683T47   791.43ʹ028ʹ0924 [B]   73-20573
ISBN 0-394-48728-1

Manufactured in the United States of America
98765432

Contents

Author's Note

Many people have been kind enough to share with me their memories of Marlon Brando for the preparation of this biography. Among them:

Steve Allen, Peter Bart, Laslo Benedek, Bernardo Bertolucci, Richard Boone, Red Buttons, James Caan, Eric Carpenter, Francis Ford Coppola, Katharine Cornell, Hume Cronyn, Jack Cummings, Francisco Day, Nick Dennis, Edward Dmytryk, Robert Downing, Robert Duvall, Robert Evans, Henry Fonda, Carl Foreman, Sidney Furie, James Garner, George Glass, David Golding, Frances Goldwyn, Buck Henry, John Houseman, Kim Hunter, John Huston, Arthur P. Jacobs, Eddie Jaffe, Elia Kazan, Howard Koch, Henry Koster, Stanley Kramer, Joshua Logan, Sidney Lumet, Alfred Lunt, Karl Malden, Joseph L. Mankiewicz, Kevin McCarthy, Dorothy McGuire, Lewis Milestone, Harry Morgan, Edmond O'Brien, Albert Ruddy, Aaron Rosenberg, Frank Rosenberg, Eva Marie Saint, John Saxon, Dore Schary, George Seaton, Walter Seltzer, Stanley Shapiro, Irene Sharif, Sam Shaw, Ray Stark, Herbert Steinberg, Harry Stradling, Jr., Robert Surtees, Jessica Tandy, Robert Towne, Jack Webb, Michael Winner.

I am also grateful to the following persons for aiding my research in these areas: Omaha, Ed Nicholls; Libertyville, Gene Mustain, Kathleen Naureckas, H. E. Underbrink, M. J. Bergfald; Shattuck Military Academy, the Rev. Canon Joseph M. McKee; Tahiti, Betty Lamm. The facilities of the library of the Academy of Motion Picture Arts and Sciences and the New York Public Library theater collection at Lincoln Center proved invaluable, as always. And special thanks to Nancy K. Thomas, my in-house researcher, and to Bob Loomis, for his sympathetic and astute editing.

Marlon
Portrait of the Rebel as an Artist

1

The Mooning of Marlon

*"I am myself,
and if I have to hit my head
against a brick wall
to remain true to myself,
I will do it."*

THERE IS SOMETHING ABOUT AMERICA THAT DOESN'T LIKE A REBEL. Although the Republic was founded in rebellion, its citizens have feared and reviled those who preach nonconformity and disturb the status quo. And so the great majority of Americans has never felt comfortable with Marlon Brando. Perhaps he is, as his peers have proclaimed, the country's best actor. But why couldn't he accept his fame with equanimity instead of using it to attack traditional values?

His could have been the ideal American success story. He came to films with a face as from a Roman coin and the figure of a fullback. His first half-dozen screen roles more than fulfilled his promise; four were nominated for Academy Awards. He acted with a wit, intensity and animal energy that had never been seen in films before.

For almost a decade, his status seemed secure. Astonishingly, he became even more mature as an actor, demonstrating his versatility in comedy, musical and Shakespearean films. His eccentric personal life was reported in newspapers and magazines for the fascination of reading millions. He was the golden figure of the 1950s. But the same qualities that lent fascination also proved disturbing

1

to a great many people. Their basic principles were upset by his free-living ways, by his espousal of radical causes.

The downfall came in the 1960s. The white-hot career cooled down. His movies turned bad, and critics blamed him as the cause. They were partly right. The big studios abdicated their power and handed it over to stars and their agents. Marlon Brando, who had resisted discipline throughout his lifetime, found himself responsible for shooting schedules and film budgets in the millions of dollars.

The string of flops began, and critics used their reviews for vituperation. Andrew Sarris wrote: "When Brando has been forced to appear with comparable talents like the incomparable Magnani *(The Fugitive Kind),* Trevor Howard and Richard Harris *(Mutiny on the Bounty)* he kills their performances by going up in his lines, take after take. More often he manages to keep big names out of his pictures, even though they would profit him commercially."

Dwight MacDonald on Brando's role in *Bedtime Story*: "A better actor might have made this heel amusing—seducers and con men have their comic aspects—but Brando makes us detest him as a slob and a bully; the pious smirk he puts on when he goes into the soldier-boy act is unappetizing, as well as being amateurishly 'indicative' acting."

Pauline Kael in the *Atlantic Monthly*: "Brando, our most powerful young screen actor, the only one who suggested tragic force, the major protagonist of contemporary American themes in the fifties, is already a self-parodying comedian."

Jerry Tallmer in *Playboy*: "The decline and fall of the artistry of Marlon Brando is a classic case straight out of what is by now almost the American myth on the fate of the creative person in our society. . . . The myth runs as follows: As the career goes up, and the fame, the man and his integrity must go down."

The most personal of the attacks came in 1967, when an actor named William Redfield, a one-time friend of Brando's, wrote in the *New York Times*: "A number of critics worship boredom in an actor (they confuse it with relaxation) but the audience despises it on balance, and Brando can no longer fool a *theater* audience for five minutes. Unhappily for the American conviction, Scofield, Finney, Burton, Richardson, Guinness and Olivier are our remaining first-rank actors. Brando is nothing of the kind. He is a movie star. A little more than kind (Rock Hudson) and a little less than kin (Spencer Tracy)."

2

The Redfield attack stirred a few other actors to write letters to the *Times* in support of Brando. They provided only a brief respite in the anti-Brando campaign.

The one-time friends and the savage critics were joined in the celebration of Brando's failure by the entrepreneurs and agents who controlled the film industry. They had always distrusted him as an enemy of the Hollywood system, and they were pleased with his downfall. Once they had grudgingly placed him at the top of their lists of stars to be sought for important film projects. Now he was no longer considered.

Brando seemed to do nothing to fight back. If anything, he appeared to be giving comfort to his enemies. His choice of films was inexplicable; failure seemed to be written on each of them. His performances were such that even the dwindling Brando enthusiasts found little to commend. He seemed destined for the long downhill race of the rejected movie star.

In 1971, at the age of forty-seven, Marlon Brando elected to play the role of an aging, paunchy, remorseless chief of a Mafia family in *The Godfather.* The film, which restored him to eminence, placed him in daily contact with a new generation of actors. Brando quickly dispelled their initial awe, and the filming was marked by a spirit of horseplay and camaraderie. Two of the most boisterous members of the cast, Robert Duvall and James Caan, introduced to Brando a prank called mooning. A Rabelaisian gesture of defiance, it consisted of lowering pants and exposing naked buttocks. When Duvall and Caan mooned on *The Godfather* set, Brando was convulsed.

For the wedding-reception sequence of *The Godfather,* five hundred extras, as well as most of the principal actors and a full production crew, had been summoned to a Staten Island estate. Before the entire company and with camera rolling, Brando mooned.

The symbolism seemed entirely fitting. Marlon Brando was once more at the height of his powers and at the forefront of his profession. He remained the defiant, uncompromising figure he had always been. As proof, he showed his ass to the enemy world.

2

The Prairie Years

*"I'm always getting in trouble with
those who live by fatuous rules
and conventional patterns.
If you challenge their patterns,
they resent you.
If you tell them, 'What you believe in
is boring, shallow and childish,'
they crucify you."*

THE YOUTH OF MARLON BRANDO IS A BIOGRAPHER'S MINEFIELD. WITH his penchant for fantacizing and putting on, Brando over the years has told interviewers such outlandish tales about his boyhood that the boy Brando would appear to have been a combination of Huck Finn, Holden Caulfield and Oliver Twist.

There can be no doubt that he was an unusual boy. His family, teachers and friends attest to that. And if the true facts are not as colorful as he would have his listeners believe, enough eccentricity remains to presage Brando the man.

He sprang from the American Midwest, reputedly the heartland of conformity, yet the place that provided such originals as Ernest Hemingway, Spencer Tracy, James Thurber, F. Scott Fitzgerald, Adlai Stevenson, Clark Gable, Carl Sandburg and John Dillinger. Marlon Brando, Jr., was born on April 3, 1924, in Omaha, Nebraska. Marlon Brando, Sr., and his wife, the former Dorothy Pennebaker, had two daughters, Frances, eighteen months, and Jocelyn, three years old. Mr. Brando was a salesman for a limestone-products and cattle-feed company, and he earned enough salary and commission to afford a servant for the house. The family lived at 3135 Mason Street in a comfortable four-bedroom frame house that sat back on a bank above the street.

The elder Marlon Brando was a taciturn man imbued with the mid-American principles of industry, thrift and conservatism. He came from solid American stock of French, English and Irish derivation; the name was originally Brandeau. His steady, sure manner aroused confidence in his farm customers, and he was well liked in middle-class Omaha society. His features were clean and handsome, and friends said that all eyes turned to his tall, elegant figure when he entered a crowded room.

Dorothy Brando—she was called Do or DoDo by her friends, Dodie by her children—was small and willowy and alive with creative energy. Of Dutch origin, she had a long American heritage, but she resisted the fettered thinking of the Midwest. She painted and sculpted, read the latest novels, conducted discussion groups and sought to enrich the cultural life of Omaha. She became a leader in the Omaha Community Playhouse, serving as a member of the board of directors, a recruiter of talent, and a frequent actress in such plays as *Anna Christie, Liliom* and *Pygmalion.* On one occasion she even convinced her husband to take a role; he portrayed the bartender in *Outward Bound*—creditably, according to witnesses.

Mrs. Brando's family were active in the Christian Science church, as were the Fondas, who lived in the Dundee section of Omaha. One year young Henry Fonda came home from college, determined not to return. Do Brando telephoned him with a plea: "Henry, we need you desperately at the Playhouse. We've lost our leading man for *You and I,* by Philip Barry. You'd be perfect for the role."

"Good God, Do, I don't know how to act!" Fonda protested. But she was insistent. At loose ends, he decided to try his hand at acting.

Fonda later appeared opposite Mrs. Brando in *Beyond the Horizon* and remembered her as "a goddam good actress. I think she could have made it on Broadway, but she didn't have the ambition to tackle it. Besides, she was married and had two daughters and Bud. There was no way that she could pursue a career." Fonda remained with the Omaha Community Playhouse for three years, then left to seek a career in the Broadway theater. He returned as a stage star a few years later and appeared at the Playhouse in *A Kiss for Cinderella.* The play marked the debut of another Omaha

Marlon 6 years old

native whose acting career had been encouraged by Mrs. Brando—thirteen-year-old Dorothy McGuire.

Do Brando invited actors, directors, artists and writers to the family home, and her three children grew up in an atmosphere of genteel bohemianism that contrasted with normal life in Nebraska. Bud Brando—he was always called Bud among friends and relatives to avoid confusion of two Marlons—enjoyed listening to the artistic talk. His mother encouraged him to express himself creatively, and this proved a source of conflict between the parents.

"That boy needs discipline," Mr. Brando remarked when he returned from his sales trips. But the father's attempts to enforce discipline usually met with failure.

In his early years, Marlon displayed an actor's sense of mimicry. "Who can sound the most like a train?" he would ask at the dinner table, and then provide the best imitation. He competed fiercely with his sisters. "Who can tap their fingers fastest on the table?" he would challenge, or, "Who can hop the farthest?" His sisters found him almost uncontrollable. It was Jocelyn's chore to see that Bud appeared at kindergarten on time. Inevitably, he wandered off to chase a cat or climb a tree, and both he and Jocelyn would arrive late for school. She solved the problem by leading him to school on a leash.

He was forever playacting, even in sports. "Whenever we played football, he beat me—not only because he was stronger," his sister Frances recalled. "He came down the field with the ball, making such terrible faces that I didn't dare tackle him."

A chunky, almost plump boy with broad shoulders and thick chest, he was full of competitive energy. He also had his mother's compassion for all living things. In later years his father recalled an incident when Marlon was five years old: "Bud had a pet rabbit then. The rabbit died, and we buried it in the backyard with a funeral service. But the boy kept digging it up. He dug it up five times. He refused to accept the fact that death could part him from an old friend."

When Bud was six years old, his father's work caused the family to move to Evanston, Illinois. For Mrs. Brando it meant leaving behind her friends and associates at the Omaha Community Playhouse. Her daughters and son were faced with saying good-bye to all their friends and moving to a strange town.

After the Brandos settled in Evanston, Bud struck up an ac-

*At seven, with sisters
Fran & Jocelyn*

quaintance with another new student at the Lincoln School, Wally Cox. They were an incongruous pair: Marlon, tow-headed, brash and physical; Wally, a year younger, introverted and shy, a studious child. Marlon loved to box; Wally didn't. They boxed. They also devised adventurous games, mostly of Marlon's invention. During one of them, Wally portrayed a missionary captured by cannibals. Marlon tied him to a stake and left him bound until early morning.

Wally and Marlon formed a friendship that would extend for a lifetime. They shared a common fear of being uprooted from friends and familiar surroundings; Cox's family moved many times before he was grown. "You get the idea that any attachment you form will be shattered," he remarked in later life.

Marlon was eight when he first evidenced his feeling for society's outcasts. One day after school he arrived home with a shabbily dressed woman of faded beauty. "I found her down by the lake," he explained to his mother. "She's sick and homeless. Can't we take care of her?" Mrs. Brando was touched by his request, but she convinced Bud that it was impractical. She rented a room for the woman at a local hotel.

After a few years in Evanston, the family moved to Santa Ana, California, and finally to Libertyville, a farm community of two thousand near Waukegan, Illinois. Each new move proved a wrench to Marlon and his sisters; to their mother it was even more unsettling to leave friends newly made. Mr. Brando was convinced that the move to Libertyville would be beneficial for his son. Bud had become more and more difficult to manage. He was repeatedly in trouble at school; his father's discipline, both physical and verbal, had no effect. Mr. Brando bought an eight-acre farm on St. Mary's Road, and he reasoned that taking Bud out of the city and submitting him to the country life would help "straighten him out."

The treatment didn't work. Instead of milking the cow and weeding the vegetable patch, Bud spent hours riding the family horse, named Pea Vine Frenzy, through the woods and fields.

Bud Brando's relations with schools did not improve in Libertyville. He once related an incident that happened when he was fourteen: "The previous evening I had been courting a girl down by the river. I'd left my glasses there. During the French period I asked the teacher if it would be all right if I went to get them. She said sure. I didn't tell her that they were four miles away. It took

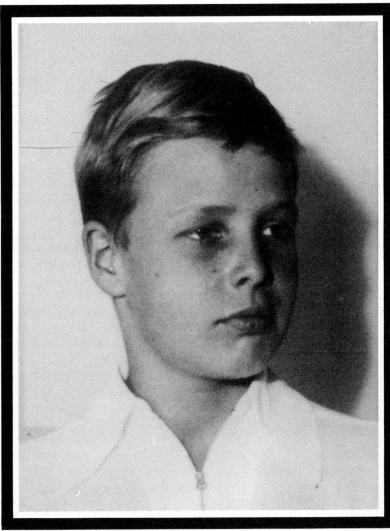

Marlon at 8 years old   Movie Life

me almost all day to amble through the sunshine to the river and back. The next day I was expelled."

The expulsion didn't last long, and Bud seemed to learn nothing from it. To some, he appeared to behave with pure exuberance. Those who were closer to the family suspected he was bidding for attention.

Bud's father had become more distant. He had been earning a good living, but he hadn't achieved the success that had been predicted for him when he was a handsome young salesman. His absences from home became longer; when he returned, he was increasingly peevish with Bud's poor grades and schoolboy pranks.

Bud also seemed to be losing the intimacy with his mother that he had known in his younger years. She was growing strange. Like her husband, she had reached her middle years without achieving the promise the friends in Omaha had predicted for her. At first she had become active in the Libertyville drama group, the Village Players, which met in people's homes, then in a small workshop above the hardware store. She appeared in some of the plays, which were presented in the Libertyville High School auditorium. But gradually she withdrew. She made trips by herself to Chicago, to see the shows and to shop and to lunch with friends from Evanston. Much of the time she was home alone, and she drank.

"The Brandos were strange people," said one long-time Libertyville resident. "They viewed this area like the provinces when they first came here. If they had any social activities, they were confined to the St. Mary's Road crowd. They never came into town. Just Marlon. He was on his own quite a bit, and he was always hanging around and asking someone to drive him home."

Bud developed his own methods to get rides. His close friend was Bob Hoskins, son of the local banker. Bud induced Bob to lie down in the middle of the road. When the first car came along, Bud waved his arms frantically, indicating the prone body. As soon as the car stopped, Bob leaped up and joined Bud in the automobile.

Glenn G. Hoskins, president of the First Lake County National Bank, had mixed feelings about his son's friend. Bud spent almost as much time at the Hoskinses' house as he did at home, and he could be likable or maddening. A favorite trick was to shake hands with a raw egg in his palm.

Bud's playacting became so frequent and so convincing that even he had trouble differentiating between myth and reality. Once he was relating a tale so fanciful that Mr. Hoskins exclaimed, "Bud, that's a damn lie!" The boy looked at him thoughtfully and replied, "Well, maybe it is. But I've told it so many times that I don't know whether or not it happened."

His gift for dramatic invention was recognized by the teacher of drama at Libertyville Township High School, M. J. Bergfald. He saw how Marlon could hold the class enthralled with his pantomimes; his most memorable performance depicted the death of John Dillinger. Marlon also performed scenes from plays, and the teacher was impressed by the boy's natural diction; he avoided the overarticulation that afflicts amateur performers.

Marlon never appeared in the class plays because he was not available for the after-school rehearsals. He was too often in the "3:15 special"—the detention period for those who misbehaved.

Mrs. Brando had already recognized indications that her son might pursue the acting life. One summer the family had journeyed to California, and the Brandos paid a visit to Henry Fonda at Twentieth Century-Fox, where he had become a star. As the former Nebraskans were conversing, Mr. Brando noticed that Bud was missing. He was found on the movie set, studying intently the preparations for the next scene. "What's with Bud?" Fonda asked. "I don't know," said Mrs. Brando, "but I think he wants to be an actor."

He wanted recognition, if not as an actor, then as a drummer. His idol was Gene Krupa, the great swing-band drummer, and Bud pestered his parents until they bought him a set of drums. He practiced all afternoon and into the night, causing a flood of complaints from neighbors. Although those who heard his drumming did not recognize it, Bud was convinced that he was going to be discovered for a big-time band.

One night at the dinner table the Brandos were talking about sending messages on drums. Jocelyn asked, "What message would you send, Bud?" He thought for a moment and replied, "Oh, I don't know—probably 'Whiteman come!'" Paul Whiteman was the famed discoverer of musical talent, and "Whiteman come!" became a repeated phrase in the Brando family.

As he continued with his drum practice, Marlon pondered his first step to musical greatness. The local swing band was the Seven Pork Chops, and he yearned for the position of drummer. He hoped that some illness would befall the drummer, Carlyle Ras-

Marlon 8 years old
Movie Life Magazine

mussen, to force him to leave the band. But Rasmussen proved to be a healthy young man, and Bud waited two years before the drummer resigned. Bud auditioned for the Seven Pork Chops and lost out to another Libertyville drummer.

Bud was desolate. Two years of strenuous practice, of dreaming of his ascent to fame as the greatest of all swing drummers—all had come to nothing. And he had suffered the humiliation of trying out for the band and being found inferior.

Bud Brando became more unmanageable after the defeat of his drumming ambitions. When a teacher gave him a lecture about applying himself to his studies, Bud said "Oh, damn!" and walked away. As soon as he learned to drive, he cracked up the family car. Arguments with his father became more acrimonious, and Bud spent more time away from home. One summer he disappeared for three days. He telephoned his mother that he and Bob Hoskins had hitchhiked to Wisconsin and had run out of money. Her husband was on one of his road trips, and Mrs. Brando called the high school principal for advice.

"I suppose you'll send him the money," Mr. Underbrink said. "But if I were you, I'd let him get home the same way he got up there." Mrs. Brando sent Bud the money.

Mr. Brando's patience came to an end. "There's only one way to straighten that boy out," he told his wife. "That's military school."

It was the standard solution for problem boys of that generation. In September 1941 Bud was enrolled in Shattuck Military Academy at Faribault, Minnesota; it had been the school of his father.

"I hated it every day I was there," Marlon recalled later. "The authorities annoyed me. I had to show respect to those for whom I had no respect. I also hated clocks. I love the kind of life where time doesn't matter, but the bell at the Academy chimed every quarter hour and I loathed it because it reminded me of things I had to do. One night I climbed to the top of the tower and worked the clapper loose. Then I buried it in the ground."

The Academy officers countered by posting buglers on the grounds to signal each quarter hour. Marlon found that more bothersome than the bell.

He enlisted for the football team, but his knee was smashed during practice. An operation removed a cartilage and ended his football career; the damaged knee plus his near-sightedness kept him out of the Army during World War II.

He found only one activity at Shattuck that interested him: close order drill. It was curious that he would have enjoyed such an extreme example of regimentation, but he liked swinging a Civil War rifle with the rest of the "crack squad" and performing maneuvers in precise rhythm. He appeared in two plays at Shattuck, but his dramatic opportunities were limited; in one play he was cast as a gallows corpse, in the other as an Egyptian explorer. The only other acting he did during this period of his life was in March 1942, when he appeared with his mother in an impromptu performance of *Curse You, Jack Dalton* with the Libertyville Village Players.

Shattuck Military Academy dismissed Marlon Brando, Jr., on May 21, 1943, shortly before the end of his junior year. He often repeated his version of the cause for dismissal: "I made a bomb of firecrackers and placed it against the door of a teacher I didn't like. Then I poured a trail of hair tonic from the bomb to my room and set fire to it. I figured the flame would burn the alcohol away, leaving no evidence to spoil my alibi that I had been quietly studying in my room at the time of the explosion. The hair-tonic fuse worked all right, but it left a trail of scorched flooring to my door."

Shattuck authorities had a different story: Cadet Brando was expelled for smoking. A minor offense, perhaps, but one of a long series indicating that the boy simply would not submit to the discipline of the school.

Marlon's father was furious. He berated Bud for his failure and for his disgrace at his father's own school. What would become of him now? He hadn't even finished his senior year of high school. The country was at war, and military service might "make a man out of him." But Marlon was 4-F.

Marlon listened to his father's complaints. There was no turning to his mother; drinking had become her solace. And now his friends were leaving, too. One by one they were shipping out to fight the war.

His best friend, Bob Hoskins, came home in the uniform of a naval flying cadet. He and Bob enjoyed a frivolous weekend with a pair of Libertyville girls, then the time came for Bob to return to the naval air station near Milwaukee. The two couples drove to the train station, and Marlon sent the girls home with the Hoskins family car. He boarded the train with Bob.

Marlon had no fare for the train ride to Milwaukee. He assumed the role of a war veteran who had been crippled in battle, but the

The model cadet at Shattuck Military School, age 15

Movie Life

railroad conductor insisted that he pay the fare. Servicemen riding the train were convinced by the young man's story, and they contributed enough for his fare.

When the two young men arrived at the naval air base, Marlon staged another performance to convince the sentries that he was a cadet flier. He remained in the barracks overnight and then his identity was discovered. "It was so important to me to *belong* to something," he said afterward, "if only for one night."

3

New York

*"I don't know what I want to do.
I don't know if I want always
to be an actor.
I've thought I want to be a writer;
perhaps I'll be a director.
But one thing I know I've got to do:
I've got to educate myself."*

IN THE SUMMER OF 1943, BUD BRANDO WENT TO WORK FOR A DITCH-DIG-
ging company. His father arranged a job with the Tile Drainage
and Construction Company of Libertyville, a firm that specialized
in draining farmland. Bud followed a huge digging machine and
laid tiles to help remove excess water. After six weeks of damp,
dreary work, Bud quit the job and left abruptly for New York City.

According to family legend, Marlon on his first day in New York
tipped a bootblack $5 because he was so affected by the man's pov-
erty. Since Marlon himself had little money, he moved in with his
sister Frances, who had arrived earlier to enroll at the Art Students
League. Soon they were joined by Jocelyn, who planned to study
acting. All three children sought escape from the ordeal of watching
their mother sink deeper into alcoholism. It was punishing for all
of them to see her blithe and gentle spirit become dulled by drinking; the one hurt most by the tragedy was Marlon, youngest and
closest to his mother.

Marlon arrived in New York nineteen and—as his father had
often reminded him—a failure. He could succeed at nothing:
school, drums, athletics. He was trained for no occupation. The
only talent he seemed to possess was for mimicry. He exercised it
when he returned to his sister's flat after wandering through the

subways and streets of Manhattan. With uncanny fidelity he reproduced the accents and rhythms of the straphangers and pushcart peddlers and waitresses he had heard.

The sounds of wartime New York excited Marlon. After a lifetime in small cities and towns, he was stimulated by the human diversity of a huge city. He had been liberated from the parochial thinking of the Midwest, from the nagging of his father "to amount to something." He didn't know what he intended to do with his life, but he was certain that he had made the proper choice in coming to New York.

After his money ran out, Marlon took jobs driving a truck, selling lemonade, running an elevator at Best's department store. The pressure from Libertyville continued. His father inquired over the telephone, "Marlon, what are you going to do?"

"I'm going to stay in New York and study," the son replied.

"Study what?"

"Acting."

"Acting!" the father said derisively. "Take a look in the mirror and tell me if anyone would want to see a yokel like you on a stage."

Marlon would not be dissuaded by his father's scorn. He had considered a number of professions, including the Protestant ministry. All had been discarded, but he had thought many times about becoming an actor. Friends and teachers had often told him that he would be good at it, since he was acting much of the time anyway. He had enjoyed his few occasions on the stage. His only knowledge of the theater came from his mother's activity in community playhouses; he had seen only two professional shows, *Life with Father* and *Oklahoma!*

Jocelyn had enrolled in a dramatic class taught by Stella Adler at the New School for Social Research and was enjoying her study. Marlon's decision to join her would be of vast importance to his later life. The liberal, even radical atmosphere of the New School was entirely suited to his temperament. Indeed, if he had been subjected to the same kind of progressive schooling earlier in life instead of the rigidity of small-town schools and a military academy, his career might well have taken a different course. He had the intelligence and talent to succeed in a number of endeavors. Not until the New School was his potential realized and nurtured.

Stella Adler recognized the Brando promise early. She was herself a successful actress, member of an accomplished acting family with roots in the Yiddish theater. Stella Adler had impeccable credentials for teaching dramatics: she had studied with Richard Boleslavsky and Maria Ouspenskaya, who had brought to America the techniques of Constantin Stanislavsky of the Moscow Art Theater.

After a week of working with Marlon, Stella Adler proclaimed, "Within a year, Marlon Brando will be the best young actor in the American theater."

Soon Marlon was appearing in plays directed by the head of the Dramatic Workshop of the New School, Erwin Piscator, a German emigré. He was an impresario in the Max Reinhardt style, imperious, dedicated to elevation of the theatrical art. He conducted rehearsals with an iron hand, and Marlon at first acquiesced to his will, so eager was he to succeed. But he simmered with the same rebellion against authority that had brought his ouster at Shattuck.

Others were beginning to notice the raw talent of the remarkable student actor. George Freedley, drama critic of the New York *Morning Telegraph,* wrote that Brando's performance in Gerhart Hauptmann's *Hannele's Way to Heaven* on May 24, 1944, was the best in the play. Two nights later, Freedley reviewed a New School performance of *Twelfth Night:* "Marlon Brando handled the tiny part of Sebastian satisfactorily, though it would have been interesting to see what he might have done with Feste or Orsino." Marlon also appeared in a program of Molière plays.

In the summer of 1944 Piscator and his wife managed a theater in Sayville, Long Island, intending to bring classical plays to vacationing New Yorkers. The impresario invited Brando and other New School students to join the company.

Marlon remained aloof from the other students, sitting by himself at the end of the railroad car on the trip to Sayville. He ate his breakfast alone in the hotel dining room, studying a script a few inches from his nose—he refused to wear glasses in spite of his poor vision. His detachment was understandable. He had been out of the Midwest only a year; now he would be going onstage in difficult plays, facing critical audiences. Would he fail, as he had failed in everything else? He remembered his father's words: "Tell me if anyone would want to see a yokel like you on a stage."

Audiences responded to Brando. Not only responded; they seemed at times astounded by the virile presence of the twenty-year-old actor. At one point in *Hannele's Way to Heaven,* he was revealed to the child Hannele as an angel. He would fling off his black teacher's coat and stand in the spotlight in a suit of golden satin. Each night the scene drew gasps from the audience.

As Marlon gained more assurance onstage, his aloofness melted. He joined the other performers at the beach during the day. But he declined to accompany them to the nightly cocktail parties given by social figures of Sayville. The free food and drink were welcomed by the other actors, but Marlon refused to be put on display for the entertainment of Sayville society.

Inevitably, the Brando temperament ran afoul of Erwin Piscator's Teutonic discipline. Marlon enjoyed needling Piscator in subtle ways that confounded the impresario and delighted the other actors. The company was being served meals by the theater management, and Piscator considered himself guardian of the larder. Each night a chain was looped around the door of the huge refrigerator and secured with a lock. Each night Marlon managed to unloop the chain and remove a cheese or a chunk of roast beef. The nighttime raids infuriated the tyrannical Piscator. Every morning he inspected the refrigerator and fulminated against the phantom thief.

Young Brando's insolence finally became more than Piscator could bear. As Marlon later recalled: "He was *der Meister* and ve vere *der Shtudents,* and the girls were not supposed to see the boys after hours. So one night he caught me necking with one of the girls in the company, but all he said was 'Ja. So. Brando.' The next day it was 'Out! You are out of this company!' and I left."

With all three of her children in New York City, Dorothy Brando found her life in Libertyville unbearable. Against her husband's wishes, she decided to join the two girls and Marlon in New York and keep house for them. They were now leading the big-city life in the arts that she had dreamed of as a younger woman, and she wanted to share it with them. The three children had misgivings, because of her drinking, but when she arrived in New York, she seemed much improved in her mental outlook, and they had hopes that escape from the stultifying atmosphere of the farming town would provide a cure.

Mrs. Brando rented a ten-room apartment on West End Avenue, and all moved in: Jocelyn, Frances, Marlon and an assortment of friends who came and went. Those months brought good times, with each of the children sharing with their mother the involvements of Manhattan life. Marlon, who had known cruel disappointments because of his mother's drinking, was pleased to see her so happy. He watched for evidence that she was regressing to her former ways, but he found none.

Marlon's own behavior was as unpredictable as it had been in Libertyville, and he still liked to play pranks and games with his sisters. One day he placed Frances in a large grocery carton and began pushing her along the sidewalk when he saw a familiar figure come walking along West End Avenue. He was small, slight and wore horn-rimmed glasses; it was none other than his old chum Wally Cox.

Wally explained that he had come to New York to study industrial arts at New York University; someone had told him the Brando girls were in New York and had given him their address. Marlon was so delighted to see his childhood friend that he threw Wally in the grocery box and pushed him down the street.

Marlon's appearances at the New School and in Sayville had attracted the interest of talent agents. One of them was Maynard Morris, who suggested that Marlon audition for a new play that Richard Rodgers and Oscar Hammerstein II were producing, *I Remember Mama.* Marlon took the script home, and Dodie Brando read it aloud to the three children. Marlon fell asleep. "The play *does* seem dull," Mrs. Brando conceded.

Stella Adler, predicting that *I Remember Mama* would be a hit, insisted that it was time for Marlon to test his talent in the Broadway spotlight. After the histrionics of Piscator's classic theater, he had little interest in the role of the timid, gentle Norwegian-American boy of fifteen. Another reason for his lack of enthusiasm: he would have to audition. He was terrified at the prospect of standing up before producers and offering his naked talent for approval. The most punishing disappointment of his life had come when he tried out for drummer in the Libertyville swing band and was rejected. He didn't want to risk such a defeat again.

Stella Adler's arguments persuaded Marlon to report to the Rodgers and Hammerstein office for the audition. He was introduced to the two producers and to John Van Druten, who had written the play and was directing it. Marlon's delivery of the script was miserable. He read the lines without feeling and inserted words that the playwright had not intended. That was certain to alienate Van Druten.

Marlon plays part of Nels, one of the
sons in "I Remember Mama"
on Broadway

Rodgers and Hammerstein were ready to dismiss the young man after the reading. Van Druten was not. He insisted on hiring Brando for the role of Nels.

I Remember Mama opened at the Music Box Theater on October 19, 1944. Stella Adler had been right; it was a resounding hit. But the role of Nels provided little advancement for Marlon's career. Reviews in the *Times, Sun, World-Telegram* and *Daily News* failed to mention him by name. The *Post* and *PM* cited him among other players as doing well. Only Robert Garland of the *Journal-American* made a specific mention: "The Nels of Marlon Brando is, if he doesn't mind me saying so, charming."

The demands of *I Remember Mama* were not great, and Marlon used the spare time to further his education. He took courses at the New School and read such books as *The Dialogues of Plato,* Kant's *Critique of Pure Reason,* Kafka's *Metamorphosis* and *The Penal Colony.* One day producer Rodgers dropped by Brando's tiny dressing room and was impressed to see the books the young actor was studying.

Following the Broadway ritual, the press agent for *I Remember Mama* interviewed Marlon and produced these notes:

> Born in Calcutta, India, but left there at 6 months of age. Educated in several California schools and Shattuck Military Academy at Fairbolt [sic], Minn. He enlivened the military atmosphere by so many pranks that he was kicked out of school. . . . At his first reading of Nels for Messrs. Van Druten, Rodgers and Hammerstein, Brando says he was so scared that he was just one jump ahead of a blood clot. When not busy at the Music Box Theater, Brando reads a lot. At present is delving into philosophy, "getting a smattering of Schopenhauer and Spinoza," he says. Likes music, particularly primitive African music. Plays the drums on which he received instruction from a drummer who traveled with the East Indian dancer, Shan Kar. . . . Has a Great Dane which he insists is a perfect apartment pet and thrives on dehydrated cubes of dog food.

4

Broadway

"If you're successful,
acting is about as soft a job
as anybody could ever wish for.
But if you're unsuccessful,
it's worse than having a skin disease."

DODIE BRANDO COULDN'T KEEP HER PROMISE NOT TO DRINK, AND HER
dream of a colony of talented Brandos in New York City was destroyed. Her melancholia could only be dulled by alcohol, and
Marlon and his sisters could no longer endure the misery of watching her disintegrate. Marlon moved into a Fifty-seventh Street
apartment with Wally Cox, and Jocelyn and Frances found their
own quarters. Their mother returned to Libertyville and her
husband.

During his year in *I Remember Mama*, Marlon drew attention
from Hollywood studios. The film companies, desperate for leading men to supplant their name players serving in the war, wanted
him to make screen tests. He refused. The prospect of testing for
movies was no more appealing than auditioning for stage roles.
He announced that he had no interest in Hollywood.

Talent agents foresaw a future for the handsome young actor of
I Remember Mama, and they sought to represent him. Among
the most persistent was Edith Van Cleve of the Music Corporation
of America. He told her, "I don't want an agent."

"But supposing you get movie offers," she said.

"I've already had them. I don't want to go to Hollywood—unless
I can choose the film I want to do."

"Then you need someone to tell the studios that," she advised
him. In time he succumbed to her persuasions, and he began his
long and profitable association with MCA.

In 1946 Brando began a collaboration that became the most significant of his acting career. Stella Adler had convinced her husband, Harold Clurman, to cast her protégé in the play he was producing with Elia Kazan, in association with the Playwrights' Company. It was a contemporary drama by Maxwell Anderson, *Truckline Café,* concerning wayfarers at a diner-motel on the Coast Highway between Los Angeles and San Francisco.

At the first reading, Marlon was inarticulate.

"Speak up, Marlon!" Kazan shouted from the back of the theater. "Stop mumbling! If this thing is going to lose money, I want to hear what I'm losing it on."

Marlon spoke up. He became acquainted with the dark, tough-minded Kazan, a Greek-American who had been an actor himself in the Group Theater and in films before turning director. The two men found they could agree on many things, particularly the style of acting that was drawn from within, that reflected human feelings rather than mere recital of an author's words.

Kazan and Clurman had assembled a competent cast of veterans and newcomers, including June Walker, David Manners, Virginia Gilmore, Karl Malden, Ken Tobey, Richard Waring and Kevin McCarthy. Some of the actors bore resentment against young Brando because they believed he had won his role through the influence of the producer's wife—as indeed he had. But their reservations melted when he began playing the role of Sage McRae.

Portraying a war veteran who drowned his faithless wife, Brando was required in Act Three to enter weeping—a feat most actors would consider impossible to do convincingly. Brando did it every night, and his fellow performers stood in the wings to watch his accomplishment.

Truckline Café opened on February 27, 1946, at the Belasco Theater to such bad notices that the playwright castigated the critics as "the Jukes Family of Journalism." The phrase was remembered longer than *Truckline Café.* The play lasted thirteen performances, and Marlon Brando was once again unemployed.

Brando's brief, electrifying scene had drawn praise from the critics, and again the film studios sought him for contracts. Edith Van Cleve talked Marlon into appearing for a film test at the Twentieth Century-Fox studios in New York. He exhibited his detestation of auditions by playing with a yo-yo through the test.

When Alfred Lunt and Lynn Fontanne were casting *O Mistress*

Mine, Miss Van Cleve suggested that Marlon appear for an audition. He agreed to do so, and later he told a story that became part of Broadway legend:

When Marlon arrived at the theater he was handed a script with instructions to study it briefly and do a reading. He hated quick readings even more than prepared auditions, and stood dumb upon the stage.

Lunt's voice intoned from the darkness of the theater: "Say something—anything."

Marlon stared toward where the voice had originated, then began, "Hickory dickory dock, the mouse ran up the clock . . ."

"There is no truth to the story," Alfred Lunt wrote in 1972. "We met Marlon Brando but once—in November, 1945. We were casting *O Mistress Mine* and thought he might be interested in playing the son. He was not, and quite rightly. There was no audition. The meeting lasted about five minutes. It was pleasant, and that was that."

Director-producer Guthrie McClintic, Katharine Cornell's husband, had attended a performance of *Truckline Café* and was impressed by the young actor playing Sage McRae. He gave Brando a small role in Jean Anouilh's *Antigone,* starring Miss Cornell. The play did not draw well, and McClintic decided to alternate it with Shaw's *Candida,* one of his wife's great successes. Brando was chosen for the showy role of the poet Eugene Marchbanks.

Some of the New York critics cited Brando for praise. Wrote John Chapman of the *Daily News:* "Mr. Brando achieved a believable, love-sick introvert by playing very quietly. His intensity was within him, where it should be." Howard Barnes of the *Herald Tribune* said Brando made the final act exceedingly satisfying. But Lewis Nichols of the *Times* called the performance monotonous, and Louis Kronenberger of *PM* found it not particularly successful.

Miss Cornell believed the critics underestimated Brando's performance. "He was of course very young and inexperienced and his portrayal of Marchbanks was erratic from performance to performance," she remarked in 1972, "but at the top of his form he was the finest Marchbanks I ever had. There was no question of his being a true poet—brilliant, unpredictable, brooding and touching, and even then his acting was always challenging. As a human being I found him warm and friendly and interesting. I thoroughly liked him."

Candida lasted only twenty-four performances. Edith Van Cleve sent Marlon a copy of a new play by Noël Coward, *Present Laughter*, which John C. Wilson was producing. It was a typical exercise of the Coward wit, devoid of social content, and Marlon was repelled by it. Miss Van Cleve suggested that he return the script with a brief note of explanation. The message: "Dear Mr. Wilson. Don't you realize people in Europe are starving?"

Brando's next Broadway performance after *Candida* was in *A Flag Is Born*, a pageant written by Ben Hecht and presented by the American League for a Free Palestine. Marlon shared with the Jewish friends of Stella Adler's circle the excitement over the creation of a homeland for Jews, and he agreed to join the company at a salary of $48 a week.

The director of *A Flag Is Born* was Luther Adler, Stella's brother, and he grew impatient with Marlon's seeming indifference to rehearsals. Marlon walked through his role as David, the Jewish soldier, delivering his lines without the fire the author had intended. "Wait—just wait," Stella Adler counseled her brother. More than anyone else, she realized Marlon's inability to slip easily into a role; he required time and thought before he could breathe life into the character. She also understood his dislike of trying out before those who could pass judgment on his performance.

Ben Hecht grew impatient with Brando's pedestrian rehearsal, and the playwright himself assumed the role of David in an intense scene. "See!" Hecht said to the actor. "That's the way it should be done."

"I don't think so," Marlon said quietly. "That was terrible." He then delivered his own interpretation of the scene, astounding both Hecht and Adler with his depth of feeling.

A Flag Is Born opened on September 5, 1946, at the Alvin Theater for a limited run. A spectacle tracing Jewish history from Jerusalem to Nazi Germany, it afforded Brando the opportunity to observe at close range the acting technique of Paul Muni. In later years Marlon cited Muni as the American actor he admired most.

After *A Flag Is Born* came the foredoomed encounter with Tallulah Bankhead in *The Eagle Has Two Heads*. Bankhead played the queen, on stage and off, and Marlon was cast as Stanislas, her lover. He did not relish the role, nor the involuted Cocteau dialogue, and he declined Bankhead's proposals to join her for champagne in her room. "I don't drink," he said blankly.

The Eagle Has Two Heads opened in Washington, D.C., in early 1947 with disastrous results. Brando was fired and replaced with Helmut Dantine, and the play closed after twenty-nine performances in New York.

The experience proved devastating for Marlon. Even though he had been miscast, he felt that he had failed—and failure in the theater was something new and disturbing to him. He went through periods of depression and suffered headaches that sometimes lasted four days. The perceptive Elia Kazan recognized the emotional imbalance in the gifted young actor, and since Kazan himself had undergone analysis, he suggested that Marlon consult his psychoanalyst, Dr. Bela Mittelman. Thus Marlon began the therapy that would continue through his twenties.

"People are usually willing to blame somebody else before they'll blame themselves, or even look at themselves," he said in later years. "I was the same way. But I was blessed with enough sense to realize that if I wanted well-being, psychoanalytic help was just about the only, and last, way I could get it."

5

Life
in
Manhattan

*"I put on an act sometimes,
and people think I'm insensitive.
Really, it's like a kind of armor
because I'm too sensitive.
If there are two hundred people in a room
and one of them doesn't like me,
I've got to get out."*

MOST ACTORS ADJUST THEIR LIFE STYLES TO FIT ASCENDING FAME. MAR-lon Brando never did. His basic pattern of living has remained the same as it was during his years as a rising young actor of the theater.

He liked to eat. More gourmand than gourmet, he could eat anything, and sometimes his consumption filled an emotional need: "If I'm unhappy, I eat cream puffs and candy and shoot up from a hundred and sixty-five to a hundred and eighty pounds."

When he dined out, it was usually in cafeterias or cheap cafés: "I never go to fashionable places; I despise them. People don't need that; their aesthetic needs aren't so great that they have to eat pheasant under glass. That's an affectation, that's overindulgence."

He drank little or no liquor: "I used to drink, but in an alcoholic way, so I stopped. I feel if I can't have a good time and enjoy life without it, then there's no point in my life."

He made few acquisitions, even when he could afford them: "I don't have any burning desire to buy a Mercedes-Benz or a combination washing machine–icebox–television set."

There were many girls in his life: "I'd like a harem of girls. A nice round fat pink one I would chase around the room and pinch.

One for roller-skating. One for an afternoon in a barn. All kinds of girls. All sizes. All shapes. All colorings." He was fondest of small, dark ones. They did not need to be real beauties, although some of them were. Often they were homely girls who attracted Marlon's sympathy.

In social relationships he functioned best with a single person, or two or three. He could not cope with crowds. Playwright Clifford Odets recalled encountering Brando at a time when Stella Adler was telling everyone about the acting genius she had discovered: "I saw the boy in her classroom, and the genius Stella was talking about was not apparent to the naked eye. He looked to me like a kid who delivers groceries. I tried to talk to him and he was totally inarticulate. But I could see that he was bursting to make communication. There was an enormous sense of pressure there.

"About a week later I went to a party at Stella's house. Brando was there. He had on his best clothes, but they were inadequate for the party. I could see that he felt socially deficient. He was going through hell. I tried to speak to him again, but again I got no response. All night he stood in a corner without opening his mouth. That seemed to be his permanent attitude: 'I'll stand in a corner because the wall is solid. It protects me in the rear and on two sides. Therefore I only have to protect myself from the front.'"

Marlon's psychoanalysis helped him deal with such situations. He was grateful for the help and he made no secret about his treatment: "Many people are sensitive about the fact that they have emotional problems, but I don't give a damn what anybody says. My analysis has helped me a great deal."

As Brando's fame in the New York theater grew, so did his reputation for eccentricity. The *Playbill* for *I Remember Mama* had listed his birthplace as Calcutta. The program for *Truckline Café* stated he was born in Bangkok; in other programs and interviews he declared his birthplace was Mindanao or Rangoon. His comment: "Oh, I just did that to amuse my father when he came to New York to see me in a play."

As legends accumulated about the young actor, case-hardened Broadway veterans suspected that he was cultivating the oddball reputation for publicity purposes. As evidence, they cited his friendship with Eddie Jaffe, an affable young press agent with a well-developed sense of independence and a taste for the bizarre.

They met through a beautiful young lady who brought Brando to Jaffe's apartment one evening. The actor mumbled a greeting.

While Jaffe and the girl engaged in conversation, Brando poked through Jaffe's jumbled belongings, played some quiet tunes on the piano and muttered "Good-bye" on parting. Because Jaffe's attitude was low-keyed, he was deemed worthy of friendship. Marlon always shunned those who tried to impress their personalities on him.

Thereafter Brando became a frequent visitor at Jaffe's place. He would drop in, murmur a few words of conversation, rummage through drawers to find a clean pair of socks, put them on and leave, depositing his dirty socks in the dresser.

Brando often visited the Jaffe apartment when the press agent was making his rounds of clients and columnists. Brando sometimes answered the telephone by saying, "You want Eddie Jaffe? Poor Eddie died yesterday morning . . . Yes, it happened very suddenly. We're having the services tomorrow morning at the Little Church Around the Corner. Eleven o'clock. I do hope you can make it."

Characters came and went at the Jaffe apartment: tap-dancers, headwaiters, acrobats, panhandlers, artists, and an abundance of girls. One frequent visitor was a fencing master who played the violin. His fencing was better than his violin playing, and his constant recitals bored the others, particularly Marlon Brando. One evening the amateur violinist picked up his instrument to begin a sonata. He noticed that the fiddle was heavier than usual. He looked inside, sniffed and exclaimed, "Why, it's filled with horse-shit!"

"Yes," said Marlon, who had done the deed. "That's what it sounds like."

Marlon's own living quarters were chaotic. He and Wally Cox shared two large rooms on Fifty-seventh Street with Russell, a racoon that had been a gift from Marlon's mother. The main features of the apartment were Marlon's drums, Wally's electric train and the silversmith equipment he used for his studies at NYU. There was little furniture, and friends who stayed overnight slept on the floor. Marlon economized on electricity by running an extension cord to a socket in the hallway.

The roommates made one effort to decorate their home. They bought brushes and paint and converted one wall to jet-black before losing interest. The paint cans and brushes remained on the apartment floor for more than a year.

The boyhood friendship between Wally and Marlon became

stronger during their rooming days. Wally was beginning to exhibit a talent to entertain, and he convulsed Marlon with monologues about Army buddies and New York taxi drivers. Marlon countered with imitations of zoo animals and a worm he found in a cookie. They laughed for hours at each other's routines, and Marlon encouraged Cox to seek a career as an entertainer.

Eventually Russell came between them. As racoons go, it had a pleasant nature, but it was mischievous. Russell raced around the apartment, upsetting things and straining Wally's mild nature. One day Russell chewed a hole in Wally's only good pair of pants. Wally moved out, emphasizing that he wasn't angry with Marlon; he simply could no longer cohabit with Russell.

Another Brando apartment was in a converted brownstone house on Fifty-second Street. It was next door to Leon and Eddie's, a night club that purveyed raucous entertainment. One night Marlon paused in front of the place to study photographs of the scantily clad female entertainers. He wore his usual attire, and the doorman reasoned that the disreputable-looking young man was not the best advertisement for Leon and Eddie's.

"Move along, buddy," the doorman said. Marlon was offended and began to argue. A policeman came along and sided with the doorman, using his billy club to urge Marlon along.

Marlon plotted his retaliation. His bedroom overlooked the night-club dance floor, which was exposed to the summer night by a sliding roof. Marlon journeyed to a First Avenue slaughterhouse to fill a cardboard box, and patrons of Leon and Eddie's were startled to find horse manure raining down upon the dance floor. Marlon's warning cry: "Beware of the Flying Red Horse!"

Some of Marlon's friends believed his prankishness possessed a social commentary. One of his early New York acquaintances was journalist-publicist Robert Condon, who later recalled the weekday morning when Marlon escorted him to the subway shuttle at Times Square: "On the way he explained that the subway turnstiles which served as both entrances and exits would lock as exits if a fare was deposited on the entrance side. The shuttle, at the time, had an entrance from the street and had six turnstiles of its own.

"Marlon deftly dropped a nickel in each one—an outlay of thirty cents in those good old days. Suddenly a train came in on track one, and the riders spewed forth like a thousand Jonahs. They hit the turnstiles full force, expecting them to spin around, but instead people were pressed into long lines of gasping bodies. Marlon grinned at me triumphantly.

"'Do this often enough,' he said sagely, 'and people would stop rushing and pushing.'"

Through Elia Kazan, Marlon became associated with the Actors Studio. It was a direct descendant of the Moscow Art Theater, which had achieved greatness under the direction of Constantin Stanislavsky. The Stanislavsky Method of acting became widely known and was introduced to America by Moscow Art Theater actors who taught such Americans as Stella Adler, Harold Clurman and Lee Strasberg. Clurman and Strasberg, along with Cheryl Crawford, were leaders of the Group Theater, which brought new vitality to the American theater during the Depression years, especially with the proletarian plays of Clifford Odets. The Group Theater also produced such naturalistic actors as John Garfield, Franchot Tone, Lee J. Cobb, Elia Kazan, Frances Farmer, Morris Carnovsky, J. Edward Bromberg and Luther Adler. All were schooled in the Stanislavsky Method.

In 1947 three veterans of the Group Theater—Kazan, Cheryl Crawford and director Robert Lewis—organized the Actors Studio, a workshop that held classes in a run-down rehearsal building, the Malin Studios, just west of Broadway in the theater district. In those dingy rooms was trained a new generation of American actors: Marlon Brando, Montgomery Clift, James Dean, Paul Newman, Kim Stanley, Maureen Stapleton, Shelley Winters, Geraldine Page, Eli Wallach, Rod Steiger, Eva Marie Saint, Julie Harris, Kevin McCarthy, Tom Ewell, Tony Franciosa, Ben Gazzara, Patricia Neal, Joanne Woodward.

The Actors Studio became famous—some said notorious—for fostering the Method as an acting technique. It was explained by Harold Clurman: "The purpose of the Stanislavsky Method is to teach the actor to put the whole gamut of his physical and emotional being into the service of the dramatist's meaning. What Stanislavsky did was to observe great actors and study his own problems as an actor. In the process he began to isolate the various factors that composed fine acting. He systematized the way actors could prepare themselves for their task—the interpretation of plays. He detailed the means whereby actors might give shape and substance to the roles they were assigned."

Brando joined in the classes of the Actors Studio, which was not intended as a dramatic school but as a place for "postgraduate" study by experienced actors. With Maureen Stapleton he performed in *Reunion in Vienna*, charming his listeners with an authentic, if incomprehensible, Viennese accent. Brando also made his first attempt at direction. He changed the locale of *Hedda Gabler* to Nebraska and directed Julie Harris as a Midwestern version of the Ibsen heroine. It was a startlingly original interpretation.

Those who observed Marlon Brando at the Actors Studio recognized the uniqueness of his talent and predicted that he would electrify the theater world if cast in the right role. That role came in *A Streetcar Named Desire*.

6

Streetcar

"Kowalski was always right,
and never afraid.
He never wondered,
he never doubted.
His ego was very secure.
And he had the kind of brutal aggressiveness
that I hate.
I'm afraid of it.
I detest the character."

TENNESSEE WILLIAMS DREW THE TITLE FROM A STREETCAR IN NEW
Orleans that was named Desire. Irene Mayer Selznick was producing the play on Broadway, with Elia "Gadge" Kazan as director and
John Garfield playing the brutish Stanley Kowalski. Kazan was
looking forward to working once more with Garfield, his one-time
associate in the Group Theater, although the director suspected
that Garfield's Lower East Side speech and manner did not fit the
New Orleans locale of the play.

Garfield himself had misgivings. He had agreed to a return to
Broadway with the hope of giving new life to his faltering movie
career. But with the release of *Body and Soul* he had become an
important star again. His interest in *A Streetcar Named Desire*
waned when he reread the play; he realized that the Kowalski role
was overshadowed by Blanche DuBois.

Garfield wanted the play rewritten to build up the part of Kowalski; Williams refused. Garfield insisted on the right to leave the
play after four weeks, if he so desired; Mrs. Selznick argued that
was economically unsound. The actor's demands made it apparent
that he no longer wanted to appear in *A Streetcar Named Desire.*
He was released from the contract.

In the summer of 1947 Mrs. Selznick tried to get Burt Lancaster and other Hollywood stars to play Kowalski; none was available. Kazan sent the script to Marlon Brando. After pondering for a week, Brando decided he was unsuitable for the role. "I finally decided that it was a size too large for me," he recalled later, "and I called Gadge to tell him so. The line was busy. Had I spoken to him at that moment, I'm certain I wouldn't have played the role. I decided to let it rest for a while, and the next day Gadge called me and said, 'Well, what is it—yes or no?' I gulped and said 'Yes.'"

Mrs. Selznick agreed to take a chance on the young actor. Next, Tennessee Williams had to be convinced. The playwright was vacationing on Cape Cod, and Kazan gave Brando bus fare and directions to the Williams house in Provincetown. A few days passed, and Brando didn't arrive. Again, the terror of auditioning. Marlon postponed the ordeal as long as possible.

Williams later recalled Brando's arrival: "He appeared around six o'clock one morning with a remarkably attractive young lady. He sat around for a while and disappeared. After he'd gone, Margo Jones, the director, said, 'There must be some mistake; that boy just couldn't be an actor!' Which summed up all our feelings."

Brando returned alone late that night and found the Williams house in distress over a stopped pipe and a power failure. Brando unclogged the drain and replaced a fuse. Then he sat down on a bed and read the Kowalski role from beginning to end. His listeners were enraptured, and Williams decided on the spot that Marlon Brando should play Stanley Kowalski. Williams telephoned the news to Kazan and said Brando would be returning to sign the contract the following day. Several days passed before Marlon appeared.

In September, the company of *A Streetcar Named Desire* assembled for rehearsals in the New Amsterdam Roof Theater. The English-born actress Jessica Tandy had been hired to play Blanche DuBois. Karl Malden, who had worked with Kazan and Brando in *Truckline Café*, was cast as Mitch, Blanche's visitor. Kazan had chosen Kim Hunter for Kowalski's pregnant wife, Stella. It was her first Broadway play.

Kazan sat with his back to the auditorium, facing the semicircle of the company members. He began quietly, drawing out the actors' interpretations of their characters and adding insight of his own. Brando remained an enigma to the other actors. His rehearsal demeanor was especially perplexing to Miss Tandy, who had been trained in the disciplines of the London theater. One day she was performing a long, emotional scene with him. While she spoke her soliloquy, he noisily shifted props on the table. Finally she broke off the speech and exclaimed, "If you make noises while I'm doing this scene, the audience won't be able to hear my lines!"

Marlon apologized, and the rehearsal continued. Miss Tandy didn't understand that he was struggling within himself to grasp the character of Kowalski. He seemed distracted, even rude, because of his intense concentration. He slept overnight on a cot in the Amsterdam Theater to maintain his focus on the role. But he couldn't locate the jagged, bawdy nature of Kowalski.

"They should have gotten Garfield for the part," he muttered to Kim Hunter after a difficult rehearsal. "Garfield could handle it. I'm not the one to play Stanley."

Kazan was convinced that Marlon possessed the power and eccentric humor that the role required. Marlon began to develop the physical aspects: the self-assured swagger of Stanley, the off-center stance of defiance and challenge. The important thing was the voice, the flat, unmusical, mocking voice of Stanley Kowalski. "It was a matter of placement and diction," he explained later. "I'm an ear man. I thought in terms of coarseness. What would be effective?"

When *A Streetcar Named Desire* opened in New Haven, Kazan recalled, "It was almost a perfect play, the most perfect I've ever had—even more than *Death of a Salesman*." Williams made a few cuts in the last scene. Otherwise the changes were only directorial refinements, particularly the question of where to position the act intermissions.

Kazan tightened the pace in Boston, and by Philadelphia the final version had been achieved. It was long—only a few minutes under the deadline for stagehands' overtime. Despite the length, the out-of-town reviews had been increasingly favorable, and word spread along Broadway that *A Streetcar Named Desire* would be a hit.

Kazan was concerned about overconfidence, and he addressed the company before opening night: "What we've got here is oysters. Not everyone in the world has a taste for oysters, so don't expect the play to be liked by everyone. Just do the play and hope for the best."

For Marlon Brando, opening night meant not only the challenge of facing the drama critics in his first starring role; he had also invited his parents to come to New York for the opening. Marlon was heartened by a telegram he received before curtain time: RIDE OUT BOY AND SEND IT SOLID. FROM THE GREASY POLACK YOU WILL SOME DAY ARRIVE AT THE GLOOMY DANE. FOR YOU HAVE SOMETHING THAT MAKES THE THEATER A WORLD OF GREAT POSSIBILITIES. TENNESSEE WILLIAMS. Of greater interest to Marlon was another telegram from a friend: TRY NOT TO MAKE AN ASS OF YOURSELF. FRED STEVENS.

A Streetcar Named Desire opened at the Ethel Barrymore Theater on Wednesday, December 3, 1947. The audience was enormously responsive and cheered at the final curtain. Like Warner Baxter in Forty-second Street, Elia Kazan lingered in the alleyway outside the theater as the crowd emerged. He heard many of the first-nighters express disfavor; they had been stunned and upset by the play.

The actors had been asked to an after-show party on the top floor of "21" to await the reviews, and they huddled together self-protectively amid a roomful of celebrities. After the bizarre stories Marlon had related of his early years, his fellow actors were surprised to find his parents dignified, handsome and completely at ease with the celebrities. They exchanged pleasantries with Tennessee Williams, whom Mrs. Brando described later as "a gentle round man with a black mustache" who had "a most remarkable insight into human behavior." But she had little sympathy for the role her son had played and said afterward, "Bud has no business being thought of as the star of the show. The audience should feel no sympathy for his role; the part is a brutal one."

Except for George Jean Nathan, who was suspected of conducting a vendetta against Tennessee Williams, the drama critics praised A Streetcar Named Desire. They did not recognize the play as a landmark in the American theater, nor were they prescient enough to anticipate the impact of Marlon Brando's performance.

Brooks Atkinson (Times) devoted his biggest praise to Miss Tandy and cited Brando along with Kim Hunter and Karl Malden as being of high quality. Robert Coleman (Daily Mirror) and Howard Barnes (Herald Tribune) did the same. Richard Watts, Jr. (Post), found Brando's work excellent—though not as good as Malden's. Ward Morehouse (Sun) wrote that Streetcar was Brando's "finest work to date," and John Chapman *(Daily News)* said "Mr. Brando is magnificent."

While *A Streetcar Named Desire* became acknowledged as the dramatic hit of the 1947–48 season, Marlon Brando was faced with what he had tried to avoid all his life: discipline. He was sentenced to performing the same role eight times a week, month after month, for two years. To Marlon it was a mind-racking ordeal. He began to depart from Kazan's direction, to the despair of his fellow players. Karl Malden discovered that Marlon would pull stunts in the poker scene, throwing in ad libs and interfering with Malden's lines.

"Come on," Malden said to Marlon one night as they left the stage, "you've got fifty sides and can throw half of them away and still register. If I lose just one of mine, I've got nothing."

Marlon was contrite. "Karl, I never thought of it that way before," he said. He resumed playing the poker scene as it had been intended—for a while.

Jessica Tandy never knew what to expect from Marlon. "It was like standing on the side waiting to catch a ball and never knowing when it would be thrown to you," she recalled. At times in a highly dramatic scene she gazed stage right, where he was supposed to be; he was at stage left. When she railed at him as the distraught Blanche, he sometimes yawned or scratched his crotch.

Kazan realized that Brando's interpretation had veered from the original direction. Kazan called a rehearsal with Marlon and Miss Tandy, which Marlon forgot about. Another was scheduled. When he didn't appear after twenty minutes, both Kazan and Miss Tandy left. She then wrote Marlon a note saying that it was tragic that he was so lackadaisical about his professional duties, because he had the potential to be a great actor. He replied with touching apology, like an erring schoolboy, vowing that he would improve.

But Marlon simply couldn't manage the unvarying, night-after-night performances that were standard for Miss Tandy's colleagues of the English theater. If he arrived at the Ethel Barrymore Theater with a bellyache, he played Stanley Kowalski with a bellyache. If he was elated, audiences would see a happy Kowalski. But if he felt depressed, his lines might not be heard past the fifth row.

The most difficult scene for Marlon came after he had been beaten up in the bathroom by his cronies, then called for Stella to return from the upstairs apartment where she had escaped from him.

It was a tense moment that required his fullest concentration. One evening some girls in the audience giggled nervously.

Still in the rage of Stanley Kowalski, Marlon stalked to the footlights and screamed, "SHUT UP!"

A gasp went through the audience. It shut up—for the remainder of the performance. Marlon never used that tactic again.

Karl Malden, with whom Marlon shared a dressing room, remained the butt of Marlon's foolery. In the final moments of *A Streetcar Named Desire*, Malden had to weep as Blanche was taken away to a mental hospital. Marlon persisted in muttering obscene remarks in an effort to make Malden break his mood. Malden plotted revenge.

Malden and Brando had a fifteen-minute break during the play while the two female leads engaged in a lengthy dialogue. The Barrymore Theater was not air-conditioned, so during the summer the two actors spent the interval in the open air on Forty-seventh Street outside the theater. They chatted with the mounted policemen, then strolled back down the alley and completed the scene.

One night Malden and Brando were enjoying the outside air and Malden sauntered back into the theater. He rushed back to the street and shouted, "Hey, Marlon, you missed your cue!"

Brando raced down the alley, through the stage door and into the set, flabbergasting Miss Tandy and Miss Hunter. He had arrived eight minutes early.

"You stupid ass!" Miss Tandy muttered. "What the hell are you doing here?"

Miss Hunter managed to say, "Oh, Stanley, come back later," and Marlon slunk offstage.

One of Marlon's close friends in the cast was Nick Dennis, a former boxer who agreed to give Marlon lessons. A ring was set up underneath the stage, and Marlon relieved the boredom of the backstage routine by sparring with members of the cast and stage crew. One night he was trading blows with a young property man, Ronnie Green. Marlon lowered his guard and took a hard blow on the face. His nose flattened and blood poured from it. He wiped away the blood and made his entrance on time. Jessica Tandy was unnerved by his bloody nose, but she and the rest of the cast managed to finish the performance. Marlon was taken to a hospital, and he remained out of the cast for a week. Jack Palance, who was understudying Anthony Quinn in the Chicago production of

Streetcar, flew to New York to replace him.

The single misdirected blow had destroyed the symmetry of the Brando nose. Instead of being straight and narrow, it was now slightly aquiline, marring his perfect features. The defect could have been corrected by surgery. Marlon refused. He liked the new nose, liked the way it added character to his almost-too-beautiful face.

Marlon Brando was confused and appalled by the stardom that had been thrust upon him by *A Streetcar Named Desire.* Unlike many other actors, to whom stardom was a happy by-product of success, Marlon found it unpleasant. The adulation, favor-seeking, publicity and constant scrutiny were factors he had not anticipated when he became an actor.

Before, he could choose his own friends. Now everyone wanted to know the dynamic young actor. He clung to the friends he had known before his burst of fame, Wally Cox, Eddie Jaffe, Red Kullman and Harry Belafonte, then an unknown actor. Cox himself was achieving notice as a night-club comedian, and he and Brando sometimes shared a dinner at a restaurant before their shows.

The pair drew the stares of other diners. Cox and Brando divided the staring ones into "gawks" and "supergawks." Brando sometimes retaliated to the supergawks by studying *them* with salt and pepper shakers doubling as binoculars.

Marlon rarely consented to attend celebrity parties, but one night he agreed to visit a reception for the Italian director Roberto Rossellini, whose realistic films he greatly admired. After an evening's performance, Marlon and Kim Hunter took the subway to Gramercy Park, where the party was being held. They spoke with the guest of honor, then headed directly to the buffet table, where Marlon gorged himself.

Nearby was Clare Booth Luce, surrounded by a group of admiring young men. She saw Brando and began rhapsodizing to her listeners about his performance in *A Streetcar Named Desire* and his youthful beauty. "Look at that face," she remarked. "Have you ever seen anything so exquisite?" Marlon reacted instinctively, contorting his face and sticking out his tongue like a small boy. Mrs. Luce was not amused.

Many of Marlon's friends were obscure people who inhabited the Broadway scene, including misfits and outcasts. Some were homosexuals, and the false rumor quickly spread that the handsome young star of *A Streetcar Named Desire* was a homosexual. One of those Marlon befriended was a young gypsy musician who lived in Greenwich Village. Sasha, as we shall call him, came to the dressing room of Marlon and Karl Malden many nights and played his moody music before the performance. Both actors enjoyed it, his soulful melodies helping to prepare them for the play.

Malden carried a prop in *A Streetcar Named Desire*, a silver cigarette case which was important in his characterization. One night as he prepared for his entrance, he couldn't find the case. He searched the entire dressing room but it wasn't there. Fortunately, the property man had a duplicate.

A few months later Malden was taking a rest between the matinée and evening performances; he often did so on a cot behind a wardrobe rack in the dressing room. Malden heard the door open. It was Sasha. Believing himself unnoticed, he slipped his hand into all the pockets of the clothes on the racks, extracted something and started to leave.

"Put it back, Sasha," Malden said quietly.

Sasha started. "I, uh—I was just getting something that Marlon wanted," he blurted.

"Put it back, Sasha," Malden repeated. Sasha returned what he had taken and departed swiftly.

Marlon was angry when he arrived at the dressing room that night. "Why the hell did you do that to Sasha?" he demanded.

"Why did I do it?" Malden answered. "The son of a bitch stole my cigarette case. God knows what else he has stolen. He's a thief."

"He's not a thief. He's got this problem: he steals things. He's been trying to cure himself of his kleptomania, and he just about had it licked. Now you ruined everything!"

"Look, Marlon, you can conduct your therapy classes on the outside. But I want a rule: Sasha is never allowed in the dressing room alone. Agreed?"

"All right. But lay off Sasha."

Marlon was embarrassed by the adulation of fans. After each performance, dozens of them, including many teen-age girls, gathered outside the stage door to ask for autographs and take his photograph. Marlon found a way to escape them: he climbed over fences and ran through lots adjoining the theater.

He wasn't as successful in eluding publicity.

The press agent for *A Streetcar Named Desire*, Ben Kornzweig, noticed that Marlon flinched every time Kornzweig spoke to him. One day Kornzweig announced proudly that a national magazine had agreed to a photographic spread on Brando.

"I would rather not," Marlon answered.

"But, Marlon, this spread will reach millions," the press agent argued. "It'll be terrific publicity for the show and for you."

"No, I'm sure I wouldn't care to do it," Marlon replied.

When another magazine proposed an article on him, Marlon not only refused to grant an interview but told his close friends to avoid the reporter, too. The writer responded, "If his friends won't talk, his enemies will." Marlon decided to cooperate. It was better to present his own viewpoints, he concluded, than to have his personality distorted by gossips and false friends. He became better acquainted with Kornzweig and grew confident that the press agent was not trying to exploit him. Marlon began agreeing to more and more interviews.

One afternoon in his dressing room he told the *Herald Tribune's* Lucius Beebe, "The rumor of my allergy to publicity, believe me, has been greatly exaggerated. In fact, it has no real basis at all. Simply, I try to differentiate between legitimate professional promotion, which is reasonable and pleasant to any professional actor, and the revolting personalized notoriety which passes as publicity in the films, and to a lesser extent, in certain circles of the legitimate stage. If people are interested in my ideas or my acting, I am flattered by it, but I don't want to make myself available to promotion as a matinée idol, which I am not, or part of preposterous romantic Broadway gossip, which is just plain nauseating."

Marlon established an attitude toward interviews that remained unchanged throughout his career. He responded to the reporter's questions with the same integrity he would bring to an acting performance, telling his own feelings, not necessarily what the reporter wanted to hear. He spoke seriously or humorously, depending on his mood or the nature of the question, and he employed an imagery and choice of words that often astounded his listeners. He was immensely quotable. He enjoyed the acquaintance of some reporters, those who treated him as a human being and not as a celebrity. He courted no one.

Marlon's most famous encounter with a gossip columnist came when Sheilah Graham came backstage at the Ethel Barrymore Theater to visit Jessica Tandy. They had known each other when both were in the London theater. Miss Graham expressed her eagerness to meet the virile young co-star of *A Streetcar Named Desire,* and Miss Tandy agreed to introduce her.

The two women walked to Brando's dressing room, and Miss Tandy knocked on the door.

"Who is it?" Marlon asked.

"It's Jessie, Marlon. I have someone I'd like you to meet."

The door swung open, and Marlon stood bare-chested, still dripping from his shower.

Miss Tandy began, "Marlon, dear, I'd like to introduce—"

"—your mother," Marlon said with a smile.

Brando had committed himself by contract to a two-year run in *A Streetcar Named Desire,* and the final year proved a punishing experience. He was helped by advice he had learned from Jacob Adler, patriarch of the acting family: "Old man Adler taught me to hold back twenty percent and you're always being honest with the audience. Try to show more than you've got to give and they catch on right away."

But no acting device could save Brando from the wearying ennui of repeating the same lines every night and twice weekly at matinées. He began to suffer memory lapses that terrified him. One night he and Kim Hunter were performing the scene that followed Blanche's birthday party. The audience, Brando and Miss Hunter realized instantaneously that a large section of dialogue had been repeated. Miss Hunter and Brando avoided looking at each other for the rest of the scene, for fear of breaking into laughter.

Brando later described another occasion: "One night I came to an absolute, complete void. I just stood there looking out at the audience with a grin on my face. I looked up at the people in the balcony and all over the house, and it seemed terribly amusing. There were fourteen hundred people waiting for me to say something and I didn't have the slightest notion of what it was supposed to be. Kim Hunter was in the scene with me, and she is inclined to come apart in such situations. Her eyes got as big as saucers, and all she could do was ask me questions like 'What did you do then?' and 'What did she say?' Somehow we managed to get through it."

Events that relieved the deadening routine could also unnerve Marlon. One night he learned that Clark Gable was in the audience. Even though he had no particular feelings toward the movie star,

Gable's presence caused Marlon to freeze. When members of the audience started shouting "Louder!" his delivery became even worse.

One night he was asked to make a curtain speech. He had just swaggered through the play as Kowalski with overwhelming confidence, but when he stepped to the footlights as Marlon Brando, he was terrified. His hand trembled so much that he almost couldn't read the speech.

The nerves of everyone in the company were growing raw as the long run continued. The actors complained that the chicken which the prop man supplied each night for the dinner scene was getting worse. One night Marlon came offstage and ranted, "That chicken is godawful. I'd rather eat dog shit." When he lifted the napkin from his plate onstage the next night, that's what he found.

Marlon sought offstage diversions. He bought a motorcycle out of his $150 weekly allowance—he sent the rest of his $550 salary to his father for investment. Marlon raced through Manhattan streets, sometimes with his pet racoon or a young woman accompanying him. One day a policeman halted him for carrying two passengers. When Marlon opened his wallet to show his driver's license, a collection of parking citations fell out. He was taken to jail, and the stage manager of *A Streetcar Named Desire* bailed him out for $500 in time for the play to go on. "What did you do that for?" Marlon said angrily. "I was meeting some wonderful people."

The two-year servitude finally ended, and Marlon Brando would never return to the New York theater. With a single role he had changed the nature of acting in America, yet he himself was dissatisfied: "I think I missed the boat on at least one element: the gaiety. I don't really understand Stanley. Nothing reaches him, other people's pain, their needs, nothing. The only way I could zero in was to say, 'This guy is a big, lusty, eating animal with no sensitivity.' I always wanted to come out laughing, but I was always too frozen."

7

Hollywood

*"Hollywood is ruled by fear
and love of money.
But it can't rule me
because I'm not afraid of anything
and I don't love money."*

BRANDO ESCAPED TO PARIS AS SOON AS HE LEFT *A Streetcar Named Desire.*
He took up lodgings in an obscure hotel, prowled the galleries and
bistros, became acquainted with the Parisian girls and toured the
French countryside with one of them. Like many Americans before
him, he found Paris beguiling, and he might have remained there
except that his money ran out.

His agents at MCA were eager for him to return and begin his
movie career. Strangely, there were not as many film offers as
might have been expected in the wake of Brando's Broadway success. He had made it known that he would not consider the standard
term contract, which subjected actors to the dictates of the studio;
he would only undertake roles of his own choosing.

The film bosses distrusted such a show of independence. Some
were offended by Brando's statements about Hollywood. In one
interview he commented, "The films are, I think, the most powerful single influence available to the American public today—much
more than either the church or formal education. I do not think
that anybody connected with the films in the United States has ever
made a sincere effort to avail himself of their fullest potentialities
the way they do, say, in France. I should like very much sometime
soon to be associated with the making of some pictures in France
where the product is so much more mature and sensitive as to be
beyond all comparison with what is made in American films.
French films are not removed from all reality whatsoever, as ours
are. I just feel dead inside, coming away from most Hollywood
screenings."

Most of those seeking to hire Brando were independent film makers. One of them was Lewis Milestone, the distinguished director of *All Quiet on the Western Front, The Front Page, Of Mice and Men* and *A Walk in the Sun.* He was in Paris, working with a couple of French writers on a script. Learning that Brando was also in Paris, Milestone called on the actor at his hotel. They had coffee at a sidewalk café.

"The script's not ready yet, so I won't show it to you," said the director. "But when it's finished and if you're available, I'd like very much to work with you."

Another film maker who wanted Brando was Stanley Kramer. Brando was receptive. He had seen and admired such Kramer films as *Champion* and *Home of the Brave,* and recognized the producer as independent-minded and concerned with making commentaries on American society. MCA sent Brando an eight-page synopsis, including some dialogue, of a film Kramer proposed to make about paraplegic war veterans. Carl Foreman was to write the script, Fred Zinnemann would be the director, and United Artists would distribute the film.

Brando read the synopsis while walking down a Paris street. He was intrigued by the dramatic situation of a husband and wife trying to adjust to his physical helplessness. He sought advice from Lewis Milestone. "I think you're goddam lucky," said the director. "Kramer has integrity, and Fred Zinnemann is an honest man. You can't go wrong."

Brando sent word to MCA that he would accept *The Men,* as the Kramer film was called. His price: $40,000. That was big money for an actor who had never made a movie, and it was more than Kramer wanted to pay. But Brando would take no less.

On a hot September day in 1949 Marlon Brando stepped off the train in Alhambra, a small Santa Fe railroad stop east of Los Angeles. He was greeted by Jay Kanter, an ambitious young agent whose career with MCA had been aided by his friendship with Marlon Brando, and by Mrs. Betty Lindemeyer, sister of Marlon's mother. Marlon was driven to Eagle Rock, another Los Angeles suburb, where Mrs. Lindemeyer lived with her husband, Oliver, in a small two-bedroom wooden house typical of Eagle Rock. This was to be Marlon's headquarters during his three months in California. Since his grandmother was also visiting the Lindemeyers, Marlon slept on the living-room couch.

With Teresa Wright and Everett Sloan, The Men, *1950*

The grandmother, Mrs. Elizabeth Myers, knew of Marlon's obstreperous ways from his earliest years, and she expressed her concern for her grandson's future in Hollywood: "I do hope that Bud comes through all this without too much scandal. I love him more than anything on this earth, but I never know when I'm going to hear from him in San Quentin."

Marlon reported to Birmingham Veterans Hospital in Van Nuys, where producer Kramer had gained permission for members of *The Men* cast to live as paraplegic veterans. For four weeks Marlon was a resident of a thirty-two-bed ward where he ate, slept and trained as if he were a paraplegic. At first the ex-soldiers were wary of the husky actor's presence; they were used to visits of many performers who breezed through the wards with plastic smiles and words of cheer. The paraplegics soon discovered that Brando was different. Everything they did, he did. He learned to lift himself out of bed, using only his arms; to operate a wheelchair; to drive a specially built Oldsmobile with hand controls; to do the rope climb; to think like a paraplegic. "Everywhere you think of going, you have to plan your course in advance and figure: Are there steps there? What about doorways? Are there elevators? Is there a parking space?" His impersonation fooled hospital attendants. Introduced as a "D-10" (paralyzed from the tenth dorsal vertebra downward), he was fitted for braces by a medical officer who was unaware that the young man could walk. He was also outfitted with a urine bottle strapped to his leg, but orderlies rebelled and said he would have to walk to the toilet.

The president of the Paraplegic Veterans Association remarked, "The guys have accepted him more as a paraplegic than as an actor." They even took him to their favorite nighttime hangout, a bar on Ventura Boulevard called the Pump Room. One night the men were gathered near the bar in their wheelchairs when a tipsy woman noticed them. Another drink turned her from lush to evangelist, and she began lecturing them on the power of faith.

"You don't have to sit there in those wheelchairs all your lives," she exhorted. "If you have faith in the power of God, you can walk. Jesus said to the lame, 'Take up your beds and walk.' You can do it! All you need is faith."

Marlon was studying her intently. "I can do it?" he said, his hands gripping the steel arms of his wheelchair.

"Yes, you can do it," she replied. She stared in alarm as his grip tightened and he struggled to rise on his shaky legs. He stood tottering for one minute. Then he did a buck-and-wing and raced out of the bar crying, "I can walk! I can walk!"

On another occasion Marlon had to pick up a script at the film studio. He telephoned for a taxi and wheeled himself out of the hospital to wait for it. When the cab arrived, Marlon pulled himself out of the chair and into the back seat, folded the chair and placed it beside him.

When the cab arrived at the studio, Marlon said, "Wait right here, I'll be back in a minute." He flung open the door, raced across the street and disappeared inside. He returned with the script and they drove back, with the taxi driver shaking his head most of the way. His perplexity was compounded when he delivered his fare at the hospital and watched him put the wheelchair outside the cab, unfold it and lift himself into it, then wheel his way into the hospital barracks.

Marlon Brando had come to Hollywood with an iron resolve to preserve his integrity against the publicity mill that he detested. As with *A Streetcar Named Desire* in the theater, he first viewed the publicity man with suspicion. But he quickly recognized that Kramer's press agent was not the Lee Tracy type he had expected.

George Glass was a veteran of movie publicity, but he was more than a publicist for Kramer. He, Kramer and Carl Foreman were partners in the independent film company, and Glass's brilliant selling campaigns for *Champion* and *Home of the Brave* had been a major part of the company's success. A short, stubby, ebullient man, he performed his craft on the basis of telling the truth. Brando was disarmed by Glass's iconoclasm, and amused by the press agent's definition of an actor: "The kind of a guy who if you ain't talking about him ain't listening." Brando quoted the remark many times.

Brando agreed to do any interviews that Glass suggested, provided reporters did not visit the movie set when heavily dramatic scenes were being filmed. Glass explained that the two press queens, Louella Parsons and Hedda Hopper, rarely went to the studios, preferring to conduct interviews in their homes or offices.

"I won't go," Brando said. "If they want to come on the set, I'll talk to 'em."

Mrs. Parsons would not accept his terms, but Mrs. Hopper agreed to come to *The Men* set. Brando seemed transfixed as she delivered a twenty-minute monologue. Finally she snapped her fingers as if to waken him. She asked if he had been listening; he said he had.

"Do you care to answer my questions?" she asked.

"I don't believe so," he replied.

"Then may I tell you that I didn't want this interview? Your producer, Stanley Kramer, insisted that I do it. You needn't submit yourself to any further agony. Thanks for nothing—and good day."

Brando had come to Hollywood expecting film acting to be easy after the deadening grind of a long-run play. He discovered that working in films "is the toughest form of acting, and anyone who can come through it successfully can call himself an actor for the first time. When you have to portray a shattering emotion while realizing at the back of your mind that if you move your head an inch too much you'll be out of focus and out of frame, that's acting."

The mechanics of filming baffled him. He was especially perplexed by the practice of shooting out of sequence—performing later scenes in the script before earlier ones. The director, Fred Zinnemann, explained that this had to be done to make the most economical use of sets and shooting time. Such a practice was alien to Brando's training at the Actors Studio and his own instincts as an actor. He needed time to develop a character and plot its progression through the story.

In rehearsals, Brando exhibited none of the dramatic power to substantiate his Broadway reputation. He delivered his lines woodenly, often inaudibly. His first important scene came when the paralyzed veteran was confronted by the sweetheart he did not want to see. The scene called for him to lash out at the girl, played by Teresa Wright, in an attempt to dissuade her from a life with a crippled husband. Brando had rehearsed his dialogue in a monotone, but when filming began, he poured forth an intensity that brought real tears from Miss Wright, and some of the movie crew as well.

Brando was dissatisfied. "I didn't feel it," he muttered. "I just didn't feel it."

Watching the scenes in the rushes the following day, he was convinced that he had missed the emotion. He had recently seen Charlie Chaplin in *City Lights:* "A brutal reminder of forgotten proportions; Chaplin has breadth and scope that no other actor has." Brando was so disturbed that he never again watched the rushes.

Under Zinnemann's sensitive direction, Brando learned the mechanics of film acting, and the shooting of *The Men* proceeded swiftly, as was the custom of a Kramer production. Marlon arrived on time each morning, coming to the studio or the Birmingham Hospital location by taxi from Eagle Rock. His offstage costume was always the same: T-shirt, blue jeans and sneakers.

When the filming of *The Men* was completed, Kramer told Marlon that he was giving a party for the cast and crew, as well as the forty-five paraplegic veterans who had appeared in the film. "And say, Marlon, maybe you ought to dress for the party," the producer suggested. "Just as a courtesy to the guests."

"You mean you don't want me to wear T-shirt and jeans?" Marlon said.

"That's the idea."

When Marlon appeared at the party, he was wearing white tie and tails.

After three months in Hollywood, Marlon returned to New York. He enrolled in courses at the New School for Social Research and continued living in his bare, one-room apartment. He had agreed to help Kramer publicize *The Men,* and the United Artists publicity department arranged press interviews and television and radio appearances. While being interviewed by Wendy Barrie on her television show, he fell asleep.

"Only had two hours' sleep," he explained when Miss Barrie prodded him awake. "Went motorcycling with Wally Cox up to the Palisades." When Miss Barrie asked him when his first film was being released, he shouted to the United Artists publicist in the audience, "Hey, Mike, when's *The Men* opening?"

In his publicity appearances, Brando seemed to satirize the traditional movie-star interview, replying to the insipid questions with outlandish comments. The satire was a convenient defense against the violation of his privacy, which he resented.

He continued his unorthodox behavior during his appearances in other cities on behalf of *The Men.* He arrived in Chicago accompanied by his pet racoon, Russell. The United Artists publicity man asked if he could do anything for him. Marlon thought for a minute and replied, "Yeah. Can you tell me where I can get my racoon fucked?"

Marlon returned to Libertyville and was interviewed by a reporter from the *Independent-Register*. Having left town as a ne'er-do-well, he enjoyed posing as the successful actor of Broadway and Hollywood. "It was a tough grind," he expounded, "and I worked very hard like every other person who advances in the movies or on the stage. After you succeed, it is an easy life, but until then it is hard—very, very hard." He observed that the restful hours of his vacation in Libertyville had benefited him very much. But of course he couldn't play it straight all the way and dropped the information that among his accomplishments was winning the Pulitzer Prize for something called *The Critics of War*.

The Men was praised for the purity of its intentions and for Brando's portrayal of the crippled veteran. But the theme was too grim for a nation still recovering from the agonies of the World War and embarked on another war in Korea. It remained for *A Streetcar Named Desire* to establish Marlon Brando as a film star.

Despite its huge success on the stage, the screen rights to *Streetcar* had not been eagerly sought. The major studios had been dissuaded by the statement of the industry's chief censor, Joseph Breen, that the play could not be filmed in its original form. According to Breen, Kowalski's ravishing of Blanche and dialogue about homosexuality would have to be eliminated to comply with the Production Code. Nevertheless Charles Feldman, head of a successful talent agency, bought the film rights to *A Streetcar Named Desire* and hired Elia Kazan to direct and Tennessee Williams to adapt the screenplay.

In accordance with the Code, Williams eliminated the profanity and the reference to homosexuality in the death of Blanche's young husband. But in a letter to Breen, the playwright pleaded for permission to retain the rape: "*Streetcar* is an extremely and peculiarly moral play, in the deepest and truest sense of the term. . . . The rape of Blanche by Stanley is a pivotal, integral truth in the play, without which the play loses its meaning which is the ravishment of the tender, the sensitive, the delicate, by the savage and brutal forces of modern society. It is a poetic plea for comprehension."

Breen capitulated on the rape, but he insisted that Kowalski had to be punished for his lust. In the play, Stella refuses to believe her sister's story of the rape, and she and Stanley resume their marriage. Williams finally agreed to have Stella tell her newborn baby that she was not returning to the house.

A Streetcar Named Desire, *1950*

Jack Albin

With the censorship problem apparently solved, Feldman made a deal with Warner Bros. to release *Streetcar* and began preparations for filming.

Kazan insisted on using the original New York cast, but he was enough of a realist to know that if he wanted Marlon Brando, he would need a big-name star as Blanche. The choice was Vivien Leigh, who had played the role for eight months in a London production directed by her husband, Laurence Olivier. Feldman offered Brando $50,000 to repeat the role of Kowalski. Brando turned it down, finally agreed to $75,000.

Brando joined the other Broadway cast members—Kim Hunter, Karl Malden, Nick Dennis, Rudy Bond, Peg Hillias, Richard Garrick, Ann Dere, Edna Thomas—for rehearsals at the Warner Bros. studio in Burbank. All felt the absence of Jessica Tandy, whose sympathy and professionalism had been the unifying force during the long stage run. Vivien Leigh quickly erased their resentment. She refused formality and worked hard and intimately with the other players.

As the rehearsals began, Kazan realized the advantage of working with a cast that was totally familiar with the material. But there were also drawbacks. He did not agree with Olivier's interpretation of Blanche, and Kazan had to reshape Miss Leigh's depiction of the role. And during the two-year run, Brando and Miss Hunter had strayed from Kazan's direction.

"Now we'll get back to the original relationship of Stanley and Stella," he told the pair. "You two become like a pair of fishwives."

When the Kowalski apartment had been constructed on the movie stage, Kazan told Brando, "Now, this is Stanley's place. I want you to go into it and place things around the way Stanley would live."

The rest of the company watched as Marlon entered the set and began rearranging things, a chair here, a bottle there. The process took several minutes, then he surveyed the place and walked out of the set.

"Is that it?" Kazan asked.

"Yes," said Brando.

"Okay," the director announced to the crew, "I want everything kept this way. Nothing is to be changed."

Kazan had ordered a mock-up of the apartment set constructed in a corner of the stage. When production began, Kazan occupied

With Vivien Leigh, A Streetcar
Named Desire

the time between filming with rehearsals in the mock-up set for the following day's scenes. Thus the actors came prepared, and shooting went swiftly.

After Kazan had completed his editing of *A Streetcar Named Desire,* it was granted a Production Code Administration seal. But its censorship problems were not over.

The film was booked to play the Radio City Music Hall in the spring of 1951, then it was withdrawn. The Legion of Decency threatened to place *Streetcar* on its condemned list, making it a sin for Catholics to attend the film. After lengthy negotiations a Catholic layman suggested to Warner Bros. cuts which would make *Streetcar* acceptable. Eliminated was Stanley's remark to Blanche before the rape: "You know, you might not be bad to interfere with." The words "on the mouth" were removed from his line "I would like to kiss you softly and sweetly on the mouth." Other changes were made to stress the goodness of Stella, the meanness of Stanley, and the waywardness of Blanche. Also removed was Alex North's music as Stella came down the stairs after her quarrel with Stanley. The music was deemed "too carnal."

The cuts were made over Kazan's protest, and *A Streetcar Named Desire* was released. It was a critical and commercial success. But it was more than simply a hit film, as Kazan noted at the time: *"Streetcar* is the first nonsentimental film we have ever made over here. It is a landmark. Its issues are not oversimplified, and you're not in there 'rooting for somebody'—all that old shit the motion picture industry is built upon. There is no hero, no heroine; the people are people, some dross, some gold, with faults and virtues—and for a while you are muddled about them, the way you would be in life."

Film acting in America would never be the same after Brando's performance as Stanley Kowalski. The naturalism that he had created on the stage was now preserved on film, and it would influence a whole generation of actors.

Despite the historic quality of Brando's performance, it went unrewarded by the Motion Picture Academy. Vivien Leigh, Karl Malden and Kim Hunter won Oscars, but the award for best actor of 1951 went to Humphrey Bogart for his performance in *The African Queen.*

8

The
Slob

*"I don't know what people expect
when they meet me.
They seem to be afraid
that I'm going to piss in the potted palm
and slap them on the ass.
Can't they get used to the fact
that I'm a human being?"*

ELIA KAZAN FOUND ANOTHER CHARACTER FOR BRANDO TO PLAY. THIS
time it was Emiliano Zapata, leader of an agrarian uprising in Mexico during the early 1900s.

For six and a half years, Kazan had worked with John Steinbeck
on a movie script about Zapata. They finally achieved a version
both were satisfied with, and Kazan started plans to film *Viva
Zapata!* in Mexico. The picture was to be made for Twentieth Century-Fox, with Darryl F. Zanuck as producer. Both Kazan and
Steinbeck had wanted a Mexican actor to play the leading role,
but they couldn't find one with sufficient dramatic power. Steinbeck
suggested Marlon Brando, and Kazan readily agreed. So did
Zanuck, although he hesitated to pay the $100,000 fee demanded
by MCA. But the studio head acquiesced—after exacting options
for Brando's future services.

As with Stanley Kowalski, Brando approached the role warily.
Emiliano Zapata was even more divorced from his nature—a fierce-
blooded man of action, a zealot who could arouse masses to revolu-
tion. Marlon questioned whether he, product of the Midwestern
middle class, could impersonate the fiery Mexican peasant. But
bolstered by Kazan's confidence, Brando lived for a while in a small
village in Sonora to study Mexican manners and talk. Returning
to Hollywood, he worked on a make-up to disguise his obvious

gringo looks and make him resemble the mestizo revolutionary. Plastic rings were placed inside the nostrils to flare his nose, and his eyelids were glued upward. At Kazan's suggestion, Brando wore brown contact lenses to disguise his slate-gray eyes.

On the morning of the departure for the Texas location, Marlon stopped by the MCA offices to see Jay Kanter. Aware of the actor's forgetfulness, Kanter asked him, "Have you got everything you need, Marlon?"

"Yeah, it's all in here," he said, indicating a small zippered bag.

"What about the contact lenses?" the agent asked. "Where are they?"

"Right here, where they're safe." Marlon dipped a finger under his lower lip and fished along his gum until he located the tiny glass circle. He did the same on the other side of his mouth and displayed the two contact lenses on the tips of his fingers.

"Good God, Marlon," Kanter said, "aren't you afraid that—"

"It's the safest place for them," Marlon assured him.

Two mornings later Kanter was awakened by a telephone call from his boss, Lew Wasserman. "I just got a call from Kazan in Texas," Wasserman said. "Marlon swallowed his contact lenses."

"No!"

"Yes. And Kazan says he can't start shooting until Marlon gets a new pair."

"But his eye doctor is in New York. And it's a holiday weekend."

"I don't care. Those lenses have to be in Del Rio, Texas, tomorrow morning."

Kanter did not mistake the urgency of Wasserman's order. After hours of frantic telephoning, Kanter located the eye doctor on a golf course. An agent in the New York office of MCA flew to Del Rio, Texas, with two pairs of brown contact lenses, and production on *Viva Zapata!* was able to begin.

Cast in the role of another revolutionary was the young Irish-Mexican actor Anthony Quinn. Members of the company expected tension between Quinn and Brando, since their roles seemed competitive. Both had played Stanley Kowalski, and Quinn's performance in the road company of *A Streetcar Named Desire*, as directed by Harold Clurman, had earned even greater critical acclaim than Brando's performance in New York. Some members of the *Zapata* company suspected that was a sore point with Kazan;

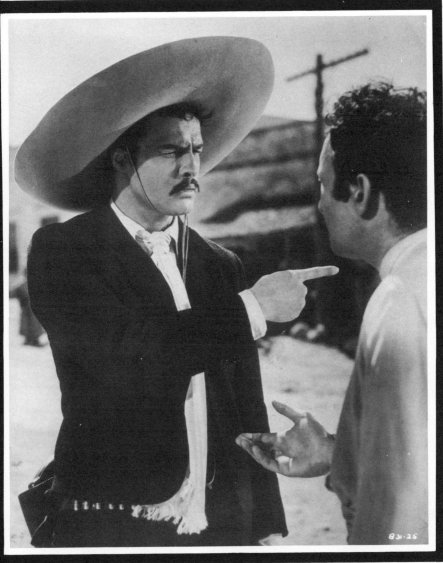

Viva Zapata, *1952*   *20th Century Fox*

With Jean Peters, Viva Zapata   20th Century Fox

Viva Zapata

they believed the director tried to pit Brando and Quinn against each other to create dramatic tension in the film.

Brando would have none of it. Initially Quinn viewed him with suspicion, but Brando disarmed Quinn with impish humor. The two actors went out for a roaring dinner together and later climbed a huge tree to serenade the film's leading lady, Jean Peters. Brando and Quinn ended up in a pissing contest on the bank of the Rio Grande.

It was Brando's first movie location, and he enjoyed freedom from the formality of studio filming. He set off firecrackers in the lobby of the hotel and engaged in running water fights with members of the crew. He struck terror in the hearts of the entire company when he played dead after the scene in which Zapata was gunned down by assassins.

Later, when such antics were reported in the press, Marlon complained to his aunt, Betty Lindemeyer, "That sure makes me look silly!"

"Darling," she replied calmly, "you *are* silly."

During the evenings, Brando dated Mexican members of the cast, especially Movita Castenada, a warm-hearted beauty who had appeared in Hollywood films since she played Clark Gable's Polynesian wife in *Mutiny on the Bounty.*

He seemed to take a casual approach to the role of Zapata, but Brando was delivering a performance that amazed his fellow actors. Kazan, too. "He is constantly doing things that surprise the director," said Kazan. "It makes you feel happy that he discovers things that you didn't know were there." Among the inspirations was in Quinn's death scene, when Zapata placed the hands of his dead comrade on his own face in an eloquent expression of anguish.

Brando was dissatisfied with his work in the film. He was twenty-six, and he felt that he lacked the maturity to play Zapata, a worn revolutionary of forty at his death. The critics and the movie public didn't share his misgivings, and *Viva Zapata!* was one of the big moneymakers of 1952. Brando was again nominated for an Academy Award as best actor; the Oscar went to Gary Cooper for *High Noon.* Anthony Quinn won as best supporting actor for *Viva Zapata!*

Brando's peasant portrayal in *Viva Zapata!*, following his Kowalski of *A Streetcar Named Desire*, reinforced the public's view of him as an insensitive, ill-mannered slob. The image had been promulgated not only by the film roles, but by the film companies' merchandizing of Brando as a commodity. A clever campaign had been conducted by Charles Feldman on behalf of *Streetcar*. The producer advertised the film with a photograph he ordered after the film had been completed. He asked photographer Sam Shaw to reproduce a scene in the movie which showed Brando's muscular back, clad in a torn T-shirt, as he embraced Kim Hunter. The actress was unavailable, so Shaw posed Brando with a model in a New York photographic studio. Brando protested that the photograph was vulgar—"It has a bad smell about it." But he agreed to the pose.

It became the butt of comedy for Sid Caesar and Milton Berle and other television comedians. The slurred Kowalski speech joined the standard repertoire of night club impressionists. Movie columnists, especially those for whom Brando had no esteem, equated him with Kowalski. *Time* magazine published a cover story which declared: "Where Barrymore was 'The Great Profile,' Valentino 'The Sheik,' and Clark Gable 'The King,' Marlon Brando is known to millions who read about Hollywood every day as 'The Slob.'"

Marlon seemed to do little to offset such a reputation. He dressed according to his own comfort and convenience. Several times Stanley Kramer was turned away from Hollywood restaurants when he tried to dine with the informally clad Brando.

Marlon continued to make New York his home; in Hollywood he stayed with Jay Kanter. When Marlon needed a suit for a special occasion, he borrowed one of Kanter's. Finally the agent said to him, "Look you're a well-known actor. You should have some clothes. Why don't you just go out and buy some? Then you'll have something to wear when you go back to New York."

"I've got a better idea," Marlon replied. "I don't like to wear new clothes; they're uncomfortable. Sell me three of those suits of yours that I've been wearing."

"All right, anything so you'll look decent," said Kanter. "I'll sell them to you for half of what they cost me."

"No, no," Brando insisted. "I'll pay you the full price. They're worth that to me, just so I don't have to break them in."

The press reported such stories in detail and with an undercurrent of derision.

Mugging for the studio cameraman

Cosmopolitan told of a Brando friend who saw the actor driving down Hollywood Boulevard with his head hanging out the window, mouth open. "Were you ill?" asked the friend. "No," Brando replied. "I was just drinking in the wind." *Life* wrote of a complaint that Brando had expressed to a girlfriend: "Your mother is the kind of woman that if I was dying of syphilis she'd give her last ten dollars to cure me." The *Saturday Evening Post* stated that he made a practice of dangling imitation black-widow spiders on the shoulders of visitors to his movie set.

In the beginning years of his Hollywood career, Brando played along with the press, contributing his own brand of whimsy to the inane queries of interviewers. When a woman reporter asked him how he bathed, he replied, "I spit in the air and then run under it." Where did he sleep? "On the bathroom floor, usually."

One wary interviewer listened to a half-hour of literate answers and concluded, "I must say that I'm grateful and surprised with this interview, Mr. Brando."

"What did you expect me to do—this?" He stood on his head and started talking gibberish.

He expounded on such fantasies as the time when he accompanied his father on a business trip to Africa and partook of a delicacy made of gazelle eyes: "They mix them in a paste and cook them in a casserole." This was the same Marlon who had delighted in tantalizing his grandmother with an offhand remark: "They're coming alone fine with that tunnel they're digging under the Atlantic."

But now he was not merely playing games with his gullible grandmother. He was exposing himself before millions and began to feel like a geek—"the lowest form of show business, the guy in the carnival who bites the heads off chickens. Geeks usually get paid off in cheap whisky. Press agents made me a geek who gets a hundred thousand dollars per chicken head."

Seeking escape from his reputation as The Slob, Marlon turned to Shakespeare.

Producer John Houseman had proposed a new version of *Julius Caesar* at MGM. Shakespeare had never before succeeded in Hollywood, but Houseman, who had teamed with Orson Welles in memorable classics at the Mercury Theater on Broadway, offered a sensible proposal: *Julius Caesar* could be filmed for $1.7 million, employing a prestigious cast and costumes and scenery left over from *Quo Vadis*. Production chief Dore Schary gave his approval to the project.

Houseman engaged Joseph L. Mankiewicz to adapt the play and direct the film. The studio favored the casting of Stewart Granger, a contract player, as Mark Antony. Mankiewicz preferred Marlon Brando, but he realized that he would have trouble convincing the MGM executives, who thought of Brando as the crude mumbler Kowalski.

"I think Brando is a marvelous actor," Dore Schary told Mankiewicz, "but I just can't see him for this part. How could he possibly play Shakespeare?"

Mankiewicz was determined to prove that Brando could. When the director proposed the role of Mark Antony to Brando, the actor was intrigued. He liked the idea of playing a classical role after Kowalski and Zapata. But could he pull it off? He asked for a couple of weeks to consider.

Marlon purchased Shakespearean recordings, studied them and made his own recordings of *Julius Caesar* speeches. He invited Mankiewicz to his New York apartment to hear the results.

"You sound just like June Allyson," the director commented. "There's nothing of Marlon Brando in the recordings."

The two men talked for hours about Mark Antony, whom Mankiewicz termed "the only twentieth-century man that Shakespeare ever wrote." He urged Marlon to seek an understanding of the character and then approach the speeches in a natural way. Brando locked himself in his apartment and spent days recording a new set of tapes. They were sent to California and played for Dore Schary.

"I can't believe that's Marlon Brando!" said the production chief.

Schary asked the actor to come to the studio for a conference. Wary of Brando's reputation, Schary emphasized the need to make *Julius Caesar* on a tight schedule. "If you do the picture, I want to get one thing straight," said Schary. "If you have any doubts about anything, tell John Houseman or Joe Mankiewicz so we can resolve them early and not hold up shooting."

Brando grinned. "Don't worry—there'll be no trouble. Because you've got no script problem."

MGM's casting of Marlon Brando in *Julius Caesar* was greeted with incredulity on both sides of the Atlantic. Television comedians issued a new round of jokes about Stanley Kowalski playing Shakespeare, and rumors circulated that the Brando tapes were not Brando at all, but Laurence Olivier. Keenly aware of the challenge he faced, Marlon underwent six weeks of training with Gladys Fogoler, a white-haired Bostonian who was vocal coach at MGM. Houseman assembled an Anglo-American cast. John Gielgud was assigned to play Cassius and James Mason Brutus, with Greer Garson as Calpurnia and Deborah Kerr as Portia; both actresses were under contract to MGM. Brando was joined by fellow Americans Louis Calhern as Caesar and Edmond O'Brien as Casca. Calhern was a veteran of Shakespeare, and O'Brien had played classics with the Mercury Theater and had appeared in *Hamlet* with Gielgud.

All gathered for the first day's rehearsal on a bare stage on the main lot of MGM. The cast members sat down at a long rectangular table with Mankiewicz at one end. Brando sat at the far end. After the preliminaries, Mankiewicz began a reading. Most of the other actors knew one another and had worked together, but Brando was a stranger to all of them. He had remained silent through the preliminaries.

Veteran of a thousand rehearsals and familiar with every role in *Julius Caesar,* John Gielgud declaimed his lines as Cassius, the words ringing through the stage. When Brando's cue approached, all eyes turned toward his end of the table. He sat hunched over the script, both elbows on the table, his eyes eight inches from the page. Ears strained to hear his words. Only the faintest of sounds emerged.

Producer Houseman later termed it "Marlon's secret performance."

Brando's delivery changed little during the three weeks of rehearsal. At the start of filming, the major speeches were delivered by the other actors. Brando remained apart, sitting in a corner of the stage playing solitaire chess or listening to recordings of Shakespeare by Laurence Olivier in his dressing room. When he wasn't needed on the set, he went to a nearby rehearsal hall and recited Antony's funeral oration for Caesar in full voice.

Brando was sometimes joined in the rehearsal hall by Mankiewicz. Together they studied the lines, which Mankiewicz sought to interpret without the religious line-scanning of traditional Shakespeare. "It should be part dance, part song," Mankiewicz emphasized.

Marlon arrived at an approach which was new to him. The words, he concluded, were everything. In modern plays, the text could be ignored, but in Shakespeare "you can't play under it, or above it, or around it, as we do in the contemporary theater. The text is everything."

He and Mankiewicz puzzled over the beginning of the funeral oration: "*Lend* me your ears." What did it really mean? They arrived at a solution that seemed both logical and playable.

When the day arrived for the funeral scene, five hundred extras were assembled in tunics and togas on MGM's Stage 27, which had been converted into a replica of the Roman Forum. Brando appeared in gray slacks, corduroy jacket, polka-dot scarf, and a black homburg which he claimed had once belonged to John Barrymore. "I hope it rubs off," cracked Mankiewicz.

The director instructed James Mason to deliver Brutus' speech to the Romans with fervor, and Mason did so. Then came the time for Brando's first big speech, and everyone in the company waited with anticipation. Although he did not appear in the scene, John Gielgud appeared on the stage; he was careful to remain out of Marlon's view.

Brando began his speech as he and Mankiewicz had planned. "Friends, Romans, countrymen . . ." The mob remained inattentive, still stirred by Brutus' eloquence. Again: "Friends, Romans, countrymen!" Then, at a shout: "*Lend* me your ears!" The mob quieted, and Brando continued the speech with "I come to bury Caesar, not to praise him . . ." through its thirty-four lines, his voice mounting with emotion as he reached the climax. "Cut!" said Mankiewicz, and the extras and crew broke into applause.

The scene was repeated seven times until Mankiewicz expressed his satisfaction by saying "Print it!"

"I think I can do it better, Joe," Marlon remarked.

"Okay, once more," said the director. The eighth take was the last.

The reservations of the British cast members were melted by Brando's conscientious attitude toward his role. So impressed was John Gielgud that he offered Brando a position in repertory at Hammersmith. Marlon was pleased with the offer, but he declined because of his film commitments. The position was taken by Paul Scofield.

With James Mason,
Julius Caesar, *1953*

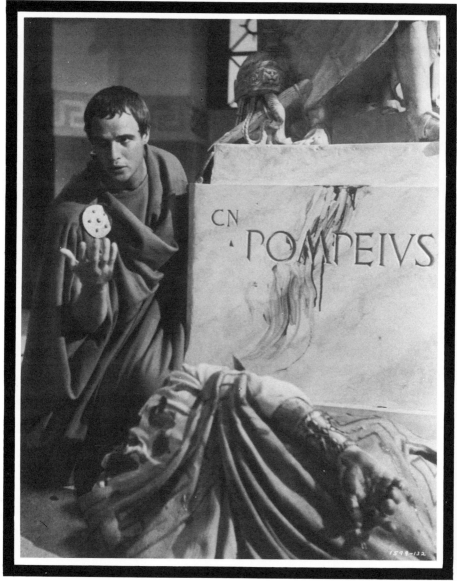

Julius Caesar

*With Louis Calhern
and Greer Garson,*
Julius Caesar

Julius Caesar produced a modest profit for MGM in its first release and proved to be a moneymaker for the company in later years. The film drew another Academy nomination for Brando. He and Gielgud were equally praised by the English critics. It was a rare achievement for an American actor, particularly one with a previous reputation for portraying slobs.

9

Pinnacle

"An actor is at most a poet,
and at least an entertainer.
You can't be a poet
by really trying hard.
It's like being charming.
You can't be charming
by working at it."

WHATEVER RESPECTABILITY THE BRANDO IMAGE ACHIEVED WITH *Julius Caesar* was negated by his fifth film, *The Wild One*. It was a project for which he had little enthusiasm. Stanley Kramer had proposed a social film based on a real-life happening—the invasion of a small California town by marauding motorcyclists. Brando was intrigued with the psychology of the alienated youths, but he saw the danger in portraying one of them: he would be deposited once more in the Kowalski mold.

He undertook the film out of deference to the man who had produced the first Brando movie. After signing a contract with Columbia Pictures, Stanley Kramer had made a series of commendable but unsuccessful films. His relations with the Columbia boss, Harry Cohn, had turned sour, and Kramer was searching for a subject that would change his luck.

For director, Kramer considered Laslo Benedek, a Hungarian who had directed *Death of a Salesman* for him. Kramer set up a meeting between Benedek and Brando in Benedek's office at Columbia. The conversation was circuitous, dealing with families and films—everything but *The Cyclists' Raid*, as the project was called. Brando was satisfied with Benedek's sensitivity, and the two of them agreed to work together.

Kramer assigned John Paxton to write the script, and it pleased everyone—except the Breen Office.

"You can't make this picture," an official of the Production Code told Kramer. "It's antisocial, if not downright Communistic. The idea of a bunch of roughnecks coming into a town and taking it over! You make them seem like heroes. By God, if they tried to do that to a town where I lived, I'd shoot 'em first and ask questions later."

Kramer was dismayed. His feud with Harry Cohn was worsening, and he couldn't withstand the ignominy of abandoning an ambitious project that had been widely publicized. He was forced to make changes in the script, shifting the emphasis from the town's intolerance of the motorcyclists to the invaders' rampage itself. Thus an attempt to understand the growing restlessness of youth became another mindless exercise in violence.

Brando was disturbed by the changes in the script. The new version eliminated the social commentary which had been the principal reason for his acceptance of the project. He tried his own hand at rewriting scenes to restore the original elements. But time was short; *The Cyclists' Raid* had to begin on schedule.

Another disappointment. Kramer and Benedek had planned to film the picture in California towns like Riverside and Hollister, where raids of motorcycle gangs had actually taken place. Harry Cohn vetoed the plan. The movie would be shot on Columbia's backlot in Burbank, using standard sets that had been seen in scores of films.

Brando prepared for his role as Johnny with customary thoroughness. He renewed his cycling technique so he could do his own riding, and he selected his wardrobe of boots, jeans, leather jacket and cap which he wore to and from the studio. Kramer had hired real-life motorcyclists to mingle with the actors, and Brando spent time talking with them to absorb their mannerisms and ways of speech.

One scene bothered Brando. It was one between Johnny and Kathie, the local girl, played by Mary Murphy. In the original script Kathie had asked Johnny why the cyclists went on their weekend rampages, and he had explained their need for release from their meaningless jobs. The speech had been rejected by the Breen Office as socially dangerous, and an innocuous explanation was substituted.

"We can do that scene the way it's written," Brando protested to Benedek. "We've got to explain why these guys need to break out and *be* somebody." He expounded on how he interpreted the feelings of the motorcyclists, and the director told him: "You say it better than the script. Let's not talk about it any more. When we get to the scene, we'll ad-lib it."

On the day the scene was to be filmed, Benedek instructed Mary Murphy: "Now, go along with Marlon as you would in real life. Ask questions. If you don't understand what he's getting at, ask more questions. Keep the scene going. We'll probably only shoot it once, so we have to get it right the first time."

Benedek ordered the camera to roll, and the following dialogue developed:

KATHIE   Where are you going when you leave here? Don't you know?

JOHNNY   Oh, man, we're just gonna go.

KATHIE   Just trying to make conversation. It means nothing to me.

JOHNNY   Well, on the weekend we go out and have a ball.

KATHIE   What do you do? I mean, do you just ride around, or do you go on some sort of picnic or something?

JOHNNY   A picnic, man! You're too square. I'm . . . I've got to straighten you out. Now, listen. You don't go to any one special place. That's cornball style. You just go. A bunch gets together after all week, it builds up. You just . . . the idea is to have a ball. Now, if you gonna stay cool, you gotta wail. You gotta put somethin' down, you gotta make some jive. Don't you know what I'm talkin' about?

KATHIE   Yeah, yeah. I know what you mean.

JOHNNY   Well, that's all I'm sayin'.

KATHIE   My father was going to take me on a fishing trip to Canada once.

JOHNNY   Yeah?

KATHIE   We didn't go.

JOHNNY   Crazy.

Brando's inarticulate eloquence provided a rare, insightful moment. The rest was violence. Brando was pitted against Lee Marvin as competitor for gang leadership; their rivalry as performers added credulity to the depiction on the screen. For their fight scene, Benedek choreographed the basic outlines by running it through with stunt men as Brando and Marvin watched. He showed the actors the physical limits of field by the three cameras that would shoot the scene. The cameras rolled with full magazines, and Brando and Marvin began the fight, trading barely missed blows (which would seem real on film with sound effects added) and rolling in the dirt. Brando was the winner, in accordance with the script, but Marvin added a clever touch by saluting the crowd like a vanquished gladiator.

Brando and Marvin spoke little to each other during the filming. Toward the end of it, Marvin walked up to Brando and said, "You know, I'm thinking of changing my name."

Brando eyed him suspiciously and replied, "Yeah? What to?"

"Marlow Brandy," said Marvin.

Brando made a sour face and started to walk away. Then he turned and said, "I think I'll change my name, too."

Marvin asked, "To what?"

Brando replied, "Lee Moron."

Filming went swiftly, necessarily so, because Cohn had imposed a twenty-four-day shooting schedule. Benedek and Brando agonized over a remaining scene to follow after Johnny rescued the girl from the attempted rape by gang members (the Breen Office would allow nothing more explicit than showing the girl encircled by her would-be rapists). A scene was needed in which Kathie thanked him for the gesture but Johnny found he was unable to respond. The scene was rewritten several times, never successfully. Benedek postponed it until the end. Finally, at five in the morning on the twenty-fourth day of shooting, the love scene was completed. But it didn't work. Brando had tried to explain the feelings of Johnny, and he did it more articulately than Johnny could have expressed himself.

When Harry Cohn saw the completed picture, he hated it. The Columbia sales department was perplexed by it. A new title was sought, and George Glass suggested two, *Hot Blood* and *The Wild One;* Columbia chose the latter.

Critics and audiences alike were disturbed by the raw violence of *The Wild One.* In England, where censorship was more concerned with violence than sex, the film was banned; it remained unseen by English audiences until 1968. *The Wild One* was not a commercial success, and a decade passed before its value as a social document would be realized. A new generation of film makers copied *The Wild One* in a series of motorcycle-gang movies that became part of the film idiom. Belatedly, the defiant character created by Brando found identity with youth throughout the world.

"*The Wild One* was a failure," Brando remarked afterward. "We started out to do something worthwhile, to explain the psychology of the hipster. But somewhere along the way we went off the track. The result was that instead of finding why young people tend to bunch into groups that seek expression in violence, all that we did was show the violence."

Brando was disturbed by the contribution of *The Wild One* to his public image; now he was identified with the leather jacket of a social renegade. But the film had one salutary effect; it helped resolve Marlon's own violent feelings. He was acutely aware of the violence in his nature. In later years he told an interviewer, "I once tried to kill my father. Really. Otherwise, I always used to imagine I was killing him by pulling out his corneas." Marlon learned to deal with his innate violence during his long psychoanalysis; the drums, motorcycles, boxing and pranks were part of the sublimation.

"Acting has done as much as anything to make me realize my violence and get rid of it," he told a friend. "*The Wild One* was the most helpful experience of all."

Next came the supreme achievement of Marlon Brando's early film career, *On the Waterfront.*

The project had a long history. In 1951 Budd Schulberg wrote a script about corruption on the New York–New Jersey waterfront, based on the Pulitzer Prize-winning series of articles by Malcolm Johnson. An independent film company planned to make the picture in the East, with Robert Siodmak as director. But the company was unable to arrange financing; potential backers considered the project too controversial. If longshoreman unions were controlled by gangsters, as the Johnson articles and the Schulberg script claimed, filming on the docks might be risky.

Rights to the script reverted to Schulberg. One day in 1952 he met with Elia Kazan to discuss a film project over lunch. Schulberg mentioned his *Waterfront* script, and Kazan said he had also tried to initiate a film about the docks, with no success. They agreed to collaborate. Schulberg rewrote the script to include more recent events, and in the spring of 1953 the two men went to Hollywood to conclude a deal with Twentieth Century-Fox.

The studio backed out at the last minute with the explanation that the script was too grim for theater audiences. Kazan and Schul-

With Mary Murphy,
The Wild One, *1954*

The Wild One

Columbia

The Wild One   *Columbia*

berg received the same response from other studios. Across the hall from Schulberg's room in the Beverly Hills Hotel was Sam Spiegel, the international film entrepreneur. He inquired about the project, and Schulberg related the story to him. "I will do the picture," said Spiegel.

The producer announced his plan to film *Waterfront* (the title was later lengthened to avoid conflict with a television series) for Columbia. Harry Cohn insisted that the picture be made in California, where he could maintain surveillance. Kazan refused. The film had to be photographed on the Eastern docks, where the events had taken place.

Spiegel's original choice to play Terry Malloy, the slow-witted, heroic ex-boxer, was Frank Sinatra, whose fortunes had revived with *From Here to Eternity.* Negotiations were broken off at the last minute, and Sinatra later sued Spiegel for a half-million dollars, charging breach of contract.

Kazan had forgotten about Marlon Brando's affinity for the boxing world. When Brando's name arose as a possibility for Terry Malloy, the director agreed he would be a good choice. Brando was signed. He recalled afterward, "Ten minutes before we started shooting in New York on that picture, I turned to my stand-in and said, 'I've got to find a characterization.' Ten minutes to figure out a way to play a part that won an Oscar! I didn't know if I was Mutt, or Jeff, or Falstaff."

Kazan admitted that the development of Terry Malloy was Brando's work alone. The basis was there, of course, in the dozens of would-be-great boxers that Brando had studied in the gyms of Manhattan. But the dimensions of Terry Malloy were provided by Marlon.

During one scene at the meeting of Malloy and the convent-educated sister of the longshoreman he had betrayed, the actress Eva Marie Saint accidentally dropped a glove. Marlon picked it up and continued his dialogue as he gently drew the glove over his own hand, thus telling in more than words his growing tenderness toward her.

It was the first film for Eva Marie Saint, who had studied at the Actors Studio and had performed in television dramas. Brando sensed her terror at being thrown in with a group of experienced actors on a film that was being photographed in bone-chilling cold on the docks of New York harbor. He gave her special attention, lunched with her every day, bolstered her wavering spirits.

With Eva Marie Saint,
On The Waterfront, *1954*

With Marlon Brando, Sr.,
Sam Spiegel, Mrs. Brando,
On the Waterfront

Columbia

"Marlon had an incredible sensitivity to everything that was around him," she recalled. "He was like an open wound. What he was never got in the way of the role that he had to play. It became such a natural part of him that he didn't have to put it on. When you work with other actors, something happens in the eyes as they start to assume their characters. The eyes grow gray and glassy, the way a snake looks just before it is going to shed its skin. Actors *start acting*. But Marlon never did. He *was* Terry Malloy."

Brando was less considerate with Rod Steiger, who played Terry Malloy's crooked brother. They had a scene in the back seat of a car in which Terry rebukes his brother for having ruined his boxing career: "Oh, Charlie. Oh, Charlie . . . you don't understand. I coulda had class. I coulda been a contender. I coulda been *somebody,* instead of a bum, which is what I am."

Kazan directed Brando and Steiger in the master shot of the scene. When single close-ups are photographed, most film actors remain on the set to feed lines to the on-camera actor. But when the time came for Steiger's close-up, Brando had disappeared. Steiger was faced with playing the scene with a script clerk. He never forgave Brando's breach of etiquette.

Little publicized and filmed in black-and-white for $820,000, *On the Waterfront* made an astounding impression when it was released in 1954. Brando's was the superior performance, in an extraordinarily well acted film; Lee J. Cobb, Karl Malden and Rod Steiger were all nominated for an Academy Award as best supporting actor, and Eva Marie Saint won the Oscar for best supporting actress.

Marlon Brando was nominated for best actor for the fourth year in a row, and it seemed impossible that Academy voters could deny him the prize any longer. The question arose: would he attend the ceremonies, and if so, would he wear a tuxedo? He attended, and he wore a tuxedo.

And he won. His acceptance speech was in character: "Thank you very much . . . uh, it's much heavier than I imagined"—weighing the Oscar in his hand—"uh, I, uh, I had something to say, and, uh, I can't remember what I, uh, was going to say, for the life of me. I don't think that, uh, ever in my life have so many people been so directly responsible for my being so very, very glad. It's a wonderful moment and a rare one and I am certainly indebted. Thank you."

*Grace Kelly & Marlon
on Oscar night*

Brando happily went through the post-ceremonies in the basement of the Pantages Theater, posing for endless photographs with the other winner of the evening, Grace Kelly. "Kiss him!" shouted the photographers, and Miss Kelly replied primly, "I think *he* should kiss *me.*" He obliged.

Walking down the corridor from one press room to another, Brando encountered Louella Parsons. She reported later that he seemed so euphoric over his victory that he almost bent down to kiss her. He shook her hand instead.

A celebration party had been planned that evening at the home of Jay Kanter. The guests waited patiently until Marlon arrived, and then they poured forth their congratulations. Marlon shrugged them off. He grabbed a magnum of French champagne and plopped himself down on a couch. Placing the Oscar on the coffee table before him, he unloosened his necktie and removed his shoes. He poured the champagne into a coffee mug and toasted the Oscar until he fell blissfully asleep.

10

Personal

*"I don't want to spread
the peanut butter of my personality
on the moldy bread
of the commercial press."*

WITH HIS SIXTH AND MOST TRIUMPHANT FILM, MARLON BRANDO SEEMED
to epitomize the American success story. He was thirty, acknowledged the best of a new generation of American actors, assured of
riches beyond human need. But psychoanalysis had not removed
the scars of his childhood, and he remained a disturbed man. The
first public evidence of this came with *The Egyptian* affair.

During his final weeks of work on *On the Waterfront*, Brando had
been required to perform climactic scenes in the freezing cold of
the Hoboken docks. The company had been racing against time,
because Marlon was committed by contract to report to *The Egyptian*. Darryl F. Zanuck had planned a lavish production which
would serve as a showcase of his inamorata, Bella Darvi. She was a
Polish-born, French-educated actress whose talents seemed invisible to all but Darryl F. Zanuck.

Each of Brando's previous films had contained some degree of
comment on the human condition. *The Egyptian,* based on Mika
Waltari's much-read novel of ancient Egypt, seemed to have none.
Yet Brando agreed to it as one of his commitments with Twentieth
Century-Fox. The reason was money. His father had been invest-
ing Marlon's movie salaries in a Nebraska cattle ranch incorporated
under the name of Marsdo (Marlon's dough). Now the senior
Brando reported that the investment could be completed with an
additional $150,000. That was what Darryl F. Zanuck was willing to
pay Marlon to appear in *The Egyptian.*

It was the first such compromise he had ever made, and guilt
weighed on him as he journeyed westward in January 1954 to report for the film. His misgivings grew as he met Bella Darvi and

the director, Michael Curtiz, who had made a long series of commercial films for Warner Bros. Marlon's fears were confirmed when he appeared for the first reading of the script.

Zanuck was there, chewing an enormous cigar and watching Bella Darvi from behind massive dark glasses. Under Curtiz's direction, Marlon read from the script with Miss Darvi, Jean Simmons, Victor Mature and other members of the cast. Marlon's usual rehearsal performance became even more muted as the reading continued. That night he boarded a train for New York.

After the train had left, an agent of MCA telephoned Zanuck at his Santa Monica beach house to say: "Marlon has decided he doesn't want to be in *The Egyptian*."

"But why?" Zanuck demanded.

"Marlon doesn't like Mike Curtiz. He doesn't like the role. And he can't stand Bella Darvi."

Zanuck was incensed. A million dollars had already been spent on *The Egyptian*, and Twentieth Century-Fox was planning to invest three more millions. Not only was money involved. Brando had insulted Bella Darvi, whom Zanuck had vowed he would build into his greatest star.

Brando disappeared. His psychiatrist, Dr. Bela Mittelman, announced in New York that the actor was under his care, "a very sick and mentally confused boy." He could certainly not report to work for at least ten weeks—the amount of time scheduled for the completion of *The Egyptian*. The studio offered to pay Dr. Mittelman's expenses to remain with Brando during the filming, but the psychiatrist said he could not leave his practice in New York. The studio asked permission for its own doctors to examine Brando and his medical records. No reply.

Edmund Purdom, an English actor under contract to MGM, assumed Brando's role. *The Egyptian* went on—to eventual box-office disaster.

Marlon remained locked inside his Manhattan apartment. One day a knock came at the door, and a voice called, "I'm here to tell you that you've just won an Academy Award nomination."

"Fine!" said Marlon. "Wait and I'll open the door."

When he unlocked the door, he was handed a summons for a lawsuit in which Twentieth Century-Fox was asking $2 million in damages.

*Brando
has paid his fine*

Marlon was undergoing another of the periodic emotional crises which were known only to Dr. Mittelman and a few of Marlon's closest friends. Six years of pressure from a white-hot career had depleted him. The pranks and the sardonic manner masked an emptiness and confusion that he felt about his own identity. He was wary of relationships, even with those he had good reason to trust.

He became increasingly distant. He sat in his apartment and allowed the telephone to ring without answering it. Sometimes he lifted the receiver and listened silently as a caller left name and number with the answering service. Then Marlon set the phone back on the hook gently. Messages piled up unanswered.

Even such a close friend as Elia Kazan had trouble contacting Brando. When Kazan was in California, he left message after message with Brando's answering service. There was never a reply, and the director gave up. One morning at two, Kazan was wakened in his hotel room by a knock at the door. It was Marlon. "I got your messages," he admitted, "but I didn't feel like calling you back."

Kazan once sent Marlon a script that he proposed for a film project. For a long time there was no answer. Then the man who had directed Brando in *A Streetcar Named Desire, Viva Zapata!* and *On the Waterfront* received the script from Brando's agent with a letter saying that it didn't seem suitable.

Such treatment confused and offended Marlon's old friends. Whenever he saw them he was as wryly cordial as always. But he had grown less visible. He became more vindictive for what he considered were breaches of friendship. The most heinous offense was to discuss Marlon's personal life with reporters. Those who failed to protect him from the prying of the press were banished from favor. Marlon's acquaintanceship was wide and varied, but his personal friends narrowed in number, the closest being those he had known from his early New York days and whose silence could be trusted. They included Sam Gilman and Carlo Fiore, Marlon's make-up man, Phil Rhodes and Rhodes's wife, Marie Squires (who later became Marlon's stand-in). And, of course, Wally Cox.

Already beset with emotional troubles, Marlon was now faced with the ordeal of his mother's death.

Frail, fragile Dodie Brando had left Libertyville with her husband in early 1954 for a visit with her sister in Pasadena. She fell ill, and Marlon hurried from New York to see her in the hospital. She had been disturbed by the wave of critical publicity that had followed her son's walkout on *The Egyptian.*

"Bud, I want you to get along with people," she told him from her hospital bed. "I want you to love people instead of fighting them. Don't fight with the studio, Bud. Don't fight with anyone. Try to get along."

She died on March 31, 1954, at the age of fifty-four. On the following day Twentieth Century-Fox announced that it had settled its dispute with Marlon Brando. He would appear in *Désirée,* and the $2 million lawsuit for damages on *The Egyptian* would be dropped. Marlon admitted that he had followed his mother's wishes in seeking a settlement with Fox.

He talked about his mother to Clifford Odets one evening after her death. The two men had dinner in Hollywood, and as Marlon was driving home along a dark, narrow street, he told the playwright, "When I was a boy, she was beautiful and tender, and I loved her. But when I needed her and reached out for her, she wasn't there. I thought I could help her solve her problem through her love for me, but she was weak, and when she didn't respond I thought that meant there *was* no love for me. I turned my back on her, but gradually, through psychoanalysis, I learned to understand both my mother *and* my father.

"It was just in time. Mother got sick, and she was in a hospital. One night when I was away from the hospital, she got bad and began to die. But she told the doctors, 'I won't die until I can hold my son's hand.' Somehow she managed to stay alive until I got there—and then she held my hand, and she died."

As Marlon told the story he was overcome with tears. He raced the car down the dark street at sixty-five miles an hour, and with his vision almost blinded, he swerved the car from side to side. Odets feared they would both be killed, but Marlon regained control of the car and himself. Odets believed at that moment Marlon seemed able to make his own terms with his life's conflicting forces.

Dodie Brando remained a strong influence in her son's life, and for years afterward his home was dominated by a portrait painted of her at thirty-seven, when she was still vital and lovely. He wanted to remember her that way, but too often the memory of her tragic failing returned.

A friend once took Marlon to see *Long Day's Journey Into Night* during its New York run, with the prospect that he might appear in the film version. Marlon sat stolidly as the play depicted the deterioration of Eugene O'Neill's mother through drugs.

"This is a lousy play," Marlon muttered, leaving before it was over.

Désirée brought an end to the series of stunning film performances by Marlon Brando. He was cast as Napoleon, a role that has long defied interpretation by dramatists and actors. Marlon himself was baffled by the role.

"How do you see Napoleon?" Brando asked Henry Koster, the German-born director of *Désirée*.

"I see him as a great extrovert—loud, bombastic, commanding," said Koster.

Brando grinned. "That's hardly my style."

"But perhaps you can get some of that quality," Koster continued. "I think a man who made such history must have had spectacular presence. He must have had a gift for presenting himself to his court, to his troops, to the people."

Koster showed Brando likenesses of Napoleon, and the actor was struck by the resemblance to himself. "Do you see any other dimensions in the man?" Brando asked.

"You can read ten different books and get ten different interpretations," said Koster. "But I believe he was self-conscious about his size. He was only five feet, six inches, but he didn't want to be considered a small man. I think it's significant that so many of the great men of history have been shorter than average. Maybe there's something to being short and ambitious."

If the interpretation made any impression on Brando, it wasn't apparent. He concerned himself with the physical aspects, building up his nose with putty for a more Napoleonic profile, and combing his forelock forward. He mastered the resemblance, but Marlon never approached an understanding of the character. The ignominy of performing an unwanted role caused something in his creative instinct to rebel. Midway in the filming he found himself unable to remember his lines. He froze in the simplest scenes, and Koster called for take after take. In one scene Brando was required to issue a command to an officer. On the twentieth take, Brando finally delivered the line correctly. Koster printed the scene, even though he was dissatisfied with it; he feared he would never get another one.

As filming of *Désirée* continued, Marlon made an effort to remedy the situation. He locked himself inside his dressing room and composed new dialogue for himself. Koster managed to convince him it was no improvement. Marlon then tried to satirize his dialogue, but that didn't help, either. He realized it was an empty, meaningless costume drama, and so did the reviewers. "Just a fancy (and sometimes fatuous) façade," said Bosley Crowther in the *New York Times*.

Marlon remembered *Désirée* as "a serious retrogression and the most shaming experience of my life."

During the filming of *Désirée*, Marlon was visited daily by his guest in California, a nineteen-year-old French girl named Josiane Mariani-Berenger. It was remarkable that the gossip columnists

With Michael Rennie, Désirée, *1954*   *Norman Michaels Productions*

made no mention of Miss Berenger's presence; they had devoted space to his dates with others: Rita Moreno, Movita, Susan Cabot, Pier Angeli, Charlotte Austin. But the columnists were unaware of the French beauty, who would soon be linked with Marlon Brando in newspapers throughout the world.

As was true of most of Marlon's girls, she was petite, dark-haired and foreign. Born in the village of Bandol on the Riviera, she had gone to New York to become tutor to the children of a psychiatrist. One day she was in the psychiatrist's office when a door opened, and Marlon Brando entered. He was visiting Dr. Mittelman in the same office, and he exchanged a few pleasantries with the well-formed French girl. He saw her again when a college student brought her to a party at Stella Adler's house. Marlon cut in and monopolized Josiane for the rest of the evening. After they had been acquainted for two hours, she told interviewers later, he proposed marriage. At least he proposed that she accompany him to Hollywood while he made *Désirée*.

As soon as the film was completed, Marlon flew to France with Josiane. He vacationed in Paris for a couple of weeks, then journeyed southward to the little fishing village of Bandol, west of Toulon. There he met Josiane's mother and stepfather, a stolid fisherman. Marlon and Josiane spent two days speeding between Marseilles and Toulon on a motorscooter, and he ate huge quantities of bouillabaisse made by her mother from sea food Josiane's stepfather had caught. Marlon awoke one morning to discover that the Bandol newspaper had published an announcement: "Mr. and Mrs. Paul Berenger are happy to announce the betrothal of their daughter, Josiane, to Mr. Marlon Brando."

The news became headlines in the international press, and it came as a surprise, especially to Marlon. But he played the gallant role. When reporters gathered at the Berenger home on a cliff overlooking the Mediterranean, Marlon greeted them with Josiane and declared, "I consider myself engaged to this lovely girl, and I gave her an engagement ring I bought for her. I wanted to make it official because I know in small towns when a man is staying with the family of a lovely girl, the people start to talk immediately." He noted that his fiancée was crying, and he remarked, "She is a shy girl and not used to having her innermost feelings exposed to everyone."

When asked if the American actor really intended to marry his stepdaughter, the fisherman Berenger replied ominously, "He had better."

Brando remained in Bandol for four days, then left for Rome. He arrived, according to press reports, with a blond Italian beauty. But he said rumors that he had abandoned Josiane were "spittoon rubbish." "I love Josie," he declared. "This is not a one-night stand." She went to church in Bandol to pray for his early return. She told reporters, "I love him and he loves me, and there is nothing else."

When Marlon arrived in New York aboard the S.S. *United States,* he scoffed at hints the engagement was publicity-inspired: "If it were a big publicity stunt, I would be stupid to admit it. If it weren't, it speaks for itself. It's stupid to deny it. People will think what they want." Josiane arrived by air, and they posed for photographers at his apartment above Carnegie Hall. He side-stepped questions about the differences between American and foreign girls: "Nationality is not important. In choosing a wife, I don't think it very important to question her nationality, provided she's not Joe Stalin's cousin." The wedding, he said, might be the following month. Well, maybe next summer.

Maybe not. He returned to Hollywood and she followed along, with talk of becoming an actress. She saw Marlon less and less, though he still insisted in interviews that they would be married. The affair drifted into limbo, and Josiane eventually returned to France.

It had been a strange, circuslike chapter in the public life of Marlon Brando, one which ran counter to all that he had claimed about the sanctity of his privacy. Never again would he be a party to spreading his private life on "the moldy bread of the commercial press."

11

Something
a
Little
Lighter

*"I got tired of those intense pictures
where I had to beat people over the head
with a crocodile,
yelling and screaming all the time."*

"A SONG AND DANCE IS PART OF AN ACTOR'S TRADE; HE SHOULD BE ABLE
to dance a jig or tell a joke as part of his bag of tricks. I've always
played lugubrious, heavy things and neglected this side of the
entertainment business too long."

That was Marlon Brando's rationale for accepting the role of Sky
Masterson in *Guys and Dolls*. He had originally declined the offer,
but the producer, Samuel Goldwyn, was Hollywood's most relent-
less persuader. After failing with various pressures on Brando,
Goldwyn enlisted the help of Joe Mankiewicz, who had agreed to
direct *Guys and Dolls*. Mankiewicz, who was in Europe completing
The Barefoot Contessa, cabled Brando: UNDERSTAND YOU'RE APPRE-
HENSIVE BECAUSE YOU'VE NEVER DONE MUSICAL COMEDY. YOU HAVE
NOTHING TO WORRY ABOUT BECAUSE NEITHER HAVE I. LOVE, JOE.
Brando decided he would play Sky Masterson after all.

He trained for the role. The frustration of *Désirée* had caused
him to overeat, so that he weighed a hundred and ninety pounds;
he trimmed down to a hundred and sixty-five on a diet of steak
and vegetables. He took dancing lessons with the choreographer,
Michael Kidd, who commented that Marlon "moves like a prize

105

With Sheldon Leonard, Stubby Kaye,
Frank Sinatra, Guys and Dolls, *1955*

Samuel Goldwin Productions

fighter—very light on his feet; a little heavy for ballet." Marlon spent forty-five minutes daily with a vocal coach who praised his "singer's palate." But Marlon's singing was barely passable; sound men had to splice together pieces of various sound tracks to achieve a complete song.

Brando thoroughly enjoyed the song-and-dance training and the freedom from the pressure of establishing a heavily dramatic character. He socialized, both on the Goldwyn lot and at parties, and other members of the company were surprised to find him both gay and gallant. Samuel Goldwyn gave a barbecue dinner at his house, and his wife was concerned because she had never tried to barbecue before. Brando appeared in a well-tailored suit and spent an hour helping her light the coals, adjust the fire and cook the steaks.

He also attended a party at the house of Jean Simmons, who was playing Sarah Brown in *Guys and Dolls*. During the evening he spent some time conversing with Irene Sharif, who was designing the costumes for *Guys and Dolls*. She suddenly noticed that a large costume-jewelry ring was missing from her finger and started searching for it. Marlon helped her, then said, "Look in the bottom of your glass." She gazed into her highball glass and there was the ring. She hadn't noticed that he had removed it.

Frank Sinatra had asked Mankiewicz for the role of Nathan Detroit in *Guys and Dolls*, and the director was willing. Sam Goldwyn immediately saw the box-office appeal of Brando and Sinatra in the same film. Sinatra realized his mistake after he signed a contract for *Guys and Dolls;* Brando's role as Sky Masterson was more romantic and appealing. Sinatra began to sulk.

Brando had hoped to borrow some musical expertise from Sinatra. When the two met, Brando remarked, "You know, Frank, I'm new at this musical racket. So I'd appreciate it if you'd rehearse with me beforehand. I'll come to your dressing room, meet you in the rehearsal hall, anywhere you say."

Sinatra eyed him coldly. "Look, Brando," he snapped, "don't give me that Method-actor shit."

Brando was stunned. He couldn't believe that one actor would turn down another's request for help. The tension between the pair grew, and when they appeared for their first scene together, everyone on the set was aware of their lack of cordiality. Marlon reacted characteristically: he blew his lines. The scene was a simple exchange of Damon Runyon banter, but Marlon failed again and again. After twenty times, he finally completed the scene. Sinatra, who dislikes more than two takes of any scene, was furious.

Their relations did not improve. Sinatra suspected Mankiewicz of favoring Brando, with whom he had worked in *Julius Caesar.* The *Guys and Dolls* company divided into two factions, with Brando, Mankiewicz and Jean Simmons on one side and Sinatra and his entourage on the other.

Brando seemed to delight in needling Sinatra. During musical numbers, he mouthed the lyrics to the prerecorded music and performed perfectly until the last line, forcing a repeat of scene. By the end of production, the two stars barely spoke to each other off camera. The Goldwyn publicity chief, David Golding, arranged for Richard Avedon to come from New York to shoot special photography for *Vogue* magazine. Avedon wanted to photograph Sinatra and Brando together, and negotiations continued for days. Finally Golding convinced the two actors to pose outside the studio stage on a Saturday morning. Avedon set up his camera, and Golding knocked at Sinatra's dressing room.

"Where's Marlon?" Sinatra asked.

"In his dressing room," Golding said. "I'm going to get him."

"When he's there, *then* I'll come," said Sinatra.

Golding knocked on Brando's dressing room.

"Where's Frank?" Brando asked. Golding went through the same routine. Finally the publicity man arranged a signal so that Sinatra and Brando could emerge from their dressing rooms simultaneously. They posed for Avedon with seeming camaraderie, then promptly returned to their respective dressing rooms.

At the conclusion of filming, Sam Goldwyn gave a party for the cast and members of the press on one of the *Guys and Dolls* sound stages. Marlon arrived early and stayed throughout the evening, dancing with Mrs. Goldwyn and other female guests and playing the drums in the orchestra. Frank Sinatra did not appear.

On the day that Marlon was collecting his belongings to leave the Goldwyn lot, he was visited by the producer. "Marlon, my boy," said the producer grandly, "you have been such a vonderful performer in the role of Sky Matterson that I vant to give you a token of my appreciation. Come outside." Goldwyn escorted him to the studio street and gestured toward a shining new Thunderbird convertible.

Brando responded with boyish glee. He jumped into the car, raced it around the studio area, then took secretaries for terrifying rides through nearby streets—he declined to wear his corrective lenses while driving.

"And to think," he marveled, "Mr. Goldwyn gave me this out of gratitude. He doesn't want anything from me."

Not true. When *Guys and Dolls* was ready for release, Goldwyn pleaded with Marlon to attend the premieres in New York and Chicago. It was counter to Marlon's principles—but how could he refuse the kindly old producer who had given him the Thunderbird?

Rain was pouring out of the neon-tinted sky on the night of the *Guys and Dolls* premiere at the Capitol Theater in Manhattan, but a youthful crowd was packed deep on both sides of Broadway. As Marlon's limousine inched southward toward the theater, fans clambered on the hood and roof and tried to break the windows; to Marlon it was like being trapped in a submarine.

When he stepped into the brilliant light in front of the Capitol, a human roar reverberated through Times Square. Suddenly the throng on the opposite side of Broadway broke through the rope barrier and rushed toward the theater. "It was the most terrifying moment of my life; I thought surely I was going to die," Marlon said afterward. Two mounted policemen galloped into the void between the mob and Brando. The onrush stopped immediately, and foot officers pushed the crowd back across the street.

Police surrounded Marlon in front of the theater and almost carried him through the lobby to the backstage area. When he got there, he discovered a document in his hand. It was a summons to appear in a lawsuit over a script that Sam Spiegel was alleged to have stolen.

"Before I die," Marlon said, "I want to meet the ingenious man who served me that summons. A truly remarkable man."

With the aid of Goldwyn's selling campaign and the box-office draw of Marlon Brando and Frank Sinatra, *Guys and Dolls* was a huge commercial success. But the production was heavy-handed, and the charm of the Runyon fable remained unrealized. Brando was determined never to attempt another musical.

Marlon said when he first saw *The Teahouse of the August Moon* in New York, "I laughed so hard I almost ended up beating the hat of the lady in front of me." He returned to see the play three times and decided he wanted to do *Teahouse* as his next film. MGM, which had purchased the film rights, readily agreed. "If Marlon had wanted to play Little Eva," said production chief Dore Schary, "I would have let him."

It had been assumed that Brando would play the role of Fisby, the Army captain who tried to introduce American ways to occupied Okinawa. But Marlon preferred Sakini, the shrewd native interpreter. Converting himself to a Japanese was a punishing process. After hours of experimenting, make-up artists devised a rubber lid that was cemented around Marlon's eyes, filling in the tear ducts. He was coated with a yellowish make-up and outfitted with protruding teeth and a black wig. He placed himself on a rigid diet to rid himself of his well-fed appearance.

A veteran MGM producer, Jack Cummings, was assigned to produce the movie. He suggested that Brando be sent to Japan two months before locations were to begin so the actor could absorb the language and Oriental mannerisms. The studio declined the extra expense, and it proved to be poor economy. So Marlon arrived in Japan shortly before production was to begin and encountered enormous difficulties with the language. Not understanding either the meaning or the cadence of Japanese, he had to learn all of his Japanese dialogue by rote, listening hour after hour to a tape recorder. He refused the shortcut of having his Japanese dialogue dubbed.

His English dialogue was also a problem. He listened to Japanese speak English, noted their rhythms, their difficulty in pronouncing *r, l* and *f.* But if he reproduced their speech precisely, his English dialogue would have been unintelligible to American audiences. So he had to adapt his own variation of Japanese English.

Brando, whose contract included director approval, agreed to Daniel Mann, whom he had known as a teacher at the Actors Studio and who had directed such films as *Come Back, Little Sheba* and *The Rose Tattoo.* For the role of Captain Fisby, MGM cast its most serviceable leading man, Glenn Ford. A Japanese actress, Machiko Kyo, was hired as Lotus Blossom, Eddie Albert as Captain McLean, and Louis Calhern as Colonel Purdy.

The American film makers arrived in the ancient Japanese capital of Nara and encountered trouble immediately. The language

With Machiko Kyo and Glenn Ford,
TeaHouse of the August Moon, 1956

difficulty was not only Brando's; it existed at every level of production. The hurry-up methods of the Hollywood crew could not mesh with the meticulous ways of the Japanese. Tensions rose.

Louis Calhern strove to keep up the company's morale. "Don't get upset; this is going to be a marvelous picture," he counseled his short-tempered co-workers. But Calhern himself was coming apart. He had been sent to Japan early, and except for two days of tests with Brando and Ford in Tokyo, he hadn't worked. He brooded about the recent failure of his marriage to a young wife. When the film company came back to the Nara Hotel after the day's shooting, Calhern was on the verandah, drinking glass in hand. He listened to accounts of the day's travails and advised patience. By the end of the evening, he was thoroughly drunk.

One day the company returned to the hotel to hear the news: "Louie's dead."

That night several of the film makers gathered in Calhern's hotel room while a local Catholic priest read a service. Glenn Ford recalled that Calhern had told him a few days before: "If anything happens to me, don't let them bury me in this godforsaken place." Calhern's remains were rushed to a U.S. Army base so they could be flown to America without any red-tape delay. Paul Ford, who had played Colonel Purdy on Broadway, was dispatched to Japan to replace Calhern.

The tragedy brought further upset to the film company. Adding to the tension was the feud between Marlon Brando and Glenn Ford. It was perhaps inevitable. Ford was the studio-bred Movie Star, Brando the stage-trained Method Actor. Their life styles, philosophy and approach to film acting were totally unlike.

Some observers believed the difficulty started when Nara school-children thronged the movie location for a glimpse of Brando. Ford seemed disturbed that so much attention was being paid to Brando by the Japanese, and by members of the *Teahouse of the August Moon* company.

One of the first scenes on the Nara location involved five hundred extras and complicated speeches to the assembled Okinawans by Ford and Brando. Twenty-eight takes were needed. Ford's remarks in English had to be rendered in Japanese by Brando, and Ford somehow fed Brando the wrong cues.

During another scene with extensive dialogue, Brando interrupted the shooting and asked the director, "Danny, do you see where I am?" Mann realized that Ford had gradually altered his position so that Brando, in order to play to him, was facing away from the camera. Later during the filming of the same sequence, Ford complained that Brando had done the same thing.

Mann tried to call a halt to the upstaging. He invited both actors to conference and told them, "Look, fellows, there's a kind of competition going on here, and it doesn't make sense. You're just creating additional problems to what is already a difficult picture. Now, why don't we quit this silly childishness and get down to business?"

Both actors seemed chastened by the lecture, and their demeanor improved—for a while. A cherished tale recounted by *Teahouse* veterans concerned the Battle of the Cookies. One day Brando was passing Ford's dressing room.

"Marlon," Ford called.

"Yeah?" said Brando.

"Marlon, did you take some of my cookies?"

"Huh?"

"Did you take some of my cookies from my dressing room?"

"Your cookies?"

"Yes. I have them flown over from the States. And some of them have been missing. If you want some of my cookies, just ask me and I'll give them to you. But don't take them without asking."

"Glenn, I didn't take your goddam cookies. Honest to God, I didn't."

The matter seemed settled. Then one day Marlon was passing Ford's dressing room. Ford was not inside, and Marlon noticed on his dressing table a package of cookies newly arrived from the United States. Marlon glanced around and noted that no one was watching. He entered Ford's room, carefully strewed the cookies on the floor and methodically stamped them into crumbs.

Bad weather afflicted *The Teahouse of the August Moon,* and after thirty days of steady rain, the company was ordered back to Culver City. The teahouse and other sets were transported to the back lot of MGM, but somehow the fragile comedy did not survive the journey. The movie did well at the nation's box offices, but the delicacy of wit and the subtle encounter of American do-gooders and Oriental realists had been lost somewhere along the way.

Twice Joshua Logan had almost directed Marlon Brando. Irene Mayer Selznick had sent Logan the script of *A Streetcar Named Desire,* and he was enthusiastic about directing the play. But at the same time Tennessee Williams had solicited Elia Kazan as director, and the playwright's choice prevailed.

When Logan was planning the film version of *Mister Roberts,* which he had directed and co-authored on the stage, the producers felt that Henry Fonda was too old to repeat his role on the screen. Fonda was willing to play the role of the ship's physician, and Marlon Brando was to play Roberts. But Brando became unavailable because of his embroilment with Twentieth Century-Fox over *The Egyptian.* The producers assigned Fonda as Roberts and John Ford as director.

When Josh Logan acquired the film rights to his friend James Michener's novel *Sayonara,* the director—as did most film makers at that time—thought first of Marlon Brando as star. But Logan feared the leading role would seem unrewarding to Brando. Michener's hero was a priggish Air Force major whose Southern prejudices would not allow him to marry the Japanese actress he loved. The role was overshadowed by Joe Kelly, another Air Force man, whose own devotion to a Japanese girl led him to suicide. To Logan's surprise, Brando seemed intrigued by the role of Major Lloyd Gruver. He had become profoundly interested in the Japanese during his *Teahouse* location, and he saw *Sayonara* as a possible bridge of understanding between the United States and Japan.

Brando conferred with Logan on the balcony of the director's New York apartment. "Any actor can play the Joe Kelly part," said Brando. "It's all written out. But this Southerner is a challenge. It'd be interesting to play someone who was pompous and superior and square."

Their talks continued at Logan's country place, where the director occupied the time by pruning the flower bushes in his garden.

"One thing about the script bothers me," said Brando.

"What's that?" asked Logan.

"The ending, where Gruver leaves Japan and the Japanese girl goes back to the theater. I don't like it."

"But if he marries her, then it becomes a typical Hollywood happy ending. There's no truth to the story."

"Why not? People of different races are marrying all the time. Why avoid the issue? Face the fact that an American Southerner could marry a Japanese girl."

Brando didn't say so, but he made up his mind to undertake *Sayonara* after watching Logan prune his garden. "Anyone who cares that much about living things must be a sensitive person," he later said.

Although he was inwardly agreed to the film, Brando continued his discussions with Logan and the producer, William Goetz. The three men met at Goetz's home in California, and Brando stated flatly, "I won't do the part unless I can marry the Japanese girl."

"As far as I'm concerned," said Goetz, "you can marry her."

"I think we should consult Paul Osborne," said Logan. "After all, it's his script, and we shouldn't make a major change like this unless he agrees."

Logan telephoned the writer, who expressed hearty agreement: "Why didn't we think of that before? The other ending was *Madame Butterfly* all over again. Marlon's suggestion is a wonderful idea."

Logan relayed the information to Brando. Goetz added that Brando would be consulted on all major casting. "All right, Marlon," the producer said, "will you play the part?"

"I'll talk to you again tomorrow," Brando said, starting to depart. His exit was halted by an anguished cry from Josh Logan: "No, Marlon! I can't wait another second!"

The astonished Brando mumbled, "All right, I'll do it."

Brando embarked on preparations for *Sayonara*, assisting in tests for the other roles. Miyoshi Umeki had previously been signed for the role of Joe Kelly's sweetheart, and Red Buttons was under consideration for Kelly. Buttons was known as a borscht-circuit comedian who had had a brief career as a television star, but Logan knew he had appeared in Broadway plays. Brando observed the filming of a test with Buttons and Miss Umeki and agreed with Logan that the comedian was right for Joe Kelly.

The biggest casting problem was Katsumi, the Japanese sweetheart of Major Gruver. She would have to be Japanese, beautiful, tall enough to play male roles in an acting troupe, able to speak fluent English and sing soprano, and knowledgeable in such Japanese customs as the tea ceremony.

It seemed impossible to find such a girl. Logan traveled to Japan, Honolulu and San Francisco to interview candidates. Film tests were made of Japanese girls in England. At one point Audrey Hepburn was considered as a substitute Japanese. Finally, Goetz and Logan decided on Shirley Yamaguchi, an actress in Japanese movies.

Then one day a Warner Bros. talent scout spotted a tall, lovely Japanese girl at a Nisei festival in Los Angeles. She was Miiko Taka, a second-generation Japanese who worked in a travel bureau. She went to the studio for an interview with Logan, and he tested her alone on film, then arranged for another test with Brando. First, Brando conversed with her in her dressing room. He talked quietly with her for half an hour. When he emerged from the dressing room, he nodded his assent to Logan. Within three weeks, Miiko Taka was playing her first movie scene, running along the banks of a Kyoto canal.

During the filming Brando devoted special attention to Miiko Taka and to the other newcomers in the cast. James Garner, who had recently been signed to a term contract at Warner Bros., found himself doing his first scene in *Sayonara* with Marlon Brando in the back seat of a taxi. Brando noticed that Garner's palms were sweating.

"What's the matter?" Brando asked.

"I'm scared," Garner admitted.

"What about?"

"This is my first important picture. I'm scared to death."

"Don't be afraid. Relax. You got any problem, just ask me."

Brando advised Garner on acting matters during their scenes together. Brando also noticed the tenseness of Red Buttons, and he passed along whispered advice: "Raise your chin a little bit; from that angle, the camera will pick up three chins."

Brando and Logan began with agreement on major matters, including Marlon's Southern accent. He had adapted both the speech and the attitudes of classmates he had observed at Shattuck; he remembered the veneer of charm over their cold-blooded bigotry. Logan, familiar with Southern accents from his Louisiana childhood, found Brando's unerring.

Logan consented to Brando's desire for improvisation. The director agreed that the role of Lloyd Gruver was not well defined in the script, and impromptu inventions could very well improve it. Logan instructed the cinematographer to light the sets so Marlon would be free to move at will. Logan also told the other actors to be prepared to reply to Brando's lines, whether or not they appeared in the script. The result was a greater sense of realism to a tale that was heavily romantic.

There was disagreement in other areas, and at times Brando seemed to be testing the strength of his will against that of the director's.

One of the last scenes in *Sayonara* took place in the wig room of the Japanese theater, when the major came to tell the actress that they would marry. When the rehearsal began, Marlon stormed into the room, grabbed Miiko Taka and shouted his intention to marry her.

Logan was astonished at the fury of Brando's performance. "Marlon, this isn't right," the director commented. "We can't have you behave in such an inhuman manner."

"Why the hell shouldn't I?" Brando demanded.

"Because it destroys the mood of the scene!" Logan declared. In a moment the two men were shouting at each other while the film crew stared in silent amazement. Logan noticed the effect on the

With Miiko Taka, Sayonara, *1957*

With James Garner, Sayonara

Warner Bros.

With Miiko Taka, Sayonara

movie workers and suggested that he and Marlon continue the argument in his dressing room.

The actor was no less adamant in private: "Goddammit, that's the way the scene should be played!"

"Marlon, you're supposed to be playing a mature man," Logan argued. "You must be in charge of the situation at all times. If you come charging in like a bull elephant, you'll alienate the audience."

"Bullshit! The audience expects it of me. I haven't played a violent scene in the whole picture."

Logan continued his persuasion that the major could be strong, but in a calm way. Brando finally agreed to play the scene somewhere between his own version and Logan's, and it was masterly.

"I never could have told Marlon how to play that scene; it had to come from the flame within him," Logan remarked later. "I realized afterward that the son of a bitch made *me* get mad at him so he could find out the way to do it."

Another vital scene came when the major arrived at the scene of the double suicide of Joe Kelly and his Japanese girl friend. As Brando started to slide open the shoji door, Logan commented, "Oh, Marlon, I don't think you ought to open the door without knocking."

Brando stared at him. "Why should I knock? They're dead."

"You know that, but still, you're a Southern gentleman, and no Southern gentleman would enter someone else's bedroom without knocking, whether they're dead or not."

Brando exploded. "That's the goddamnedest thing I ever heard!"

Again, a furious argument before the entire crew. Finally Marlon said, "All right, I'll do it if we shoot it both ways."

Logan agreed, and Marlon played the scene by removing his shoes, hesitating, tapping lightly on the screen, then slipping the door ajar. It was perfect.

"All right, let's take the other shot," Logan said.

"What for?" Marlon asked.

"So we can shoot it your way."

"Forget it." Again, Logan concluded that Brando was employing argument to help him locate the right way to do the scene.

Logan gave no instructions for the scene when Marlon entered the bedroom and saw the bodies of his two friends. He ordered the camera to roll, and Brando walked into the room. Overcome with emotion, he muttered, "Oh God, oh my God, oh God, oh God!" He knelt beside the bed and lifted a lifeless hand.

"There's no blood on this hand," he said to Logan.

"Cut!" said the director. "No, Marlon, there's no blood."

"Why not? There must be blood."

"Marlon, do you know what the blood would do? It would destroy the scene. It would distract the audience from the romantically sad deaths of these two people."

"I can't play the scene without blood."

The argument continued until a compromise was reached:

Marlon would lift the hand above the frame of the camera so the audience wouldn't know if it was bloodied or not.

When Marlon wasn't involved in power struggles with Logan, he was relaxed and affable. He demonstrated his prankishness one night in Kyoto when he telephoned William Goetz and posed as a drunken American newspaperman. He said he was planning to release a story exposing the American film company for paying substandard wages to Japanese workers. The producer grew apoplectic until Brando revealed his true identity.

The company returned to Burbank to complete *Sayonara* at the studio. It had been a long, tedious film, and everyone was looking forward to its conclusion. With four days to go, Logan arrived on the set one morning to find Brando looking sheepish. His arm was in a sling.

"Listen—don't blame him," Brando said.

"Don't blame whom?" Logan asked, his concern growing.

"My stand-in. It wasn't his fault. We were just sparring around, and I happened to slip, that's all. I don't think it's broken."

"Have you seen a doctor?"

"Yes. He thinks I'll be able to work in three or four weeks. Six weeks at the outside. You can do all the scenes with me away from the camera."

Logan was crestfallen. "Can you do any kind of action at all?"

"Oh, I can move my arm like this," Marlon said, rotating it slightly. "I just can't do this—" He slapped his arm and pulled it upward in an obscene Italian gesture, then roared with laughter and ran away.

Sayonara ended with good feeling, and it proved to be an immensely popular film, winning Miyoshi Umeki and Red Buttons Academy Awards for their supporting performances. Marlon Brando's opinion: "There's a lot of hearts and flowers and soft violins in it, but beneath the romance it attacks prejudices that exist on the part of the Japanese as well as on our part."

Sayonara was also notable for Marlon Brando's most famous and unhappiest encounter with a journalist.

Truman Capote had proposed a piece of reportage on the Kyoto location for *The New Yorker*. Josh Logan was opposed; he remembered how Capote had lampooned members of a *Porgy and Bess* troupe in Russia for a *New Yorker* article. Brando was more receptive. "The man's got to earn a living," he reasoned.

"Not at our expense," said Logan. "He'll make idiots of us all."

One day after filming had begun, Logan saw Capote with Cecil Beaton, the photographer, at the registration desk of the Miyako Hotel in Kyoto. Logan wrapped Capote in a bear hug and carried him outside the hotel. "But I'm not going to write about the picture," the author protested; "I'm just going to do a piece on Brando." Logan counseled Brando to avoid seeing Capote, and Brando said he wouldn't.

But he did. He entertained Capote during a long evening in his hotel suite. When the article appeared many months later, it began innocently enough, with a Japanese maid showing Capote the way to the room of "Marron." Another maid was inside the Brando suite, and Marlon commented, "They kill me. They really kill me. The kids, too. Don't you thing that they're wonderful, don't you love them—Japanese kids?"

The rest of the article reported the minute happenings of the evening, interspersed with Brando biography. As Capote reported it, the encounter appeared to have been a lengthy monologue by Brando. A Brando comment: "The last eight, nine years of my life have been a mess. Maybe the last two have been a little better. Less rolling in the trough of the wave. Have you ever been analyzed? I was afraid of it at first. Afraid it might destroy the impulses that made me creative, an artist. A sensitive person receives fifty impressions where somebody else may only get seven. Sensitive people are so vulnerable; they're so easily brutalized and hurt because they *are* sensitive. The more sensitive you are, the more certain you are to be brutalized, develop scabs. Never evolve. Never allow yourself to feel anything, because you always feel too much. Analysis helps. It helped me. But still, the last eight, nine years I've been pretty mixed up, a mess pretty much . . ."

The most revelatory part of the article—and the part that disturbed Marlon most when he saw it in print—was his reference to his mother's alcoholism: " . . . I didn't care any more. She was there. In a room. Holding on to me. And I let her fall. Because I couldn't take it any more—watch her breaking apart, like a piece of porcelain. I stepped right over her. I walked right out. I was indifferent. Since then, I've been indifferent."

Marlon's friends were astounded that he had been so candid with someone who was going to report their conversation. "How did it happen?" George Glass asked Marlon.

"Well, the little bastard spent half the night telling me all his problems," said Marlon. "I figured the least I could do was tell him a few of mine."

"An old trick," observed Glass. "Is there anything you'd like to do to get back at him?"

Marlon pondered. "Yeah. I'd like to beat him to death with a wet noodle."

12

Changes

*"Before people meet me,
they feel they know me.
I'm the kid who rides a motorcycle
and wears a black leather jacket
with crossbones painted on the back.
When I'm an old man
they'll still be asking me
where my hot rod is."*

MARLON BRANDO HAD CHANGED, THOUGH NOT IN THE PUBLIC CON-
sciousness. Long gone was Russell, the spirited racoon. Marlon
had taken the pet home to Libertyville and set it loose in the thick-
ets where he had roamed as a boy. Russell was at first bewildered,
then disappeared into hibernation.

Gone, too, was the motorcycle; Marlon had given it up "because
I saw too many guys picked out of trees." It had been years since
he wore jeans and a T-shirt, yet the public still clung to the early
image of Brando as The Slob. He had been astonished to find a new
crop of actors emulating him as he was in the *Streetcar* period.
The most notable was James Dean.

The comparison was natural. Dean was also a Midwestern boy
who burst from obscurity in a role directed by Elia Kazan. With
East of Eden and *Rebel Without a Cause,* Dean had established himself as the same brand of brooding, rebellious, inarticulate figure
that Brando had first played.

Dean had continued the characterization offscreen. He adopted
the T-shirt, jeans, slouch, motorcycle and unpredictable behavior
that had been associated with the early Brando. Marlon, seven
years Dean's senior, was appalled. At a party Marlon criticized
Dean for the obvious imitation. The younger actor was unreceptive,
and Brando ended the conversation by telling him, "You ought to
see a psychiatrist."

Marlon himself was still returning to New York after every picture to continue his therapy with Dr. Mittelman. He was also searching the religions and philosophies of the East, and he consulted a California mystic named Krishnamurti. He was so impressed with a book called *The Art of Loving,* by Erich Fromm, that he distributed copies to friends. He read the works of Arnold Toynbee and other historians, and the problems of America and the world occupied his thinking more and more. His growing awareness of world affairs prompted him to seek more control over his films. MCA was prepared to oblige him.

By 1955 a tremor of change had began to alter the foundations of the film industry. The advent of television had caused a ruinous decline in theater attendance, and the steel-tight grasp of the major companies was weakening. The vacuum of power was sensed by the talent agencies, particularly the giant Music Corporation of America. With the aggressive leadership of Jules Stein and Lew Wasserman, the agency was making deals which had been impossible during the absolute monarchies of the Harry Cohns and Louis B. Mayers. Studios now agreed to partnerships with stars they had once controlled. The stars selected their own properties, oversaw production and shared in the profits.

Brando's company was called Pennebaker Productions, after his mother's middle name. His associates in the firm were his father and George Englund, a young actor-director who had become a close friend of Marlon's. Pennebaker had a choice of studios for partnership. MCA selected Paramount.

In March 1956 Brando announced that his initial movie as an independent producer would be based on the work of the United Nations in its technical-assistance program. "There is no more exciting, romantic and important work being done in the world today than that accomplished by UN technical assistance," Brando told the press. "For sheer entertainment their stories are unrivaled and will be told with all the magic and impact that motion pictures can provide." Brando, Englund and a screen writer, Stewart Stern, embarked on a twenty-thousand-mile tour of Asia to research their project.

Marlon poured out his impressions from the journey when he returned: "I found so much to stimulate me that I couldn't begin to tell you in one conversation. . . . Americans don't even begin to understand the people of Asia. The average American couldn't tell you even three of the main bodies of land that comprise Indonesia, what the capital is, what the natives' attitude toward the Dutch is. . . . American prestige is dwindling among those countries of Asia while the great masses of China and Russia are waiting to gobble them up. Our understanding of Asians will never improve until we get out of the habit of thinking of the people as short, spindly-legged, buck-toothed little people with strange customs. . . . Except in Manila, where they went mad, the film fans in Asia are the most considerate and thoughtful I have ever seen. They stand at a distance and don't bother you. Often they give you little gifts. I must have gotten hundreds of them. . . . The industry, kindness and courtesy of the Japanese made a terrific impression on me. They seem to incorporate their religion into their daily life much more than we do. . . . An example of the Asian crowds was in Hong Kong. I went into a store to buy something, and a lot of people started peering through the window. By the time I came out, there was a big crowd, but no one pushed at me or asked for an autograph. Very quietly, they parted and made a path for me to walk through. . . . The Asians are looking to us for signs of friendship. I hope my picture will help. But it must be entertainment. If it's not entertainment, I have accomplished nothing, and I may have done irreparable harm."

When Pennebaker made its first Brando film three years later, it was a Western.

Since the Pennebaker offices were located at Paramount, Marlon often ate lunch in the studio commissary. It was there that he first met Anna Kashfi.

She was playing the leading feminine role in *The Mountain,* starring Spencer Tracy and Robert Wagner, and the studio biography stated that she had been born in Calcutta to Devi Kashfi, a civil engineer, and Selma Ghose. The biography also reported that she had: been schooled in a French convent in Calcutta and in the capitals of Europe where her father was employed in engineering projects; learned eight languages; studied classical dancing in India; been discovered for Indian films while in a class recital.

In 1955 she had been working as a model in London when Paramount issued a call for an Indian girl to appear in *The Mountain.* She was one of several young women flown to Paris to audition for Edward Dmytryk, director of the film, and Spencer Tracy. Both were impressed with Anna's beauty. It didn't matter that she had never acted; during most of *The Mountain* she would be semiconscious as the lone survivor of an airliner crash in the Alps. She was hired for the role.

After the European locations, she accompanied *The Mountain* troupe to Hollywood for the conclusion of the filming. That's when Brando spotted her. He requested an introduction from A. C. Lyles, assistant producer on *The Mountain.*

Brando began dating the olive-skinned beauty. A few months later Anna Kashfi fell ill with tuberculosis and entered the City of Hope Hospital in Duarte, east of Los Angeles. She had few friends in the United States, and Brando often visited her. After five months in the hospital she was released as cured, and Anna and and Marlon resumed their dating until he left for European locations of *The Young Lions.*

Marlon Brando and Montgomery Clift had been rivals for the position as America's best young actor. Clift came to films first, establishing with *The Search* and *Red River* in 1948 a new sensitivity in movie acting, which had previously been dominated by strong, two-dimensional leading men. Clift was the most acclaimed new actor in postwar films—until the advent of Marlon Brando.

Clift was sensitive about the threat to his newfound eminence, and Brando seemed to realize that. One day when Brando was still appearing in *Streetcar,* he roared his motorcycle down Madison Avenue. Spotting a figure peering in a store window, he stopped and asked, "Are you Montgomery Clift?"

"I am," said Clift with a pleased smile. "You're Brando; I recognize you."

"People tell me I remind them of you."

"Oh?"

"I don't think so." Brando returned to his motorcycle, kicked it alive and sped off.

They met on other occasions in New York and Hollywood, and the encounters were equally unsatisfactory. Clift considered Brando clownish and insensitive. Brando thought Clift was overly serious. "What's the matter with your friend Clift?" Brando asked Kevin McCarthy, who knew both actors. "He always seems like he's got a Mixmaster up his ass."

McCarthy once invited them both to his apartment for an antic evening during which all performed in a home movie. Clift posed reading a newspaper while his cigar burned a hole in it. Brando sneaked up behind Clift and snipped off his tie with a pair of scissors. They relaxed together for the first time. But they rarely met again until *The Young Lions.*

A veteran producer, Al Lichtman, had acquired the rights to Irwin Shaw's novel of World War II. He planned to film it for Twentieth Century-Fox on a $2 million budget and a forty-six-day schedule, using such contract players as Don Murray and Tony Randall. Edward Dmytryk, who was to direct it, believed *The Young Lions* a strong enough vehicle to warrant more important casting and a bigger budget. He sent the script to Montgomery Clift, whom he had directed in *Raintree County.* Clift accepted immediately. Agents of MCA proposed Marlon Brando for the role of the Nazi soldier; *The Young Lions* would allow Brando to rid himself of a remaining film commitment to Twentieth Century-Fox. Also, Brando's Pennebaker company could become a partner in the production, providing income and a tax advantage for Pennebaker.

Dmytryk met with Brando at the actor's rented home near the Sunset Strip. Marlon greeted the director in a Japanese kimono and squatted on the floor during the conference. He had read the Shaw novel, admired it, but believed the character of the Nazi, Christian, was too villainous. Dmytryk agreed that Christian could be made less ideological. "Go ahead and make the deal," Marlon said.

The third major role was originally assigned to Tony Randall. But Clift expressed doubts about Randall, and the part went to Dean Martin, whom MCA had been pushing for a dramatic role since he left the partnership with Jerry Lewis.

Members of *The Young Lions* company gathered in Paris for the beginning of production. Marlon Brando and Montgomery Clift met for a dinner together, and it proved a social failure. Brando conversed at length on his psychoanalysis, and as he had to James Dean and other troubled persons he met, Marlon said to Clift, "You ought to see a psychiatrist." Clift was deeply offended. Aware of his own problems, he had once sought help through psychoanalysis and then rejected it. He considered Brando's suggestion rude, and the two of them had no further contact during the filming. Fortunately, they had no scenes together, since their two characters did not meet in the script.

Brando was more sociable with pleasure-loving Dean Martin, and the two actors spent time together in the company of Parisian

The Young Lions, *1958*   *20th Century Fox*

beauties. One day Brando and Martin accompanied two French girls to the bar of the George V Hotel. Martin ordered a drink, and Brando asked for tea. Martin accidentally pushed the teapot in Brando's lap.

"Jesus Christ!" Brando screamed. He leaped up, unzipped his trousers, pulled them down and played a seltzer bottle on his scalded flesh. He was rushed to a hospital for treatment of the burns. As a distinguished American patient, he received the most attentive of service. In fact, he noted that every time his dressings needed to be changed, the hospital's nuns filled the room.

When Brando's burns had healed, he returned to *The Young Lions.* He had assumed a German accent and white-blond hair, and he sought ways to justify Christian's Naziism. This proved to be a source of argument between Brando and the novelist, Irwin Shaw. Brando insisted that "no race or nationality has a corner on the mistakes that are made." Being a partner in the enterprise, he was able to make his point prevail.

The Young Lions proved to be a film of mixed values. Some audiences were confused, others outraged by Brando's sympathetic portrayal of the Nazi warrior. But the shrewd characterizations by Clift, Brando and Martin, Dmytryk's sure hand with the warfare scenes, and the box-office appeal of the stars combined to make *The Young Lions* a moneymaker. It was to prove Brando's last unqualified commercial success for a dozen years.

When *The Young Lions* company returned to the United States for desert scenes at Borrego Springs in the Imperial Valley of California, Brando was visited by Anna Kashfi. The encounter proved fateful, for in the autumn of 1957 Anna revealed that she was pregnant. Marlon decided they would marry.

He wanted secrecy. He told his wishes to his new partners in Pennebaker, George Glass, whom he had first known as Stanley Kramer's partner and publicist, and Walter Seltzer, himself a one-time publicist turned producer. Glass, who had been a Los Angeles newspaperman and was familiar with legal shortcuts, knew of an attorney in Riverside, sixty miles distant, who could arrange the license without publicity. Brando was pleased with the arrangement. But then, in contradiction to his wishes for privacy, he went to downtown Pasadena to purchase a wedding ring—dressed in a flowing Hindu robe.

Marlon and Anna, accompanied by Seltzer and Glass, made the

The wedding of Anna and Marlon,   Wide World Photos
1957

journey to Riverside and accomplished their mission without detection. On the drive back to Los Angeles, Marlon seemed unconcerned about the coming nuptials. He occupied the trip by querying Seltzer about a male star with whom Seltzer had been closely associated. Seltzer described a peculiarity of the star: he was a public urinator. He had caused a scandal by urinating in front of a crowd of fans at a girl's college, once was almost arrested after relieving himself in the vestibule of a Boston–New York train.

The party returned to Brando's house for a perfunctory celebration. As Marlon passed through the kitchen within Seltzer's gaze, he paused for a mischievous commentary on Seltzer's story: he pissed into a sink full of dirty dishes.

The wedding was held at the Eagle Rock home of Marlon's aunt, Betty Lindemeyer—the same modest residence where he had stayed when he arrived to film *The Men.* Marlon's father was present, and a few friends of the family, and the brief service was read by the minister of a nondenominational church in North Hollywood. Marlon wore a dark-blue suit, white shirt and tie; his hair was still bleached from his role in *The Young Lions.* His bride was in a pale sea-green sari with a gold-embroidered white brocade blouse. They posed for a rather grimly smiling portrait that was released to the newspapers on the same day, October 11, 1957. She was twenty-three years old, ten years younger than the bridegroom.

The Hollywood establishment, through its spokeswomen Louella Parsons and Hedda Hopper, was pleased to see Marlon Brando settling down to marriage with the lovely Indian girl. Alas, Marlon had no intention of staying married. He had taken Anna as his bride only to legitimize their child. He intended to seek a divorce after a year of marriage.

While Marlon and Anna were honeymooning in the California desert, a factory worker announced from Cardiff, Wales, that the new Mrs. Marlon Brando was really Joan O'Callaghan, his daughter.

"Indian?" William Patrick O'Callaghan mused. "Well, I suppose she is, if you consider she was born in Calcutta. But she's our daughter, and both the missus and me were born in London."

He related a different story from the one in Anna's studio biography. He said that he had worked as a railway superintendent in Calcutta, where Joan spent her first thirteen years. Then the family moved to Cardiff, where Joan waited tables and worked as a cashier in a butcher shop. She became a model in London and changed her name to Anna Kashfi when she won the role in *The Mountain.* O'Callaghan attributed her olive skin to his French mother.

Anna countered with her own version: her father, Devi Kashfi, had died, and her mother had married O'Callaghan, whose name Anna assumed. She claimed her mother was an Indian, Selma Ghose, although reporters established that Anna's mother had been born in London and seemed unmistakably English. Then who was Selma Ghose? It turned out that a woman with the same name was the mother of two Indian girls Anna had known in her London career.

The controversy disturbed Marlon deeply. "I thought Anna had never worked before she came to Hollywood," he said to a companion, "and that she came from a fine Hindu family and background. I never doubted that she was a Hindu."

The marriage lasted less than the year he had intended. Within two months he departed for New York and Chicago, and he extended his trip. He returned to the home he had bought on top of Mulholland Drive, but he absented himself from the house for days at a time.

The baby was born May 11, 1958, at Cedars of Lebanon Hospital in Hollywood. It was a boy, and he was given the name of Christian Devi Brando. The first name came from Marlon's good friend, Christian Marquand, a French actor and director. Devi was the man Anna claimed to be her father, although researchers pointed out that the name meant "goddess" in Hindi.

Marlon Brando and Anna Kashfi separated officially on September 25, 1958. In April 1959 she appeared in Superior Court in Santa Monica to sue for divorce, charging that her husband's frequent absences left her lonely and afraid. He gave her a house and furnishings in Beverly Hills, a car, jewelry worth $9,000, $60,000 in cash, and payments of $440,000 for the following ten years. He also agreed to a $1,000 monthly support for their son.

It was an expensive finish to a marriage that had begun and ended quietly. Relations between Anna and Marlon would be less quiet later on.

13

Brando as Director

"The stage is made up of integrated groups
working toward one end.
The movies are departmentalized.
They make me feel like an exhaust pipe
running around looking for a motor."

PENNEBAKER PRODUCTIONS HAD REMAINED UNPRODUCTIVE, LARGELY because Marlon Brando could not make up his mind. George Englund, Marlon's first partner in Pennebaker, despaired of getting a decision from him for a film project and left the company. His successors, Walter Seltzer and George Glass, advised Marlon that Pennebaker would be classified as a personal service company—and hence lose its tax status—if it did not make movies.

Since Marlon could not agree on a vehicle for himself, Seltzer and Glass produced three films without him: *Shake Hands with the Devil,* starring James Cagney and Don Murray; *Paris Blues,* with Paul Newman, Joanne Woodward and Sidney Poitier; *The Naked Edge* with Gary Cooper and Deborah Kerr. *The Naked Edge* provided a good profit for Pennebaker.

But the future of Pennebaker depended on finding a vehicle for Marlon Brando. It finally came from another press agent who had turned producer, Frank Rosenberg. It was curious that Brando, who professed to abhor publicity, should become associated in his own company with three one-time press agents.

Searching for film projects as an independent producer, Frank Rosenberg spotted a brief review in *The New Yorker* of a novel, *The Authentic Death of Hendry Jones.* He read the book and saw its possibilities as a film. The author, Charles Neider, agreed to sell his book for $25,000.

At the time, Rosenberg was preparing the pilot film for a television series, and his writer was a newcomer, Sam Peckinpah. One day Peckinpah saw a copy of *The Authentic Death of Hendry Jones* in Rosenberg's office and asked to write the script. The producer agreed, despite Peckinpah's lack of experience in feature films.

Peckinpah's script seemed promising, and Rosenberg submitted it to his agency, MCA, which controlled much of Hollywood's production by submitting to the studios packages consisting of scripts, stars and directors. George Chasen, a top MCA agent, saw *The Authentic Death of Hendry Jones* as a possible vehicle for Marlon Brando.

A meeting was arranged in the garden of Walter Seltzer's house in Sherman Oaks. Brando arrived and took a chair in the sunshine, studying Rosenberg from behind dark glasses. The producer outlined his intentions for the production, and mentioned that "the script needs about six weeks' work."

"No, I love it just as it is," Brando declared. He changed his mind later, and after eight months the script was still being prepared.

During one of the early meetings, Rosenberg and Brando discussed possible directors for the film. The actor had been impressed by two films by young Stanley Kubrick. *The Killing* and *Paths of Glory.*

"We've got to get Kubrick," Brando declared.

"But do you think he can handle a big production like this one?" Rosenberg asked.

"There's no question about it. He's an extremely talented man."

Kubrick was hired. He insisted that the Peckinpah script had to be totally revised. Kubrick would write a new treatment with Calder Willingham. Weeks later they presented their treatment, and a meeting was held at Brando's house to discuss it. Present were Brando, Kubrick, Willingham, Rosenberg and Brando's agent and friend, Jay Kanter. Rosenberg began by saying, "Fellows, I don't think you can dramatize what you've got on paper."

The arguments began, and after long exchanges, Brando signaled to Rosenberg to join him in another room. When they were alone, Brando whispered, "These guys are talented; we must give them a chance to see what they can do."

Kubrick and Willingham began writing their version of the script, and story sessions were held regularly at Brando's Oriental-style home on the mountaintop. The meetings became ritual. Present were Brando, Rosenberg, Kubrick, Willingham and Carlo Fiore, a friend from Marlon's stage days who had been appointed Rosenberg's assistant. All were required to remove their shoes so they would not mar the teakwood floor. Kubrick also found it more comfortable to remove his pants, and he paced the living room in shirt and undershorts. Marlon sat on the floor with legs crossed; near him was a large Chinese gong which was part of the house's furnishings. The sessions began each morning with equanimity but became more heated as the day progressed. When a participant became overly zealous, Marlon lifted a mallet and struck the gong with two sharp blows. That was the signal for the discussion to cease and begin on a new and less heated basis.

While the script was being written, Producer Rosenberg began assembling the cast. The leading lady was to be a young virginal Mexican, and Rosenberg went to Mexico City to search for an actress who would play the role. He interviewed sixty girls until he found two sisters, Pina and Pilar Pellicer. Pina seemed especially poignant. She was brought to Hollywood and was given lessons to improve her English. In August 1958 she was put on the payroll, as was Karl Malden. Marlon had promised that he would be able to start filming on September 15.

The days dwindled down, September . . . November, and still no starting date. Calder Willingham had left the project, and Rosenberg hired a veteran film writer, Guy Trosper. "You'll like him," the producer assured Marlon. "He's expert, a real craftsman — and he's just as neurotic as you are."

The script sessions continued at Marlon's house, but the gong was being struck more regularly. It was apparent that the rapport between Brando and Kubrick was eroding with each script wrangle. The beginning of the end came during a meeting with Kubrick, Brando and the Pennebaker partners, Seltzer and Glass. When Brando was out of the room, Kubrick complained, "How can we get Marlon to stay away from the story?" The remark carried through the paper walls of the Brando house.

The break came when the film makers were discussing a Chinatown sequence which was shot and later cut from the finished film. Marlon was then enamored with France Nuyen, a French-Chinese beauty who had played Liat in the film version of *South Pacific.* "I think France Nuyen would be perfect for the role of the Chinese girl," Marlon suggested.

"I'll bet she can't act at all," Kubrick responded.

Brando's face turned to stone. He flicked his head in the direction of the kitchen. Rosenberg noted the cue and followed him out of the room.

"We gotta get rid of Kubrick," Marlon said grimly.

"Shit, he's been on the picture for twenty-six weeks, Marlon! We're supposed to start shooting in four weeks."

"We gotta get another director," Marlon said with finality. After a moment he added, "I think I'd like to direct the picture."

"Marlon, don't you think you ought to try to direct a picture that's not this big?" Rosenberg argued. "And also one that you're not appearing in? It's risky."

"Look, I can do it. If you don't move any further away from me than you are now, I can do it. Help me."

Rosenberg sighed and said, "Okay."

Brando informed MCA that Kubrick was through. Both met the following day with Rosenberg in the office of Jay Kanter at the MCA Building. There was an uncomfortable silence until Brando remarked, "I feel as though I'm sitting in a room with a ten-foot kangaroo." Kanter outlined the details for the dissolution of Kubrick's contract, and the meeting was over. The director was obviously upset by the sudden dismissal but he offered no argument. A press release declared that Kubrick had tendered his resignation "with deep regret because of my respect and admiration for one of the world's foremost artists, Marlon Brando." The reason given for his departure was that he wanted to prepare his own film, *Lolita*.

Time was now pressing. Paramount had built a huge reconstruction of early Monterey on the back lot. Other actors had been placed under contract for *One-Eyed Jacks,* as the film was now called—Katy Jurado, Slim Pickens, Ben Johnson. Locations had been prepared on the Monterey peninsula in Northern California.

On December 2, 1958, four weeks after his decision to direct, Marlon Brando began production in Monterey. Five days later he was two weeks behind schedule. A remarkable feat, accomplished because Marlon added new scenes that weren't in the script.

"I'm shooting a movie, not a schedule," he announced.

Production went slowly because Marlon was trying to adapt the Actors Studio system of improvisation to filming. He told the actors not to bother studying the script for the following day because he would be changing it. "There is nothing unusual about improvising in front of a camera," he insisted. "During the silent movies, they used to do it all the time. Actors are much freer in improvisation than when they are restricted by scripts."

Brando as director seemed far removed from the traditional Hollywood concept of the breed. One day he was directing Ben Johnson and Sam Gilman in a scene in which they murdered Larry Duran. The three actors were tense after enacting the scene several times to Brando's dissatisfaction. As Brando instructed them once more he suddenly stopped in midsentence and raised his chin so high that he could look backward. In that position he said to Karl Malden, who was sitting behind him, "Just wanted to see how you looked upside down, Karl."

Frank Rosenberg remained on the set throughout production, but his urgings could not induce Marlon to speed his pace. One day he was filming the Chinatown sequence with Lisa Lu, who had been cast as the Chinese sweetheart after Marlon had a falling out with France Nuyen. In the background was a pile of sticks, and Marlon spent an hour arranging them in the pattern he wanted.

On another day he was filming a scene without dialogue. The script called for Brando by the ocean, contemplating a necklace Pina Pellicer had returned to him because she felt his love was insincere. Rosenberg decided it was safe to leave the set, and told Marlon, "I'm driving over to Carmel for a couple of hours to buy some Christmas presents for my kids." The producer made the journey and returned to find the movie crew idle as Marlon sat on a rock overlooking the Pacific. Nothing had been filmed.

"What are you doing?" Rosenberg asked.

"I'm waiting for the right wave," Marlon explained.

Brando examined every costume, every prop. He spent hours talking quietly to the actors, urging them to act from within themselves, not merely to recite dialogue. He spent an entire day filming a single scene that lasted three minutes on the screen— 270 feet of film. He expended 11,000 feet of film to achieve it.

The movie was being filmed in Paramount's VistaVision process, which cost fifty cents per foot for film and processing. One day when Brando was expending footage with abandon, producer Rosenberg and the cinematographer, Charles Lang, stood behind the camera and chanted, "Half a buck, half a buck, half a buck . . ." They had hoped that their simple lesson in film economics might have an effect on Brando. It didn't.

Brando insisted that all one hundred and twenty members of the *One-Eyed Jacks* company be sent home from Monterey to celebrate Christmas with their families. Marlon himself returned alone to his Mulholland house, even though a brush fire was racing through the chaparral on nearby hills.

"But it's not safe to be there alone," he was warned.

"It's all right," he said. "If the fire gets too close, somebody will wake me up."

Shooting resumed at the same tedious pace after the holiday. The hierarchy of Paramount now began to express alarm. Barney Balahan, president of the company, had authorized the project and continued his support even when preproduction costs mounted to $500,000. But now it was obvious that the original budget of $1.8 million would not be met. The added cost worried the studio chief, Y. Frank Freeman, an easy-mannered but tough-minded Georgian. "I had my first heart attack on *The Ten Commandments*," said the studio head. "I had my second heart attack on *The Buccaneer*. This picture may give me my third heart attack."

"Gee Frank, it's only a movie," Rosenberg said.

"Yes, but it may break the company," said Freeman. "Barney made this deal, but I feel responsible for it. If I can't get it moving, I may resign."

Rosenberg reported the conversation to Brando, who refused to take it seriously. He continued to maintain his sense of humor. One day on location he was visited by a columnist, Erskine Johnson. For several minutes Brando peered at the ocean through a viewfinder used by directors to frame scenes. The assistant director, Chico Day, took Brando aside and told him, "Marlon, you're looking through the wrong end." Marlon grinned and said, "No wonder I'm behind schedule."

Frank Freeman was becoming more apoplectic after Marlon returned to the studio and continued shooting week after week on a fiesta sequence requiring hundreds of extras. Brando had said he planned to film three more weeks on the fiesta, but Freeman vowed in midweek: "I'm going to pull the plug on him Friday night. That's it. No more shooting."

Seltzer went to the *One-Eyed Jacks* set and told Marlon of Freeman's threat. "I think he's right," Seltzer remarked. "You've still got thirty pages of script to shoot, and you know that you can't use all that material. Why don't you shut down this afternoon and we'll

One-Eyed Jacks, *1961*   *Paramount*

have the writer compress the sequence so you can finish on Friday night?"

"Bullshit," Marlon replied. "I'm going to shoot every word in the script."

"But Freeman says he's going to pull the plug on Friday."

"I'll believe that when I see it."

Seltzer returned to Freeman and reported Brando's decision. "I may be his partner," Seltzer added, "but you're the one who made him the boss. It's your responsibility; you're running the studio. *You* tell him."

"All right, I will!" Freeman promised.

The two men marched to the *One-Eyed Jacks* set. Marlon's back was turned, but he sensed their arrival. He wheeled around, strode up to Freeman and gave him a bear hug. Freeman beamed at Marlon. "I've seen the rushes," said Freeman, "and you're doing just fine. Keep up the good work!"

They exchanged some pleasantries, and Freeman returned to his office. Marlon glanced over to Seltzer and thumbed his nose.

When would it ever end? The length of the filming of *One-Eyed Jacks* became a local joke, and producer Rosenberg added to the legend with a much-quoted remark to columnist Army Archerd: "This isn't a movie; it's a way of life."

Marlon continued to make *One-Eyed Jacks* in his own unorthodox manner. One of the sequences called for him to appear drunk. "I've never seen a really good drunk scene in a picture," he said. "I think the way to make it convincing is to *be* drunk."

And so he prepared for the scene by consuming a tumbler of vodka. He continued drinking vodka until he was unable to act or direct, and that was the end of filming for the day. He had purposely scheduled the scene for late Friday so he could sleep off the effects of the indulgence over the weekend. On the following Friday he scheduled the drunk sequence again, and the same routine ensued. He drank, filmed, passed out. At this time in the filming he was sleeping each night in his dressing room, so he did not have far to go when slumber began to overtake him.

On the day after one of the vodka Fridays, one of Brando's aides received a telephone call from columnist Earl Wilson in New York: "I got a tip that Marlon Brando was seen at Seventy-ninth Street and Madison with France Nuyen. Could that be true?"

"Impossible," said the aide. "Marlon is taking a long . . . rest this weekend after a hard week of shooting." But Marlon's bed was empty. Unknown to everyone, he had been flying to New York each weekend to see France Nuyen, with whom he had resumed a romance.

One-Eyed Jacks whimpered to an end on June 2, 1959. Filming had lasted precisely six months, more than twice a normal schedule. Director Brando had exposed more than a million feet of Vista-Vision film and had printed one quarter of that amount. Both were considered to be world records; the average movie used about 150,000 feet of film, with about 40,000 of it printed. The final cost of *One-Eyed Jacks* was $6 million.

Now Brando was faced with the responsibility of assembling the mass of film into a finished movie. The uncut film was shipped back and forth across the continent eight times while Brando contemplated whether to edit *One-Eyed Jacks* in New York or Hollywood. Finally he decided to perform the chore in Hollywood. He labored over the film until he arrived at his first cut. It ran four hours and forty-two minutes.

"That's not a picture," Rosenberg told him. "That's four hours and forty-two minutes of assembled film."

Back to the cutting room. Marlon continued trimming and trimming until he could face it no more. He walked away from it. The Paramount executives took over and cut *One-Eyed Jacks* to fit their interpretation of public taste. They imposed a new ending, which was filmed more than a year after the end of principal photography.

"Now it's a good picture for them, but it's not the picture I made," Marlon declared. "I don't feel it's what I set out to do. In my film, everybody lied, even the girl. The only one who told the truth was the Karl Malden character. Paramount made him out to be the heavy, a liar. . . . Now the characters in the film are black and white, not gray and human as I planned them."

Paramount's version of *One-Eyed Jacks* at two hours and twenty-one minutes was previewed in Sacramento, Denver and St. Louis to generally good results. When it was finally released in March 1961, the reviews were mostly commendatory ("one of the most intriguing Westerns ever made"—*Newsweek*). The film earned $12 million, barely enough to turn a profit; studios calculated that a film had to return double its cost before becoming profitable.

One-Eyed Jacks is one of the rare films that have grown in critical esteem with the passage of time. It contains some remarkably original and dramatically effective scenes, as could be expected from Brando's talent. But he was unable to maintain the overall concept of structure, the progression of character and the synthesizing of events into a dramatic whole, and that is why he could never be a film director.

14

Headlines, Family, Orpheus

*"In Hollywood, they want personalities,
not actors.
The public isn't interested
in reading about acting;
they'd rather read about
my alleged romances."*

NOTHING INFURIATED MARLON BRANDO MORE THAN TO SEE HIS PER-
sonal life splattered across front pages of newspapers. That happened often during his mid-thirties.

A year after Anna Kashfi divorced Marlon, he petitioned to cite
her for contempt of court because she did not comply with his rights
to visit Christian. He testified that Anna screamed at him and
slapped him twice when he tried to see his son. When he visited her
in the hospital, she threw a bottle of water and other objects at him,
grabbed his hair and tried to kick him in the groin. On another
visit to her house she told him, "You don't deserve to hold the
baby!" then snatched the child away. When Marlon grabbed her
arm, she slipped and sat down with the baby. When Anna tried to
call the police, Marlon slapped her twice and started to spank her.
The baby began to cry, and Marlon stopped. Anna followed him to
the kitchen, he said, "then she picked up a knife and started to
come at me. I pushed her away. She raised the knife. I told her to
go ahead if it would make her happy. She threw the knife on the
floor and came at me again, grabbing me by the hair. I freed myself and left."

Their most violent encounter came in the early-morning hours of August, 15, 1959, he testified: "I was asleep in my own house. The door burst open and the plaintiff flung herself into the room and into my bed. I tried to restrain her, but she slapped me and bit me three times. I got her out of the house and then she started to come back in. I spanked her and she went out and got in her car and tried to run over me. I went back in the house and locked the door. She threw a log through one of the windows and came into the house through the window. I held her down on the bed and tied her with a sash from my dressing robe. I then called the police and asked them to escort her home."

Anna countersued, charging that Marlon had entered her house while she was gone, had ransacked her personal papers, strewing them over the premises. She said he also "brutally beat and struck me, and once threw me to the floor of the bedroom while the baby was in my arms."

A judge imposed orders for the pair not to harass each other and established visitation rights for Brando. Within four months, they were back in court again. Brando charged he had been cheated out of thirteen visits with his son. She responded that "he is an immoral man, and I don't intend for my child to grow up in his environment." The wrangling continued, and a judge admonished them, "You are this child's parents, and you must not allow the conflict between you to warp his life." He added to Brando, "You are an artist, and you have a certain right to your eccentricities, but the child has rights, too."

"What are those eccentricities, your honor?" Brando asked. "I would like to know, so that I may eradicate them, if they do exist."

"That matter is not before us," the judge replied.

The wrangle between Anna and Marlon went on and on, occupying columns of news space. Marlon's attachment to France Nuyen also provided copy for the newspapers. She was similar to Anna: beautiful, black-haired, petite and explosive. In September 1959 Marlon and the Eurasian actress flew off to Haiti for two weeks together. When they returned to Miami, his name was listed on the airliner manifest as Dr. Miles Graham of Omaha, Nebraska. That fooled no one, and news photographers arrived to greet them. Miss Nuyen slugged one on the shoulder with her purse, then slapped him on the head. Other photographers captured the scene. A reporter asked Brando if he planned to marry France. "I don't think that is any of your business," he replied.

Five months later Miss Nuyen was in London filming *The World of Suzie Wong*, in which she had also starred on Broadway. Marlon, meanwhile, was dating Barbara Luna, a Filipino-Hungarian actress. The news distressed Miss Nuyen and she began to eat with such compulsion that she could no longer fit into her silken costumes. She was fired from the film and flew to California for a much-reported reunion with Marlon Brando.

The romance dissolved, and Marlon began dating another tempestuous actress, Rita Moreno. He made one of his rare public appearances when he took her to a theater opening in Hollywood. Associated Press photographer Harry Matosian tried to take a picture of the pair, but Marlon held up his right middle finger and said, "I don't want my picture taken and I'm going to keep my finger up until you go away." Matosian took the photograph and the AP issued it with the finger airbrushed out.

The relationship with Rita Moreno almost ended in tragedy. In April 1961 she took an overdose of sleeping pills and went to Marlon's house when he wasn't there. Her presence was discovered and she was rushed to a hospital.

Marlon continued complaining about the press's coverage of his personal affairs, to no avail. Louella Parsons huffily suggested that he seek another profession. Said she: "We Americans don't even permit our President the luxury of a private life."

Marlon remained close to his sisters. He often visited Frances —Mrs. Richard Loving—at her New York apartment and in Libertyville, where she moved later. He saw Jocelyn more often, because she was also engaged in the theater and films. She had first understudied Dorothy McGuire in *Claudia*, then had a long run as the only actress in *Mister Roberts*. She went to Hollywood for a contract with Columbia Pictures and played opposite Glenn Ford in *The Big Heat* and Edmond O'Brien in *China Venture*. Then her acting career came to a sudden halt.

Her inability to find movie jobs was a puzzle to Jocelyn and to Marlon. They discovered the reason: Jocelyn's second husband, author Eliot Asinov, who had been identified with radical causes. Through guilt by marriage, she had been placed on the film industry's blacklist.

Marlon was revolted by the spectacle of superpatriots preventing his sister from pursuing her profession because of her husband's

Jocelyn visits her brother on the set of The Wild One

politics. He pleaded with his agents at MCA to exert their influence to break the blacklist, threatening to fire them if they failed. They replied that they were powerless to find a job for Jocelyn in the studios.

Marlon turned to his partner, Walter Seltzer, who understood the Hollywood power machine. Seltzer made contact with a Hollywood official who had been a leader of the anti-Red forces.

"What does Jocelyn have to do to get a job in this town?" Seltzer asked.

"If she would write a letter telling her abject apology for being used by the Commies, that'll do it," the Red hunter said.

Seltzer supplied the letter, along with a $200 gift certificate at a department store. Jocelyn was able to work in films again, and she signed a term contract with Universal.

In 1958 Marlon Brando, Sr., married again. His bride was a twenty-eight-year-old widow, Anna Parramore, daughter of a film producer, Eugene Frenke. Mr. Brando enjoyed traveling with his wife to film locations in Europe where Pennebaker productions were shooting. On one such trip he was interviewed in Paris by Art Buchwald of the Paris *Herald Tribune.*

"The one thing I regret is giving Marlon Brando my name," said the father. "One shouldn't have that much ego to name his son after himself." It wasn't that he was ashamed of the name, he added, but "it's just too much damn confusion. When I take a plane or check into a hotel, everyone expects to see my son, and when I show up they look at me as if I were an impostor. Only last week I paid a hotel bill and when I signed it I heard the cashier say, 'He's a phony. He's not Marlon Brando.' It's even tougher on my wife because her first name happens to be Anna, the same as Marlon's ex-wife. So no matter which name she uses, everyone thinks she is Marlon's ex-wife, instead of my present one."

The confusion sometimes upset Marlon, Jr. One day his father apologized for opening a personal letter to Marlon by mistake. Marlon exploded. "Goddammit, this confusion has to stop!" he exclaimed.

"Well, what do you suggest, Marlon?"

"You'll have to change your name, that's all."

The elder Brando thought for a moment and said, "No, I don't think so. I've had the name longer than you have. You'll have to change *your* name."

Marlon, Sr., at a Dublin theater with his second wife

Marlon's feelings about his father were ambivalent. At times he seemed to display affection—an affection he had never known as a boy. But at other times he became furious over what he claimed was his father's mismanagement of Pennebaker.

"Dammit, I want you to fire my old man," he said one day to partners Seltzer and Glass.

"Fire your father?" Seltzer asked incredulously. "On what grounds?"

"Incompetence," Marlon replied. "Sheer incompetence."

"You fire him," Glass said, "and you can fire us, too." That was the end of it.

There was indeed some question about the senior Brando's capabilities in matters of finance. The question seemed settled for Marlon when he learned that the investment of his earnings in the cattle venture had turned bad. He placed the loss at $1 million, the savings from a decade of hard work. Gone, too, was Marlon's oft-repeated dream of giving up acting for his cattle ranch in Nebraska. For the first time in his career he felt compelled to work to help support Pennebaker and the growing number of persons who relied on him for their livelihood.

Marlon's next film was based on a twice-failed play by Tennessee Williams. The incentive: $1 million.

Battle of Angels, Williams' first full-length play in the commercial theater, closed in Boston in 1940. Rewritten as *Orpheus Descending,* it flopped in New York in 1957. But the playwright would not give up. With Meade Roberts, he wrote a movie script based on the play. United Artists sponsored the project, now called *The Fugitive Kind.* The producers were Richard Shepherd and Martin Jurow, two young agents.

To play the role of Lady, the bedeviled wife of a bedridden Southern bigot, the producers signed Anna Magnani, the Italian star who had won an Oscar as another Tennessee Williams heroine in *The Rose Tattoo.* Joanne Woodward, also an Academy Award winner, was chosen to play the kind-hearted housewife. Williams had long dreamed that the role of Val Xavier, his doomed Orpheus, would be portrayed by Marlon Brando.

With his keen analysis of vehicles, Brando realized that the play belonged to the female lead, even more so than in *A Streetcar Named Desire.* The role of Val was designed merely to enhance and complement the role of Lady. But Marlon needed money, and the producers were offering him $1 million. He accepted.

The director was Sidney Lumet, whom he had known from his theater years. Brando had developed a technique to test new directors. On the first day of shooting, he played a key scene two ways: first with meaning and inventiveness, then in a mechanical and routine manner. If the director out of expediency or ignorance chose the empty scene, then Brando would have no respect for him throughout the picture. But if the director recognized the creative version, then Brando would listen and try.

Lumet detected the device and printed the version in which Brando used his creativity. Their relationship proved to be cordial and productive.

Brando and Magnani clashed from the start. Self-protective as a she-wolf, the Italian used every trick in her repertoire to seek an advantage in their scenes. Marlon was astonished by her volatility; she was perplexed by his cool detachment. He found her overbearing and aggressive; she believed he was frightened by her and hated her. She was right.

Rehearsals proved useless. Both Lumet and Brando preferred to rehearse before filming; for Brando it was a process of testing and discarding. But Magnani proclaimed, "I am a spontaneous animal; I cannot rehearse!"

Locations for *The Fugitive Kind* were filmed in Milton, New York, which doubled for Marigold, Mississippi, where the action was supposed to take place. Interiors were shot at the Gold Medal Studio in the Bronx. As filming progressed, Brando grew more restive, and not merely because of relations with his co-star; he was having problems with Anna Kashfi in California. Each weekend he flew to California without the knowledge or consent of the production department.

Lumet knew what was going on, and tried to accommodate his star. The real test came late one Friday. Lumet wanted to finish a key sequence. Brando tried to force himself. Each time he reached a certain line, he blew it. Ten takes went by. Twenty. Thirty.

"Sidney," he said quietly to the director, "do you think we could leave this until Monday?"

"I think I know what's distracting you," Lumet replied. "But if we don't get it now, we'll never get it. If you take the weekend off, you'll lose everything. I'd rather bull it through."

With Anna Magnani and Joanne Woodward, The Fugitive Kind, *1960*

Brando continued until the thirty-seventh take. Both he and Lumet recognized immediately that he had succeeded, and Brando soon was racing for the airport.

The tension between Magnani and Brando grew. Tennessee Williams accused Brando of lack of consideration for an actress working in an unfamiliar language: "Brando's offbeat timing and his slurred pronunciation were right for the part but they were torture for Anna who had to wait and wait for her cue, and when she received it, it would sometimes not be in the script."

The climax came four days before the end of the shooting. Magnani broke off in the middle of a scene and began ranting against Brando in a torrent of Italian-English. She burst into tears and raced to her dressing room. Brando and Lumet stared at each other in perplexity.

"I'd better go see what it's all about," said the director.

"No, *I'm* the one she's mad at," said Brando. "I'll go see."

A half-hour passed, and Brando didn't return. Lumet ventured to the Magnani dressing room and found her still castigating Brando. Her principal complaint was that Brando's contract gave him top billing over the world, and she wanted her name above his in her native Italy. The two men managed to assuage her, and *The Fugitive Kind* continued to its unhappy conclusion.

The reviews of the film were mixed, some critics claiming it a work of art, others terming it dreary and pretentious. The public sided with the latter opinion. Tennessee Williams expressed his disappointment that the film didn't adhere more closely to the script. "It's Anna Magnani's film," he added, "but Joanne Woodward is brilliant in it, too. Marlon Brando is Marlon Brando. I just wish he didn't remember Kowalski so well."

15

Mutiny

*"I have searched my conscience
to see if I could have been responsible
for the chaotic history of this picture.
I cannot see that I have."*

AS AN EXERCISE IN HUMAN FOLLY, THE SECOND *Mutiny on the Bounty* is unsurpassed in film history. No movie project has been marked by worse executive judgments, pettier personality squabbles, and more profligacy of creative and financial resources. Along with the concurrent *Cleopatra, Mutiny on the Bounty* signaled the almost total disintegration of the studio system as the source of power in the film industry.

Marlon Brando was both the unwitting cause and the ultimate victim of the entire affair. Confronted with broken promises, deceit and incompetence, he responded in the Brandovian manner. At times he tried to use his power to remedy the ills of the production; at other times he merely acted in a peevish, childlike way. Inevitably, he was given the blame for all that went wrong.

The first deceit victimized Aaron Rosenberg, a burly one-time all-American football guard newly arrived at MGM after producing a string of well-made, successful films for Universal. He had been promised the chance to produce an epic Western, *How the West Was Won,* but it was snatched away from him. Rosenberg was furious. To placate him, the MGM hierarchy offered a remake of *Mutiny on the Bounty.* Rosenberg was understandably hesitant to attempt a new version of such a well-remembered classic, but he was persuaded.

Director John Sturges suggested to the producer that Marlon Brando would be ideal, either in the role of Fletcher Christian or Captain Bligh. Rosenberg made the suggestion to Brando, who discarded it immediately, but then he had second thoughts. He

With Trevor Howard, Mutiny on the
Bounty, *1962*

M.G.M.

studied the history of the mutiny and instructed his agents at MCA: "Tell MGM I'll do the picture—as long as it's not just a remake of the old one. I want to investigate what happened to the sailors *after* the mutiny. Why did they go to Pitcairn Island and within two years kill each other off? What is there in human nature that makes men violent, even in an island paradise? *That's* what would interest me."

A meeting was arranged between Brando, Rosenberg and Sol Siegel, a veteran producer who had become production boss of MGM after the firing of Dore Schary. Brando's interest in the project waned as the conversation continued, and he made it clear he wasn't interested. Rosenberg began thinking about other casting, and he assigned the suspense author Eric Ambler to write a script.

The Ambler script was submitted to Brando, and turned down. He was being sought by Sam Spiegel, who had produced *On the Waterfront,* to play the leading role in an epic based on the life of T. E. Lawrence. Marlon contemplated the project, then concluded, "I'll be damned if I'll spend two years of my life out in the desert on some fucking camel." Instead, he decided to accept *Mutiny on the Bounty.*

Brando told Rosenberg he would play Fletcher Christian if the script were rewritten to include a lengthy sequence about what happened on Pitcairn Island. Rosenberg agreed, and so did the MGM bosses, who granted the actor approval of that portion of the script. In early 1960 a contract was drawn up to grant Brando $500,000 and 10 percent of the gross receipts, plus $5,000 for each day the film ran over its scheduled time. Filming was to begin on October 15, 1960.

Rosenberg had already set into motion the enormous logistics of *Mutiny on the Bounty.* The major problem was the *Bounty* herself. A suitable hull could be found nowhere, so a brand-new *Bounty* had to be built. In 1959 a shipyard in Nova Scotia had been commissioned to construct the *Bounty* and deliver her to Tahiti by September 1, 1960. Trouble developed at the start. The arctic winter descended early, and lumber could not be transported by land. Wood for the hull had to be shipped from New Jersey, causing delay and running the cost of the ship up to $750,000, one third more than the estimate.

Sir Carol Reed was hired to direct *Bounty,* and he journeyed from London to California to meet with Brando. The meeting was less than successful. Marlon spent much of the time expounding on his plans to make a film on the life of Caryl Chessman, a rapist whose California execution had been fought by opponents of capital punishment, including Brando. Reed and Brando seemed ill-matched at the start. The Englishman was a cool technician who had directed such brilliant intellectual exercises as *Odd Man Out*, *The Fallen Idol* and *The Third Man*. He was accustomed to exacting unflawed performances from the disciplined actors of England. Brando was visceral, unfettered and headstrong. But the two men were polite and respectful of each other's talents. It was hoped that out of this respect would come a working relationship.

While Eric Ambler attempted a script rewrite to conform to Brando's wishes, Rosenberg, Reed, Brando, Robert Surtees, the cinematographer, and other production aides visited Tahiti to look for locations. It was Marlon's first trip to Tahiti, and the traditional enchantment of the Society Islands struck him immediately—not only the Gauguin landscapes but the innocent naughtiness of the Polynesian girls as well. His flagging enthusiasm for *Mutiny on the Bounty* began to improve.

Rosenberg assembled a cast, mostly of actors from England: Trevor Howard as Bligh; Richard Harris as John Mills, instigator of the mutiny; Hugh Griffith for the humorous character of Smith. All were contracted for the October 15 starting date.

Hints of trouble appeared. Brando was dissatisfied with Eric Ambler's interpretation of the Pitcairn episode, and Borden Chase and William Driskill were added as scriptwriters. Their efforts proved no more pleasing. The major problem was in renewing excitement after Bligh had been cast adrift; his personality had so dominated the action that it was difficult to establish a new level of interest.

The *Bounty* herself continued to be a vexation. The ship was two months late in leaving Nova Scotia. A week after she passed through the Panama Canal, the engine room caught fire. The crew almost abandoned ship before the fire was brought under control. Another fire broke out before the ship reached Tahiti. In addition, the *Bounty* proved a misery for her crew. She tossed and pitched perilously in high seas, and seasickness was endemic.

Rosenberg had planned the production to shoot in sequence, filming the shipboard scenes in gray weather, then bursting forth with color upon arrival at Tahiti. With the October starting date nearing and no *Bounty,* he was forced to change his scheme or keep eighty-seven highly paid actors and crew members idle until the ship arrived. Production began.

Reed filmed all the island scenes that were possible without the *Bounty.* He ran out of script before the ship's sails finally appeared on the horizon on December 4. Cast and crew now discovered the misery that the sailors had endured. Even with outriggers on each side, the *Bounty* rolled with each swell. On most filming days a hundred persons were jammed onto the ship, and the crew had to cram into hiding places when the camera was turning.

Charles Lederer had now replaced the first three writers on the script, and he tried to produce new pages that would satisfy the disparate viewpoints. Not even William Shakespeare could have accomplished that feat. The MGM bosses wanted an approximation of what had succeeded before: the original *Mutiny on the Bounty* script. Carol Reed disagreed; he felt that Bligh should be no black villain, that his motivations should be explored. Marlon had his own concept, which shifted with the Tahitian tide.

The *Mutiny on the Bounty* company had come to the island at a time when natives warned them not to come: the rainy season. The heavens unloaded. In one memorable day, seventeen inches of rain fell on Papeete.

The company was also afflicted with the well-known Polynesian fever, which has struck visitors since the time of Captain Cook. Americans and Britishers alike were quickly converted to the languorous pace of living and the acquiescent charms of the Tahitian maidens. The sexual playfulness of the girls was quite overwhelming for those accustomed to Anglo-Saxon traditions. One middle-aged film man was so beguiled by his Tahitian girl that he announced his engagement to her at a hotel dinner party attended by her mother and father. He was dissuaded from his plan by the end of the location, and he returned to his wife in California.

There was something for everyone. For those film workers who were not of a heterosexual persuasion, there was an ample supply of willowy and compliant Tahitian boys.

The accessibility of girls brought another hazard to the *Mutiny on the Bounty* company: the French malaise. The star himself was infected with what was termed by physicians a classic case of ancient ailment. A doctor flew from California to treat him, and after ten days of antibiotic injections, he was able to return to the cameras.

With Tarita, Mutiny on the Bounty

As if the Polynesian fever and the French malaise were not enough, the company was also subject to what Aaron Rosenberg termed "the British troubles."

From the beginning there was no rapport between Marlon Brando and his co-stars, Trevor Howard and Richard Harris. Both Howard and Harris resented the control that Brando exercised over the script, including their own parts; both were hard-drinking roisterers who were offended by Brando's aloofness. Howard was a veteran performer with standards of professionalism which Brando did not meet. Harris was an ambitious newcomer who perceived in *Mutiny on the Bounty* a chance to establish himself as an international star.

Other members of the company became aware of the conflict. One hot day a scene was being staged of the natives' welcome to the *Bounty* crew. Howard reported to the set, dressed in his officer's uniform. Marlon was sixty feet down the beach talking to three Tahitian girls under a palm tree. When all was prepared, the assistant director called over the loudspeaker: "Mr. Brando, we're ready." Marlon continued his conversation as Howard sweated in the tropical sun. "Mr. Brando, we're ready," the assistant repeated. After the third call Marlon strolled down to the camera. Howard stormed out of the scene. "Mr. Howard, we're ready," the assistant director began calling.

"I can't honestly say that I got to *like* Brando," Howard said with restraint when he returned to England. "I didn't hate him, either. I just didn't get to know him. No one ever does. The only thing I *could* feel for the fellow was pity. Yes, I really think Brando is to be pitied. He hasn't a friend in the world. He never speaks to anyone unless it's someone smaller or younger. He has a curious fondness for playing practical jokes with people like that. I saw him try a jujitsu trick one day with a young Tahitian. But the Tahitian turned the tables on him and Brando sulked for the rest of the day. As an actor he's a great politician, and as a politician he could destroy my work."

Tahiti itself resembled paradise to Brando. On the first day of shooting, he remarked to Carol Reed, "I'm sorry to see this day come; it means one day sooner that we'll be going back to the States." He told a visitor from the United States that he would hate to leave: "This is the first time in ten years that I've been able to feel comfortable among people." Many Tahitians knew who he was,

Tarita

but none bothered him. He could walk through the streets, enter a café, swim in a lagoon with no one staring. One of the movie workers saw him enter a bar one night and try to make his way through the crowd to order a drink. The frolicking Tahitians shouldered him back; he shrugged and finally found a stool. It would have happened nowhere else.

Marlon lived in a thatched house a few miles from Papeete. In the waters outside his door he went skin-diving and water-skiing but refrained from fishing; he refused to kill animals for any purpose. At night he wandered barefoot into the night clubs, where he danced the animated Tahitian *tamure* with the local girls. His only male companion was Bob Hoskins, the banker's son from Libertyville; Marlon had induced MGM to hire him for the film as "dialogue coach."

The girls came and went, but the one who stayed was Tarita.

Her full name was Taritatum a Teripaiam, and she had been second dishwasher at the restaurant Les Tropiques. Like many Tahitian girls, she danced at native festivals and for tourists at the hotels and cafés. When the call went out for dancers to appear in *Mutiny on the Bounty,* she was among the applicants. One day Aaron Rosenberg and Marlon Brando were surveying the film's dancers for a girl to play the role of Fletcher Christian's Tahitian wife. Production was soon to begin, and the role had not been cast. Both producer and star were impressed with the grace and beauty of the nineteen-year-old Tarita. Her teeth were bad, and she knew no English. But a dentist made caps for her teeth, and Marlon volunteered to coach her dialogue. She was hired.

Marlon's attentions brought a storm of protest from Tarita's boyfriend, a hot-tempered Dane who was the chef at Les Tropiques. He was placated by being hired as chief cook for the MGM location.

Carol Reed remained firm in his belief that Bligh should not be a total villain. Unable to achieve script changes, he neglected to film scenes which were contrary to his point of view. Brando continued to infuriate the British actors by changing his interpretation of the scenes after they had learned them. Then the rains came. For seventeen straight days, no camera turned. In despair Rosenberg ordered the entire company to return to Culver City for interior filming until the rains abated.

The return to MGM brought the Carol Reed issue to a head. Not only did Reed disapprove of the Bligh characterization; he also objected to Brando's portrayal of Fletcher Christian as a fop. Sol Siegel, the studio head, demanded that Reed film *Mutiny on the Bounty* according to the script. Reed replied that he couldn't continue on that basis. He wanted to resign.

"You can't resign," Siegel told him.

But that night Siegel and Rosenberg decided that Reed would have to be replaced. Brando was against the firing, but he remained neutral in the decision. Reed received word by telephone that he was being relieved. Siegel's initial reluctance to accept the resignation proved a windfall for the director. Instead of resigning and being paid nothing, Reed won a settlement of $200,000.

The search began for Reed's successor. A remarkable director was needed: one who could satisfy Brando while exacting performances from his British co-stars; who could interpret the intimate human relationships yet take command of the spectacle scenes; who could carry out the wishes of the MGM bosses without alienating the star Brando; who was available to start work immediately. Obviously no such person existed.

Charles Lederer suggested Lewis Milestone, the tough-minded aesthete who had survived the Hollywood jungle with such achievements as *All Quiet on the Western Front, The Front Page,* and many others. Milestone agreed to a conference at Aaron Rosenberg's house. Marlon Brando was there, and he failed to recognize Milestone as the man whose advice he had sought in Paris before embarking on *The Men.* After some vague questioning, Rosenberg and Brando left. Milestone and Charles Lederer remained.

"What is this all about?" Milestone asked.

"Carol Reed has quit *Mutiny,*" Lederer said.

"Did he quit or was he pushed out?" Milestone asked.

"He quit."

"If he didn't—if he was fired—I don't want the job."

Milestone called Reed and found out that the Englishman had indeed wanted to resign. Milestone met the picture makers in the office of Sol Siegel and said, "Okay, I accept—as long as it's understood that I'm coming in on trust. You need me, you want me. I'll do the best I can."

"We'll never forget you for this," Siegel remarked.

The case-hardened Milestone replied, "Don't make any promises. I know as soon as I'm out the door you'll forget about me."

Within ten days, Milestone had assumed the direction of *Mutiny on the Bounty.* The filming went well for two weeks, and then

Milestone realized his mistake. It happened one day when he noticed Brando talking confidentially to the cameraman. Milestone signaled to the assistant director to call "Roll 'em"—a traditional start of filming. Nothing happened. Brando made some additional preparations for the scene, and then he nodded. The camera was switched on.

Milestone decided to see what would happen if he didn't say "Cut!" The scene ran its course, and the camera was switched off when Brando was finished with his lines. No one asked Milestone if the scene was to be printed.

When the second take was ready to begin, Milestone picked up a copy of the *Hollywood Reporter* and sat down to read it. Within a few minutes producer Rosenberg arrived on the set. "Aren't you going to watch the scene?" he asked.

Milestone laid down his paper and asked, "What for? When the picture is finished, I'll buy a ticket and see the whole bloody mess in a theater."

"Does that mean you're quitting?" Rosenberg asked.

"Look," said the director. "I've been around awhile. If I quit, MGM can sue me; I can't afford that. But if MGM fires me, I can sue them."

The studio head, Sol Siegel, urged Milestone to remain. "Stick it out," he said. "I know it will be difficult, but stick it out to the end. If Carol Reed leaves and then you leave, it will be a disaster. No other director will take over."

"Yes, but if I stay, I'll get the blame," said Milestone. "I've been in this racket a long time. I know that when a picture is a failure, it's the director's fault. When it's a hit, everybody shares the credit."

"Milly, you must stay," said Siegel.

"Sol, this guy Brando is going to ruin you," said Milestone. Then he sighed, "Oh well, it's MGM's money. I'll stay."

The filming of *Mutiny on the Bounty* continued with director and star maintaining a strange relationship. In Milestone's view, Brando was headstrong, dictatorial and power-mad, demanding repeated rewrites and questioning every instruction by the director. To Brando, Milestone was mechanical and unfeeling; Brando even accused the director of being senile. Indeed, out of ennui Milestone took naps on the set, sometimes during the shooting. Crew members prized an announcement one day over the loudspeaker: "Will somebody please wake up the director? His feet are in the shot."

It was a sorry time in Marlon's career. He had made a choice, accepting out of greed or misjudgment a vehicle that was totally unsuited for him. He found himself doing business with weak-willed executives who had neither the sense nor the honesty to fulfill their promises to him. But he chose as victim of his wrath the man who was striving to bring the project to an acceptable conclusion—Milestone. He was an artist who had served the film medium well, and he deserved better.

Twice during the filming, Milestone stalked off the set with the intention of quitting. Each time Brando stopped him at the stage door and implored him to return. On the second occasion, the wry Milestone remarked, "You know enough about drama to realize that one exit might work, but two exits are ridiculous. Let me go."

Brando insisted he would accept Milestone's dictates if the director would return. Milestone came back, and Marlon acquiesced, for a whole day. Then he resumed the questioning of each speech, each piece of business, the demands that new pages be written to conform with his changing notions about the Fletcher Christian character.

The *Mutiny on the Bounty* company returned to Tahiti in July. The weather proved favorable for filming, but the climate of the movie troupe turned bleak. Milestone and Brando spoke to each other only when necessary, and then only to wrangle. The script was still in tatters; new pages of dialogue arrived daily by short-wave from California. Not even the legendary pleasures of Tahiti could improve the ruined morale.

The British members of the company found solace in drink. Trevor Howard was missing one morning when cast and crew were called to report on board the *Bounty* at seven, with departure at seven thirty. Nothing could be filmed without Howard, and the film makers waited. Finally, at nine a police wagon drew up beside the dock. Two gendarmes escorted Trevor Howard to the gangplank. He lurched aboard and reported below for his makeup. By the time the *Bounty* was at sea and Milestone was ready to film Howard had prepared himself, and he performed the scene flawlessly.

The Welsh sprite, Hugh Griffith, was inclined to pranks when he took to drink, which was often. On the flight to Tahiti he locked himself in the lavatory of the airliner and painted obscene signs on the walls and mirrors; MGM received a $1,200 bill for a cleanup. In Tahiti, Griffith's pranks overburdened the limited French sense of humor. Authorities one day escorted him to the airport and put him on the first plane leaving Papeete. This presented a problem to the film makers, since the Griffith character was to extend throughout *Mutiny on the Bounty.* The problem was solved by the insertion of a scene showing poor Smith being buried at sea. The nature of his death was unexplained.

Richard Harris became more pugnacious. One night he entered a bar in a blustery mood and cut in on a young man who was dancing with a native beauty. When the young man objected, Harris shot out a fist and knocked him down. He challenged others in the place. When he found no takers, he spied Marlon Brando's stand-in, who was drinking quietly at the bar. "You want some?" Harris challenged. The stand-in ignored him, and that infuriated the Irish actor. He threw a punch. The stand-in ducked and returned a blow that sent Harris crashing to the floor.

The Australian actor Chips Rafferty was a towering man of quiet dignity. He spent the evenings in the hotel restaurant drinking huge amounts of the good local beer. At the end of the evening the Australian and his wife walked to their thatched hut to retire. Then Rafferty stuck his head out of the door and emitted a loud, doglike howl. This set off a barking spree among the scores of dogs for miles around. When the noise subsided after half an hour, Rafferty emerged again to utter his howl. Again, the riotous response. This continued into the morning, and some company members changed their residence to another hotel in order to get some rest.

The Tahitian location finally came to an end, but not *Mutiny on the Bounty.* It returned to Culver City for still more attempts to locate an acceptable ending. Brando had long been earning $5,000 per day in overtime payment; he eventually would receive $750,00 beyond his $500,000 base pay. Charles Lederer had summoned the aid of his friend, Ben Hecht, in writing a new ending, and it met with Marlon's favor. He volunteered to waive his overtime while the sequence was filmed.

Lewis Milestone maintained the pretense of directing *Mutiny on the Bounty.* He reported to the set each morning at nine and retired to his office–dressing room to read magazines. The mornings passed without the turning of the camera; Brando and Rosenberg conferred about the new pages from Lederer and Hecht. By midafternoon the filming began. The action was directed by Marlon with the assistance and advice of Rosenberg. Milestone remained in his room until he considered it a legitimate time to leave. "Nobody will hire me again," he reasoned. "Since there won't be any more films, I might as well take what I can get. Nobody can spit on me after this." His eventual take was $250,000.

One day in late October 1961, more than a year after the start of the filming, *Mutiny on the Bounty* was finished. Marlon was in a foul humor. He told a visitor it had been the worst experience of his acting career.

"Yes, I know some people will crab, 'Well, what's he got to bitch about? He's being paid.' But after you have enough, money doesn't matter. . . . I have asked for a finished script for a year and a half. A year and a half! They didn't give it to me. There have been thirty different versions of the script, but never have I received a finished script. We went to Tahiti with no idea of how the final third of the picture was going to be. How can you write a novel when you don't know how it's going to end? How can an actor play a character if he doesn't know what will happen to him? A week ago I decided I'd had it, plus eight. I was so frustrated, so tied up, I was getting palpitations. I had indigestion all the time. I was snapping at aspirin like a Christmas goose pecking corn. I finally went to the front office and said, 'No more show until I get the last ten pages of script.' I was promised them that night or first thing in the morning. I didn't get them in the morning. I was promised them at two. The pages came at two, and I asked if they would be the final, unchanged version. I was told they would be. And look—" He held out a stack of revision pages.

"If I do something stupid, I expect to get rapped for it. If I give a lousy performance, I expect to get bum reviews. But I don't expect to be blamed for something I haven't done. . . . I don't care what happens now. I just want to get it over with—before I lose my mind."

Nor was it over yet. The mass of film was put together, partly by Milestone, partly by Rosenberg and the studio executives. The malady remained: there was no ending.

Months passed, and still no solution was found. The issue became so well known that President John F. Kennedy on a visit to California asked his dinner guest, Billy Wilder, "When in the world are they ever going to finish *Mutiny on the Bounty?*"

Actually, it was Wilder himself who supplied the ending. The director-writer suggested the reason for the killing on Pitcairn: Christain proposes that the mutineers return to England and face justice; his companions reject the notion and set fire to the *Bounty* to prevent escape; Christian is burned in the fire and dies.

Brando agreed to perform in the new ending. Milestone was out of the question as director, and Brando submitted a list of three directors who would be acceptable. One of them was George Seaton, who agreed to the two-week assignment on two conditions: he would not be paid; there would be no publicity.

"I've seen the film," he said to Brando, "but don't ask me what I think of it. And don't ask me to do any rewriting. I'll simply get these scenes on film the best I can. I'm coming on this picture as a technician only."

Brando accepted the terms and performed with complete professionalism. He knew his lines. He didn't argue. If he had any question about a scene, he and Seaton discussed it in private. When they came to the death scene, Seaton asked, "Have you ever seen anyone burn to death?"

"No," said Marlon.

"Unfortunately, I have," said the director. "Strangely, because the body fluid has gone, it's like freezing. The victim shivers, almost as if he were caked in ice."

Marlon's eyes glowed. "Let's do it!" he said.

"Do what?"

"I'll freeze myself."

Buckets of chopped ice were brought to the stage, and the ice was spread on Brando's bed. He lay down on it, covered himself with a blanket, and played his death scene. He remained on the ice for three takes at a time, and when he emerged from the scene his skin was blue.

The new ending took only seven days to film. It was shot in August 1962, twenty-two months after *Mutiny on the Bounty* had begun. The sanguine atmosphere surprised everyone, including Marlon. "I am amazed," he said, "that everything is so amicable after all the name-calling and backbiting and other shit that has gone on."

As *Mutiny on the Bounty* was being prepared for release, it received unwanted publicity from the *Saturday Evening Post,* which during its dying months had turned from a benign family journal into a purveyor of hoked-up scandal. The magazine assigned Bill Davidson to write an article about Brando and *Bounty,* and the reporter caught Lewis Milestone in a sour mood. The director provided the *Post*'s title: "This picture should have been called *The Mutiny of Marlon Brando.*" The subtitles: "Six Million Dollars Down the Drain . . . . A petulant superstar turns paradise into a moviemaker's nightmare. How Brando broke the budget in a marathon remake of *Mutiny on the Bounty.*"

The article accused Brando of ballooning from one hundred and seventy to two hundred and ten pounds during the production, of making outrageous demands, of malingering, of wasting millions of MGM's money, of failing in his professionalism. The only mention of MGM's unkept promises was Rosenberg's comment: "Marlon gave us a rough time, but he felt we were not living up to the agreements we had made with him about the basic concept of the picture."

The *Post* on its editorial page inveighed against both Brando and Elizabeth Taylor, who was blamed for the waste of millions on *Cleopatra* because of her marital "peccadilloes." (As in the case of *Mutiny on the Bounty,* the principal cause of the *Cleopatra* overage was corporate stupidity.) The *Post* editorialized:

> For their separate but equally extravagant performances we think this cast of two would be perfect castaways. Why not send them both to bountiful Tahiti, equip them with one movie camera apiece, an unlimited supply of film and an eternity in which to produce definitive and epic motion pictures of each other? No distractions, managerial or marital, for either. Liz, who has already lived to an overripe age of thirty, could seek a method for preserving her beauty in the tropics. Marlon could have years to polish his bongo drumming, synchronizing his own mumbled incantations to every beat. Maybe the two films could be merged and sent back thirty years from now when we might be more sympathetic to these examples of National Vulgar. The only hitch we can see is that Tahiti, once burnt by Brando and the *Bounty,* might be unwilling to accept such important emigrés. In that case, we recommend sparsely inhabited but nearby Bora-Bora, an island whose very name onomatopoetically suggests our reaction to both stars.

Brando was incensed. Except for the Truman Capote article, he had never reacted publicly or privately to anything printed about himself. Whenever an aide had tried to tell him about an outrageous article or item, he always clapped his hands over his ears and said, "I don't want to read those things, I don't want to hear those things." But after the *Post* article appeared he said, "This has to be answered."

He summoned his advisers and told them of his determination to fight back. One of them said, "I'm pleased that you're angry, Marlon, but why now? You never let articles bother you before."

"Because my son will soon be starting school," Marlon replied, "and I don't want him to have to answer questions about what a kook his father is."

Marlon flew to New York for a Saturday-morning meeting with Joseph R. Vogel, the new president of Metro-Goldwyn-Mayer, in which Vogel agreed to issue a statement absolving the star for troubles on *Mutiny on the Bounty.* Vogel declared that the articles blaming Brando were "gravely unfair," and he cited such causes as delay in ship delivery; fire aboard the *Bounty;* tropical storms; "clashes of temperament among director, producer, writer and principal players, illness and death among the cast, particularly the illness and resignation of the original director." Vogel gave credit to company members for creating a superb entertainment, "especially Marlon Brando, who performed throughout the entire production in a professional manner and to the full limit of his capabilities. . . ." Vogel's statement was later used by his enemies as ammunition to depose him as president.

Marlon next sought out Lewis Milestone, whose quotes had been the basis for a large portion of the *Post* article. The director agreed to see him. "What do you want of me?" Milestone asked.

"I'm thinking of suing the *Saturday Evening Post* over that article," Marlon said.

"The courts are free to everybody," said Milestone, adding, "Look —you never listened to me during the horrible time on the picture, so there's no reason to believe you'd listen to me now. But I think you'd be a horse's ass to sue the *Post.* They can produce all kinds of witnesses to prove that you were out of your bloody head on that picture."

"I don't think you're right," Marlon replied.

"If I'm called as a witness, I'm not going to lie. And I'm not looking for revenge, either. I'll simply tell the truth."

In January 1963 Marlon Brando sued the Curtis Publishing Company and the Curtis Circulation Company for $5 million, charging he had been libeled by the article "The Mutiny of Marlon Brando."

Mutiny on the Bounty had finally been completed, and it was premiered in Los Angeles and New York. Uncharacteristically, Marlon attended both premieres and even went to Tokyo for the opening there. The reason, he admitted, was to bolster his case against the *Saturday Evening Post.* "I am most anxious for the picture to succeed," he said. "If it didn't, I would be standing alone in the Gobi Desert. My suit wouldn't have a chance if the picture would be a flop. Everybody would be standing just below the horizon on that desert, pointing their fingers at me." (Pretrial depositions were taken, but Marlon never brought his suit against the *Post* to court.)

Marlon disputed a report by Robert O'Brien, the successor at MGM to the deposed Joe Vogel, that *Mutiny on the Bounty* would not turn a profit on its first release, but would do so when rereleased. In fact, Marlon said, *Mutiny on the Bounty* had actually cost $12 million, not the $18 million the company reported; the rest was overhead, including a $500,000 charge for the original story, which had been paid for twenty-five years before.

Mutiny on the Bounty was not a success, despite Marlon's brave claims that it would be. The *Post* article and other bad publicity had made the film an object of ridicule. The chaotic conditions under which it was made showed in the finished product; Marlon's interpretation of Fletcher Christian lacked consistency, beginning as a fop ("more faggot than fop," said one of his advisers) and ending as a mystic. Some critics wrote kindly of the film. Others used *Mutiny on the Bounty* as the basis for screeds against indulgent studios and headstrong stars.

Brando was damaged by *Mutiny on the Bounty,* both professionally and personally. The film earned about $20 million, a sizable amount, but far from enough to turn a profit. Following *One-Eyed Jacks, Mutiny on the Bounty* helped identify Marlon Brando as a loser and profligate.

Mutiny on the Bounty hurt Marlon in more personal ways. He knew now to trust no one, believe no one. His cynicism affected his dealings with producers; it influenced his work as well. He could never again portray the innocent idealism of Terry Malloy.

16

Personal
and
Politics

*"I wish I could die with some blazing conviction —
like a man in a concentration camp.
But I can't.
I haven't found it yet.
All I can do is look in the mirror
and hope to understand a little more
of what I see."*

MARLON BRANDO MARRIED AGAIN — AND FOR THE SAME REASON. BY IRON-
ical circumstance, his second wife was the actress who had played
the Tahitian wife of Fletcher Christian in the 1935 version of *Mutiny on the Bounty.*

She was born Maria Castenada in 1917 aboard a train en route
from Mexico to Nogales, Arizona. One of a family of eight daughters and two sons, she grew up in Los Angeles, went to parochial
schools and Fairfax High School. She played guitar and danced in
local theatricals and appeared in the Astaire-Rogers musical *Flying
Down to Rio.* Irving Thalberg chose her to play opposite Clark
Gable in *Mutiny on the Bounty,* and her screen name became simply Movita. She appeared in minor films like *Paradise Isle* and *Rose
of the Rio Grande* and *Wolf Call.* In 1939 she married Jack Doyle,
a colorful Irish pugilist whose temperament inside and outside the
ring had made him a noted figure. She and Doyle lasted five tempestuous years together, most of the time in England during the
war. She returned to Hollywood to pick up her career, but she could
find little except bit parts.

In 1951 Movita was playing a Mexican woman in *Viva Zapata!* when she met Marlon Brando. They dated on location and over the years in Hollywood. Early in 1960 Movita discovered that she was pregnant. Marlon, who was preparing for his role in *Mutiny on the Bounty,* flew with her to Xochimilco, Mexico, and they were quietly married on June 4, 1960. He was thirty-six, and she was forty-three. A few months later their son, Miko, was born. Marlon later said in court that he had never lived with Movita, nor had had sex relations with her after their son had been conceived.

Predictably, Anna Kashfi became furious when she learned of Marlon's remarriage and second son. Brando himself broke the news to Anna in April 1961. When Marlon tried to discuss the matter with Anna she became hysterical and began cursing him.

When Marlon sued Anna over visitation privileges with Christian, she told the press about Marlon's marriage to Movita and about their son: "He said he was interested in establishing a good relationship between this other child and our child, and that the child would be spending a good deal of time up here (at my house). He wanted to establish an atmosphere of togetherness between them. I guess he wants me to be sort of a second mother to the child. . . . Then he asked me to go with him on this trip to Tahiti and live there because of racial prejudice and the difficulty of bringing up our child here, because I am Indian and he is American.

"Somehow that just rips into me. I've had no difficulty with any racial prejudice, and I think what he said is the most terrible and devastating thing that could have happened to our child, especially since it comes from his father. I know why he wants me to go to Tahiti. He wants me to be stuck on an island somewhere, and he could come and go as he pleased. It's time he was man enough to assume the responsibility of being a father. . . . This child by Movita is his problem, and what he does about it is his own business."

Brando came back to California from the *Mutiny on the Bounty* location in Tahiti to press his suit for visitation. He admitted on the witness stand that he had married Movita and fathered a son by her. His one great wish, he said, was to establish a father relationship with Christian. The judge allowed Marlon a visit with his son before returning to Tahiti, and he admonished both Marlon and Anna to resolve their differences for the sake of their son.

Movita in her starlet days

Six months later they were in court again. He was seeking more frequent visits with Christian, and she tried to prevent him. She became so incensed that during a recess she called him a "miserable son of a bitch" and landed a roundhouse swing to the side of his head to the delight of news photographers.

The bitter court wrangles over the boy Christian continued year after year. In 1964 Anna revealed to the world that Brando had a third son, born two years before to Tarita. The boy's name was Tehotu, and Anna said she would not allow Christian to visit his father because Tarita was living at Brando's house and they were not married. Anna declared that Marlon showed no real interest in the boy, but was forever going off for "love affairs with ladies."

During one stormy encounter with Marlon, Anna testified, "He got a knife out of the kitchen drawer, pushed it in my hands and said, 'Why don't you kill me?' I said, 'You're not worth it.'"

Marlon also testified to their squabbles: "I guess it was in 1961 or 1962 when all of a sudden I was awakened by the person I was with. Then I saw Anna. She had broken into my house and jumped on the bed and started pulling the girl's hair out. The girl was terrified, and she beat it. Then Anna started wrecking the house. I let her do it. I thought it would be good to let her get it out of her system. The house was rented, and I didn't own the furniture, anyhow, and it was all insured. Then Anna heard the taxi which the girl had called. Anna ran down to try and catch the girl. I followed along, with Anna biting me, hitting me, scratching me and swearing at me. Finally I said, 'Anna, this is enough. Go home.' She refused, so I took her and I turned her over and spanked her as hard as I could. I put her back in her car and hid behind a wall as she drove off. I went back to the house and locked all the doors. It wasn't long before she came back again and threw a log through the window and started wrecking the house all over again. This time I called the police and let them take her home."

The court ruled against Anna, giving the six-year-old Christian to the custody of Marlon's sister, Frances Loving; the boy would live with his aunt for six months on her forty-acre farm near Libertyville. Said the judge: "Miss Kashfi's reliance on drugs and alcohol . . . contributed to her uncontrollable temper. The evidence here and the probation report does not label Miss Kashfi an unfit mother but it does make her emotionally unstable. With her own problems, I feel that she will have enough trouble taking care of herself."

After the decision, Anna ranted to reporters: "If you call this fairness, you can keep it. Is there anything wrong with a mother's wanting her own child? He's been given away to a woman I don't even know. God! . . . I bore this baby. Where in hell was Marlon Brando when this baby was being reared? . . . I am not through fighting. I will subpoena the judge and the whole damn court."

Anna later regained custody of Christian Devi, and the bitterness continued.

Marlon entered a period of discontent following *Mutiny on the Bounty*. He worried about the decline of his career, the recession of his hairline, Anna Kashfi's erratic ways, the wrangles over Christian, the embarrassment over the hasty marriage to Movita. The culmination of his troubles plunged Marlon into depressions he had not known since his early twenties.

During such times Marlon became incommunicado. He remained in his hilltop home, refusing to answer the telephone. One alarmed associate went to Marlon's house during a long silent period, fearing suicide. Marlon wasn't suicidal. Just depressed.

"But why?" the associate argued. "You've told me there isn't a dame in the world you couldn't lay after one hour with her. You have all the dough you need; all you have to do is commit yourself to ten weeks of work, and you could earn enough to support yourself for the rest of your life. You have a beautiful house, a fancy car, a secretary to take care of everything. You're at the top of your profession; no actor is more highly respected. Why the hell should you be so depressed?"

Marlon shook his head wonderingly. "I don't know why," he admitted. "I guess I'm crazy."

No amount of reasoning could shake him out of the depressed moods. But they passed. A new girl came along. Or a script that seemed promising. Both fancies would fade, and the depression returned. Sometimes he could make it go away by drinking. This was something new in his life; he had never drunk much before. But now he enjoyed playing the game of drinking vodka from a teacup and making people think it was tea.

After the *One-Eyed Jacks* experience, he lost interest in Pennebaker Productions. Walter Seltzer and George Glass strove to keep the company viable, with no help from Marlon. In 1962 Pennebaker entered into a contract with Universal—now owned by MCA. One of the projects was a story titled *Fluffy*. Seltzer and Glass couldn't get Marlon to read the script. So much time passed that Marlon became too old for the leading role, and it was finally played in 1964 by Michael Parks in a film called *The Wild Seed*.

Marlon became engrossed with the problems of India and he proposed a movie about India.

"All right," said Seltzer, "if you feel so strongly about India, why don't you appear in a co-production? India has a thriving industry; in fact, they make more pictures than the United States. The only trouble is that none of them gets out of India. But with your name, I'm sure a picture about India would be sold throughout the world."

"You mean I'd have to go over there and work?" Marlon asked.

"That's the idea."

"Forget it."

At another time he expressed concern over China. After hearing Marlon's comments about China's masses for days, Glass finally told him, "Look, Marlon, it's time you stopped worrying about eight hundred and fifty million Chinese and started being concerned with two Jews—your partners."

After six years with Pennebaker, Glass quit for other pursuits. There was talk of dissolving the company, and Seltzer started looking for a position elsewhere. He found one with Ray Stark, an independent producer. At five one morning Seltzer received a telephone call from Marlon. "Look," he said, "we were just kidding about folding up the company. I want you to stay on."

"Marlon, I can't afford to waste any more of my creative life," Seltzer said. "I'm not keen about coming back. But I will under one condition."

"What's that?"

"That you'll take a real interest in the company."

"I will, Walter. Honest I will."

For five weeks Marlon remained in daily contact with his partner in Pennebaker. Then Seltzer didn't talk to Marlon for two years. The producer finally quit out of frustration and disgust.

"Marlon was bored with Pennebaker," a friend explained. "That is his trouble, or perhaps it is a symptom of his genius: he gets bored easily. He gets bored with women. He gets bored with conversations. He gets bored with movies. Any kind of discipline bores him."

Places bored Marlon, too. First, New York. The excitement he had known in his youth was gone; so were the friendships he had once known there. Now his old friends were in awe of him as superstar. That bored him.

So did Hollywood. He had learned to tolerate it as the source of his income. That made Hollywood no more acceptable—or less boring.

Tahiti was the answer, the ultimate of escape for an Occidental. Beginning in 1961, Marlon found contentment there, not only in the childlike charms of Tarita, but in the French-Polynesian style of living. Marlon savored the privacy that only Tahiti afforded. It was a freedom and a fulfillment that he would always return to.

The radicalization of Marlon Brando began in the early 1960s.

Marlon's liberalism was easy to trace to his youthful rebellion against Midwestern values, the authoritarianism of Shattuck Military Academy, the political conservatism of his father. He was inclined further to the left by affiliation in his early twenties with graduates of the Group Theater, many of them former Communists. In 1948, when he was just emerging from obscurity, he made appearances at New York rallies supporting the presidential candidacy of Henry Wallace. He felt an affinity for the almost unworldly idealism of Wallace: "I'd trust him; I like him personally. I feel he's a man with strong integrity. From what I have been able to learn, Wallace comes the closest to being the kind of man I'd like to have suggest things to me as a citizen. I have no conclusions about government; I know very little about it. But I feel that any decision in this chaos is better than no decision. I must do something."

He did little politically during his next dozen years, when the pressures of his career almost precluded any other activity. He felt little enthusiasm for the candidacy of John F. Kennedy in 1960. Marlon supported Kennedy only because he was the Democratic candidate; and Marlon knew that his brand of liberalism was incompatible with the Republicans.

The first public manifestation of Marlon's activism came in 1960, when he, Shirley MacLaine and Steve Allen appeared in Sacramento to plead with Governor Edmund G. Brown for a commutation of the sentence of Caryl Chessman, a convicted rapist who was scheduled to die in the gas chamber. The governor listened sympathetically but declined to act. The stars then went to San Quentin Prison to maintain a vigil with other protesters of capital punishment. They remained until after Chessman's execution.

In 1963 Brando became thoroughly involved in the struggle for black rights. He was one of the chief organizers of a planeload of celebrities who flew to Washington for the historic march for civil rights. He appeared in Gadsden, Alabama, scene of frequent clashes between black demonstrators and law authorities, and told a gathering in a Negro church, "It's not going to be long before they realize that clubbing you and beating you and jailing you is not going to do any good." He marched with the demonstrators in Torrance, a suburb of Los Angeles, protesting discrimination in an all-white housing development.

Brando also attacked prejudice in Hollywood. Speaking at a conference organized by the arts division of the American Civil Liberties Union, he suggested that stars refuse to work if Negroes were not represented in their films. "All of us are late in joining this movement," he said. "We must do something. This is not a Negro movement. It is a democratic movement."

Making his first trip to England in 1964, Brando gained support from British actors for his proposal that stars' future contracts should prohibit their films from being shown to segregated audiences anywhere. "When you pinch a man in the nose, you impress him; when you punch him in the pocket, you deeply impress him," he said.

Brando began turning up on television talk shows. He shrugged off the usual movie-star questions and talked about political issues. "For too many years I have neglected the forum which was available to me," he said. "Well, I'm not going to neglect it any more. I'm going to use every means at my disposal to get across what I want to say."

Marlon described some of his feelings about Negro rights in a lengthy interview with *Ebony* magazine in October 1963. He was asked when he first became personally involved with the struggle. His reply:

> When this Negro woman in the South, Mrs. Rosa Parks, decided she wasn't going to sit in the back of the bus anymore. From that moment on, I think things began to change. It's very difficult to tell

when you suddenly find yourself in a movement, in thought. I think there are many Negroes now, just as there are many white people, who are not awakened to what is happening. Very few people understand what the nature of this movement is. James Baldwin, I suppose, articulated it as well as anyone. I don't know when it began for me, but I know that the end can only be won when there is hard legislation that supports all of the issues that Rev. Martin Luther King, Rev. Ralph Abernathy, the N.A.A.C.P. and C.O.R.E. people have set down. . . .

Most people don't realize what it meant for James Meredith to go through his daily life at the University of Mississippi knowing that any minute his life could be taken. I'm sure he wondered as he walked along the streets: "Has somebody got me in the crosshairs? Is there a bomb in my locker?" When I went up to Sacramento I talked about this, and I said that if a bullet had come crashing into the brain of Mr. Meredith, nobody would have been surprised. The next day, Medgar Evers was shot. . . .

This poor, dreadful little fellow [George Wallace] who stood in the door at the University of Alabama—it was such a pathetic, ballyhoo political demonstration. These guys, Faubus and the rest of them, are looking for the vote. Privately, perhaps, they know that integration is inevitable—perhaps some of them are even subtly assisting it in some way. But publicly they've got to say that, "We don't want the Negroes to come here to do this and to be with us." Otherwise they're not going to get elected, and they want to get elected. Governor Wallace knew damned well from the word go that there was going to be a bayonet in his behind and he was going to have to get away from that door.

It is amazing that one of the things I have found in common with politicians is that they are just as good actors as we are, because their business involves acting.

Brando found other causes for his energies, particularly the American Indian. He traveled throughout the West to visit Indian councils and listen to the chiefs and young people pour out their grievances with the white man. In January 1964 he went to Washington to plead the Indians' cause with congressmen, reporters, administration officials, and even the widowed Jacqueline Kennedy. He pointed out that Indians were in the lowest income group; that 45 percent of them were unemployed, 20 percent died from malnutrition. He cited a lunchroom sign in his native Nebraska: "No Indians or dogs allowed." He decried cancellation of a Seneca

Marlon marches in Torrance

With Charlton Heston, Harry Belafonte and James Baldwin at the
Lincoln Memorial during the March
on Washington

Marlon in custody of a Washington
State Game Department agent after
the "fish-in"

Indian treaty, signed by George Washington in 1794, because the government wanted to build a dam in western Pennsylvania.

Four months later Brando took more militant action. He participated in a "fish-in" with Puyallup Indians, who declared they had been granted unlimited fishing rights in the Puyallup River of Washington under the treaty of Medicine Creek of 1855. The government had banned fishing on the river.

Brando and an Indian spread a net across the Puyallup and caught two steelhead trout as two hundred Indians cheered. A State Game officer appeared and asked Brando, "Are you openly defying state law?" The actor replied, "I'm helping some Indian friends to fish. If this is defiance of state law, then I guess I'm doing it." He was arrested and booked in the county jail on illegal fishing charges; the charges were later dropped.

The Hollywood establishment considered Brando's activism simply another manifestation of the eccentricity of the brilliant actor. Only a few stars joined him. Others of liberal persuasion had witnessed the penalties of supporting unpopular causes during the 1940s and 1950s: careers had been destroyed, lives ruined.

Those frightening times would not return, but many leaders of the film industry doubted the wisdom of taking stands that might antagonize a portion of the ticket-buying public. They considered their belief confirmed when the outburst of Brando's political activism coincided with the beginning of a slow and steady decline in his movie career.

17

The Dark Years

"What has acting given me?
Money, notoriety, fame, fortune, success.
Mostly weal and woe.
What about success?
It doesn't add anything to your life,
and, as a matter of fact, it takes a lot away.
It destroys some people.
Look at Marilyn Monroe.
It never earned her a nickel's worth—
a dime's worth—of happiness."

THE ROAD TO BANGKOK WAS PAVED WITH GOOD INTENTIONS. MARLON Brando had long wanted to make a film that would illustrate his beliefs: that Americans fail to understand foreigners, especially Asians; that American politicians can be venal and stupid; that American foreign policy is short-sighted and self-serving; that the idealism of Americans abroad is foolhardy, but sometimes quite marvelous.

In 1962 Brando joined with the two young men with whom he had traveled to Asia in search of a film about the United Nations, director George Englund and writer Stewart Stern. Having failed in their first mission, the three prepared a film based on the best-selling novel by Eugene Burdick and William J. Lederer, *The Ugly American.* It was a faintly disguised tract on the mistakes of American aid to Thailand. Designed as a political piece, it lacked the necessary elements for dramatization, and so the film makers had to create their own plots, scenes and characters.

With Sandra Church, The Ugly
American, *1963*

The Ugly American proved controversial from the start. Senator J. William Fulbright arose in the United States Senate to denounce the film project, and elder statesman Samuel Goldwyn attacked it in Hollywood. Both feared the film would present America in an unfavorable light abroad.

"There are few countries left where a picture like this could be made," Brando said in defense of *The Ugly American*. "It couldn't be done in France, the one-time citadel of freedom. Certainly not in Russia. Only America, England, Sweden and a few other countries would permit such self-criticism."

In contrast to *One-Eyed Jacks* and *Mutiny on the Bounty*, *The Ugly American* was filmed on a two-and-a-half-month schedule, including a location in Thailand. Marlon earnestly wanted it to succeed, not merely because he believed in what the film had to say but also because he wanted to offset the bad publicity he had received from the two misguided epics.

Appearing in Bangkok for the world premiere, he told the press, "I feel that this film is critical of the United States. It is critical of the neutralists. And it is critical of the rightist regimes who make no reforms and are not willing to make reasonable and intelligent concessions for the establishment of democracy in their countries. It is critical of the Communists. I think there will be an enormous and perhaps bombastic reaction against this picture in some areas of America. I think it is fitting."

He launched a nationwide tour for *The Ugly American*, receiving more publicity exposure than he had ever experienced before. In Washington he explained why he had undertaken the tour: "I had two reasons. One is I wanted to push *The Ugly American*, which represents for the most part what I believe in, and secondly, I've decided there has to come a time in my life when I have to correct the preconceived notion that the public has of me. I'm not trying to change my image; I'm trying to present it. I've decided I finally want to speak out against slop-oriented journalism and the conversational scavangers who exploit for profit and libel for amusement."

Despite his efforts to publicize it, *The Ugly American* was a failure. Theater bookings were low, especially in the South, where owners feared alienating white patrons who disliked Brando's views on civil rights. Some of those who agreed with him were not prepared to accept Marlon Brando as a witty, well-tailored, pipe-smoking diplomat. Audience involvement was hampered by a

Marlon and George Englund are
garlanded by Thai beauties on arrival
in Bangkok for premier of The
Ugly American

screenplay that attempted to reflect all sides of complex political situations.

The lack of response to *The Ugly American* was tragic. Many of the things it stated about the conduct of American policy in Asia were prophetic, detailing in uncanny accuracy the tragedy of Vietnam. But no one had the prescience to foresee the parallel in 1963.

Bedtime Story (1964) was an attempt to repeat the success that Universal had enjoyed with a series of sex comedies written or co-written by Stanley Shapiro: *Pillow Talk, Operation Petticoat, Come September, Lover Come Back, That Touch of Mink.* Shapiro had been made a producer, and he wrote his next film with a radio-television gag writer, Paul Henning. Titled *King of the Mountain,* it was the story of two con men, one a former American soldier, the other a sophisticated European, who combined their talents to fleece American widows and divorcées. Among the co-stars considered: Gary Grant and Tony Curtis; Cary Grant and Rock Hudson; Gregory Peck and Tony Curtis.

The earthiness of *King of the Mountain* appealed to Marlon Brando, and he agreed to make the film as a co-production of Pennebaker. A topflight farceur was needed for the other role, and David Niven was signed. The director was a newcomer to films, Ralph Levy, who had directed television comedy shows.

Before production began, Shapiro told Brando, "I've heard some wild stories about you. I don't know whether they're true or not. But when we work together I'd like to have an understanding: one, that you'll be on the set on time; two, that you'll know your lines."

Brando was not offended by Shapiro's frankness. "Look, a lot of what you've heard was not true," he said. "A lot of what you've heard *may* be true—but I had my reasons. You don't have to worry."

His conduct was exemplary throughout the filming. His only failing was a sudden loss of memory which curiously affected him in unimportant scenes. His lines simply vanished out of his head and nothing could bring them back. It happened two or three times, and the director had to go to other scenes and return when the mental blank had passed.

The reviews for *Bedtime Story*, as it was finally called, ranged from fair to brutal ("a vulgar soporific for the little-brained ones"— Judith Crist, New York *Herald Tribune*). Business was only fair. The hidden boycott of Brando films prevented full booking of the comedy.

Brando's stance as an adherent of civil rights mitigated against the success of *Bedtime Story*. So did the Brando face. It was simply too strong, too commanding to portray a simple-minded con man who earned his livelihood by seducing rich women.

"Sometimes," Marlon Brando was telling an interviewer, "I need the money. It is like a car and the oil dipstick. You look at it once in a while, and find you need oil. Well, every so often I look at my financial condition and I find I need money, so I do a good-paying picture. You see, I have three households to support and I pay alimony to two women."

He was telling frankly why he undertook a film like *Morituri* (1965), a World War II sea-spy melodrama. There was little other reason. But Marlon agreed to do the film for his fellow veteran of the *Mutiny on the Bounty*, Aaron Rosenberg, who had moved

Bedtime Story, *1964*

from MGM to Twentieth Century-Fox. Marlon was enthusiastic about working with Bernhard Wicki, whose direction of *The Bridge* he had admired.

Within two weeks after the beginning of filming, Marlon was at odds with Wicki. The German directed in a mechanical way, devising all the camera movements and lighting with stand-ins and then summoning the actors to perform the scene. This was impossible for Marlon, who rarely knew what his performance would be —or even what his lines were—before stepping into the set.

He began needling Wicki, and he asked for rewrites of his scenes. *Morituri* fell weeks behind schedule.

"It's like pushing a prune pit with my nose from here to Cuca-monga," said Marlon to a set visitor, "and now I find myself in Azusa." He added cheerfully, "Of course if this picture is good, all the grief will be forgotten. But when a picture is bad, all you can do is stick a lampshade on your head and stand real still and hope nobody notices you."

It was lampshade time. In assessing Brando's work in the film, which was released under the unwieldy title *The Saboteur: Code Name—Morituri,* Pauline Kael wrote: "Like many another great actor who has become fortune's fool, he plays the great ham. He seems as pleased with the lines as if he'd just thought them up. He gives the best ones a carefully timed double take so that we, too, can savor his cleverness and the delight of his German accent."

Despite the smell of failure over the enterprise, Brando agreed to help promote it. In New York he received a string of visiting television reporters who taped interviews for release in their home cities. Brando was at his puckish best, particularly when being interviewed by a pretty girl. An excerpt from a tape with a girl named Metrinko from a Boston station gives an illustration of the Brando style:

With Yul Brynner, The Saboteur:
Code Name—Morituri, *1965*

20th Century Fox

METRINKO Our viewing audience would like to know why you're here and for you to tell us about your latest movie—

BRANDO How old are you?

METRINKO —*Morituri.*

BRANDO No, you? Twenty-three?

METRINKO No, I'll be twenty-one in March.

BRANDO Twenty-one . . .

METRINKO Yes, but this is supposed to be a woman's privilege.

BRANDO What is?

METRINKO Her age.

BRANDO You're talking like an American adage.

METRINKO No, please, do tell us about your new movie.

BRANDO Well, why?

METRINKO Because we're looking forward to seeing it in Boston.

BRANDO That's the thing. Are you?

METRINKO We certainly are.

BRANDO Excuse me, I didn't mean to touch your ankle. What can I tell you about it?

METRINKO Oh, if you'd like to tell us something about, oh, behind the scenes while you were making the picture, or—

BRANDO How far behind the scenes?

METRINKO Oh, just some interesting things our audience would like to hear about.

BRANDO Well . . .

METRINKO I'm sure you've run into—

BRANDO Bernie Wicki smokes the worst cigars of anyone I ever knew. I hate his cigars. And . . . he smokes cigars that were made of— They got some shoes from Italian fishermen, with rope soles, rope-soled sandals, they crushed them up and mashed them around and sent them to Vladivostok. [Publicist hands Brando a note.] She was Miss U.S.A.! Is that a fact?

METRINKO Yes, it is.

BRANDO Well, I . . . I could have guessed.

METRINKO That's very sweet of you.

BRANDO Well, you know it's unusual to find somebody as beautiful as you are who is also a college graduate, and seriously interested in world affairs and studying law.

METRINKO Well, I enjoyed being Miss U.S.A.

BRANDO She was Miss U.S.A.! What year was that?

METRINKO In '64.

BRANDO (to audience) In 1964 she was Miss U.S.A. I asked her if she was pretty and said she—well, that was a subjective opinion and she didn't really know.

METRINKO   Well, there were only six judges that decided, so I don't think that's very decisive.

BRANDO   Yes, but you went through several stages to finally arrive at the title, didn't you? So it was really more than six judges?

METRINKO   Well, six here and six there . . . and I was very honored. But Mr. Brando! Thank you so much for being our guest.

BRANDO   Good night, folks. Smoke Optima cigars.

By the mid-1960s, Marlon still viewed new movie projects in terms of their social content, but he seemed to have lost the ability to judge scripts for their dramatic impact or popular appeal. This lack of perception resulted in a series of muddled, unrealized films.

The Chase (1965) was an adaptation by Lillian Hellman of an unsuccessful play by Horton Foote. Sam Spiegel produced the film, and Arthur Penn directed a cast that included Marlon Brando, Jane Fonda, Robert Redford, E. G. Marshall, Angie Dickinson, Janice Rule, Miriam Hopkins, Martha Hyer and Robert Duvall.

The first trouble was the Hellman script, which depicted the inhabitants of a small Texas town with unrelieved meanness. Then Spiegel decided that most of the action could be photographed on the back lots of Columbia and Universal studios, thus eliminating any atmosphere of reality.

As the sheriff who tried to maintain order in the hate-ridden town, Brando had no scenes to challenge his talent. He made no secret of his contempt for the project. "Fuck 'em," he told Stanley Kramer, who visited the set. "If they're going to be so stupid, I'll just take the money, do what they want, and get out. I don't give a damn about anything."

He was moody and uncommunicative throughout the filming. As he always did when he found himself in situations he detested, he mumbled. The sound man had so much trouble recording Brando's dialogue that he hid a microphone in the sheriff's desk.

The Chase continued the erosion of Brando's reputation. "Poor Mr. Brando," wrote Bosley Crowther in the *New York Times.* "He just rides around in his prowl car. To be sure, the character assigned him is ambiguous and gross, and Mr. Brando cannot make it any more than a stubborn, growling cop." Crowther called it "a phony, tasteless movie."

The Appaloosa (1966), resulted from the takeover in 1962 of Pennebaker films by MCA, at which time Brando had received a

With director Arthur Penn and Angie
Dickinson, The Chase, *1966*

large sum of cash and his father was provided with an income
(Marlon, Sr., died in 1965). Marlon gave MCA a commitment for
five films at $270,000 apiece plus an amount of MCA stock.

In more ways than one, Marlon admitted to himself, it was a sell-
out. Gone were his early dreams of using Pennebaker to create
meaningful motion pictures about the world's ills. He had sold out
to his one-time agents, men with an obviously greater regard for

commerce than art. He had seen these men put the squeeze on producers in his behalf; would they now pressure him for their own advantage? Marlon approached *The Appaloosa* in a black mood.

MCA had chosen as his director Sidney J. Furie, a young Canadian who had been praised for his visually stylish *The Ipcress File.* When Furie first met Brando, the director commented, "I'm really looking forward to this picture."

"Why?" Brando replied. "We've got no script."

"Yes, but when I started *Ipcress,* I had no script, either. At any rate, I consider it a real privilege to be working with you."

"Bullshit," Brando replied.

The producer of *The Appaloosa* was Alan J. Miller, a long-time MCA executive who had developed the agency's television-film subsidiary, Revue Productions. He was being rewarded with his first feature production, and he prepared *The Appaloosa* with enthusiasm. His zeal diminished during the first script meeting with Brando, Furie and James Bridges, author of the screenplay. Brando threw out one quarter of the script because it involved an Indian fight. "I won't kill any Indians," he announced.

With Anjanette Comer, The Appaloosa, *1966*   Universal Pictures

Four months remained before the start of filming, and producer Miller was certain that an acceptable script could be achieved. The script sessions continued, with Brando suggesting new approaches, then rejecting them. Bridges wrote additional sequences for the script, and they were incorporated, then deleted. The date for departure to the location approached, and the script remained in fragmented form. But the start could not be postponed, because of the Brando commitment. *The Appaloosa* company departed for St. George, Utah.

Brando was apathetic from the beginning. His only interest in the script was in trying to construct a statement. "How can we turn this story into something that will help the Indian?" he asked script-writer Bridges. There was no way. The script had been altered to place emphasis on the Brando character's pursuit of his favorite Appaloosa horse. When actor John Saxon reported to the location, Brando asked him what he thought of the script. "It looks to me like 'Boy Meets Horse, Boy Loses Horse, Boy Gets Horse,'" said Saxon. Brando agreed. With the rewriting, Saxon's role became more important. One day he remarked to Brando, "You know, I've got a lot of things going for me now. I might steal this picture."

"Be my guest," Brando said.

His relations with Furie worsened. The star sometimes made suggestions for scenes; more often he played his scenes mechanically. As he sometimes did in times of stress, he overate. His belly became so distended that in the afternoons he could not fit into his costume, and he had to be excused from filming for the rest of the day. Many of his long shots were performed by his double.

The memory lapse also afflicted him. During one cabin scene with Miriam Coyle, Brando could not deliver the simplest of dialogue. It was a brief portion of the script, but it required ten days to shoot.

James Bridges finally despaired of fashioning an intelligible script and departed from St. George in the middle of the night. Another writer, Roland Kibbee, was flown in from Hollywood, and he began turning out new pages. But much of what he produced had already been superseded by scenes improvised by Furie, Brando and Saxon.

Part of Brando's dissatisfaction with Furie was due to the director's insistence on the kind of visual trickery that had helped establish his reputation with *The Ipcress File*. Many of the crew agreed with Brando; "Furie's even shooting up the horse's ass," said one of them.

The tension between star and director exploded during snow sequences at Wrightwood, California. The cumulated frustrations welled up in Furie when Brando failed to respond to direction.

"You think you're a big fucking star," Furie shouted, "but you're a failure as a human being!" Brando merely smiled.

Alan J. Miller used all his executive talents in an effort to keep *The Appaloosa* moving. But his plans were often frustrated by Brando, who saw Miller as a symbol of authority and hence someone not to be trusted. During a rare moment of light-heartedness, the producer composed a jingle to be sung to the theme from *The Appaloosa* (Brando's Spanish name in the film was Mateo):

> Mateo, his heart.
> It bleeds for the mass.
> But the people he works with
> He kicks in the ass.

Surprisingly, *The Appaloosa* was completed on schedule and within budget. Brando abruptly left for London and *A Countess from Hong Kong* without finishing the sound recording for *The Appaloosa.* He promised to do it in London. But when Miller and Furie arrived for the chore, Brando kept them waiting for weeks.

Critics showed as much apathy for *The Appaloosa* as had Brando. Arthur Knight in the *Saturday Review* said that Brando gave the impression of delivering a guest performance in someone else's picture. Richard L. Coe wrote in the Washington *Post:* "Brando's self-indulgence over a dozen years is costing him and his public his talents."

The public responded as had the critics, and *The Appaloosa* lost money for MCA. After his experience with Brando, Alan J. Miller announced that he was retiring from show business.

18

The Dark Years
(cont'd)

*"Most of the successful people in Hollywood
are the way they are for only one reason:
It's the hardest thing in the world
to accept a pinch of success
and leave it that way."*

MARLON BRANDO HELD NO ESTEEM FOR THE PROFESSION OF ACTING,
not when he embarked on his career, certainly not in mid-passage,
when he found so little reward. After dealing with actors as director of *One-Eyed Jacks,* he remarked in a baleful mood, "Acting by and large is an expression of a neurotic impulse. I've never
in my life met an actor who was not neurotic—not that it's bad to be
neurotic. It's just not satisfying. Once you've developed the faculty,
you can continue being an actor long after you're too neurotic to
be anything else. Every time I talk to an actor, I ask what he enjoys.
The answers include none of the things that you would expect. The
answers are pathetic. They start out general—'It gives me pleasure
to act'; 'I can express myself on stage and I am unable to do so in
life'; 'I can communicate'; 'I like to be appreciated.' Those are all
stock neurotic answers. I think the truth is that actors are actors
because it gives them sustenance for their narcissism. Acting en-
ables them to experience a false form of love and attention, the
same kind of attention given any exhibition. The fact is the actor
is released from the confinement of neurotic inhibitions by being,
so to speak, the part he plays.

"Acting is a bum's life in that it leads to perfect self-indulgence.
You get paid for doing nothing, and it all adds up to nothing."

That seemed to be his philosophy as he pushed into his forties. He admitted that he had no direction: "The last fifteen years of my life seem never to have happened; they've just gone up the chimney without any knowing impression or impact on me at all. . . . I still feel that Hollywood is a cultural boneyard. To a degree, anyway. This is a business, not an art. It's a movie industry, remember? True, I've become a businessman. But I'm a very poor business-man."

Even though he had been earning $1 million a picture or more, plus 10 percent of the gross profits, he was not a wealthy man. Payments to his wives and children consumed a large part of his income. Many others depended on him for their livelihood, and he was open-handed with causes he believed in.

So he had to continue making movies, although his enthusiasm for them had gone. One of the most hopeful of the projects was *A Countess from Hong Kong*. It was obviously a major film event: Charlie Chaplin's first film in eight years, the first in which he did not star since *A Woman of Paris* in 1923.

The story had been in Chaplin's mind since 1931, when he took a voyage to Shanghai. After his marriage to Paulette Goddard, he conceived a romantic comedy which would portray her as a White Russian emigrée seeking to escape from her life in China as a bar-room girl. The project was shelved with the end of his marriage to Goddard.

In 1965 Chaplin revived the plot at the urging of a young producer friend, Jerry Epstein. Chaplin asked Sophia Loren to play the White Russian emigrée, and she quickly agreed. For the American diplomat with whom she stowed away, Chaplin wanted Marlon Brando.

A Countess from Hong Kong was being organized by Jay Kanter, who had advanced in MCA to control of Universal's filming in England. Kanter urged Brando to fly to London for a conference with Chaplin. They met at the Savoy Hotel, where Chaplin was staying, and the comedian recited the entire script, assuming the identities of each role. They went out to dinner, and Chaplin spent the evening recounting stories of his past.

Chaplin's performance would have convinced anyone—except Marlon Brando. He remained skeptical of the enterprise and asked to see the script. Chaplin sent him one in California, then cabled instructions to disregard it as he was writing an entirely new one.

04-18

With Sophia Loren, A Countess
from Hong Kong, *1967*

Brando finally decided to do *A Countess from Hong Kong* "because Chaplin asked me. When a man of his stature in the industry writes a script for you, you can hardly refuse. Why he should think of me for a comedy, I haven't the faintest idea. But he said I was the only one who could play it." Marlon added with a grin, "Which makes me wonder why he has also been calling Sean Connery."

Brando flew off to London with an air of trepidation. His fears were confirmed during the first days of filming. Never before had Brando worked with a director who demanded such total control. Chaplin dealt with everyone in an imperious way; his wife, Oona, remained on the set at all times and acted as go-between, soothing hurt feelings and softening her husband's stern orders.

At first Brando was at a loss to know how to deal with Chaplin. He began with a casual approach, treating Chaplin with humor and approaching his work in the usual offhanded way. But after Brando had twice reported late to the set, Chaplin snapped, "That is the most unprofessional thing I've ever heard of—an actor coming late to work!" Thereafter Brando was on time.

He bowed to the master in other, more important ways. The Brando method had always been to search a character and the situation, and attempt to draw from within something that seemed valid and interesting. Chaplin wanted no such contribution from the actors. He acted out each scene and expected the performers to duplicate what he had mimed.

No detail was too small. During one scene Brando waved cigar smoke away from his face. He used two outstretched fingers. "No, Marlon, I think you should use four fingers," Chaplin suggested.

Marlon and Sophia Loren at first exhibited a respectful cordiality. As filming continued, a coolness grew between them, and they exchanged words only when required to do so in a scene. Loren, like Anna Magnani, was not Marlon's kind of female. "As far as I can see," he remarked to an acquaintance, "Sophia isn't very feminine." She suspected him of eating garlic before their love scenes. He was astonished by her cool-headed approach to her profession, by her businesslike attitude toward publicity. She accepted all interviewers, posed willingly for photographs. Loren dominated publicity on *A Countess from Hong Kong,* since Chaplin would talk to no one, and Brando initially said no to any interviews. But when he saw Loren starring in all the news stories, he relented. His first interview was with Roderick Mann of the London Sunday *Express,* and Brando warned the publicity man, "I can only give him an hour." Marlon accompanied Mann to a London restaurant and talked continuously, and brilliantly, for three and a half hours.

One day in April 1966 Marlon finished a scene with Loren and walked to his dressing room. He felt a sudden stab in his stomach and doubled over in pain. After lying on the dressing-room bed for an hour, he felt the agony diminishing and was able to return to his flat in Chester Square. During dinner the pain returned, and he was taken to a hospital.

Eight doctors diagnosed his ailment as appendicitis and recommended immediate operation. A ninth doctor demurred. Marlon refused to submit to the appendectomy until his own doctor arrived from California.

The pain was unremitting. He could neither sleep nor eat, and drugs provided no relief. As he lay sleepless in the hospital room, he convinced himself that he had cancer and that the doctors were trying to keep the news from him. When Jay Kanter and the Universal publicity man, David Golding, visited him, Brando told them of his suspicions. "If I should die, I want one thing clear," he said to Golding.

"What's that, Marlon?" the publicist asked.

"There will be no publicity photos of Sophia weeping over my grave."

Marlon's doctor arrived, and his analysis was reassuring. The patient had neither cancer nor appendicitis. The English had been misled because Marlon's appendix was not where it should have been; it was in his midsection. The pain was caused by a twisted intestine. He was placed on a diet to lose fifteen pounds, and soon he was able to return to work at Pinewood Studios. He finished out the picture with complete and uncharacteristic acquiescence to Chaplin's direction. One scene required Brando to drum his fingers on a dining table as he fought off seasickness. Chaplin rehearsed the finger movements time after time, and he reshot the scene four times before he was satisfied with it.

"Chaplin's a nice old gent," Marlon said in a charitable mood. "We do things his way, that's all. He shows us how; he doesn't really know how a scene works until he does it himself. So I've just been following directions. I've done that before, with Kazan, and . . ." His voice dropped away as he tried to think of other directors.

A Countess from Hong Kong didn't work. It was too much to expect that a seventy-seven-year-old man, no matter how great his one-time genius, could produce a sophisticated comedy for a new generation of moviegoers. Critics found various ways to express their sadness and disappointment, and some didn't even bother to be polite: "Chaplin's film takes us straight back to the mood of 1931"; "painfully antique bedroom farce"; "primitive in its technique, its execution, its sentiment and its humor"; "bad enough to make a new generation of moviegoers wonder what the Chaplin cult was all about."

Chaplin bristled at being called old-fashioned and insisted it was the critics who were. "I'm not worried," he said. "I still think it's a great film, and I think audiences will agree with me rather than the critics." But the audiences didn't, and another failure was attached to the dwindling career of Marlon Brando.

Marlon vanished to Tahiti after each unrewarding film. He felt the urge to stay there, but he couldn't. He was forced to continue making films, and each decision on a new project became an agony. In 1966 he considered an offer to play opposite Elizabeth Taylor in a Gothic tale by Carson McCullers, *Reflections in a Golden Eye.* Ray Stark, who was producing the film for Seven Arts, sent the script to Brando, who couldn't decide whether to accept or not. He flew to Ireland to discuss the project with John Huston, the director of the film.

Brando drove to Huston's manor house in County Galway. Huston listened for several hours as Brando outlined his ideas for *Reflections in a Golden Eye.* After Brando had finished, Huston said, "I think your ideas are very sound, Marlon, but they don't coincide with my conception of the picture. Now, I'm just having the new script retyped. Why don't you read it and then tell me what you think?"

Brando studied the script late that afternoon and commented, "I think it's very good. Let me think about it." He decided that a walk would aid his contemplation, so he strolled out of the house and into a torrential rainstorm. Night fell, and Brando didn't return. His host became concerned that the actor had become lost on the back roads of County Galway, and he sent a driver into the storm to locate Brando. The driver found him ambling down a lane, completely soaked. "Get in, Mr. Brando," said the man.

With Elizabeth Taylor, Reflections in
a Golden Eye, 1967

Warner Bros.

"No, thanks," Marlon answered. "I'm not lost; I know where I
am."

Late in the evening Brando returned and went directly to bed.
The next morning Huston asked him, "Well, what do you think?"

"I'd like to make the film," Brando replied.

Next came the matter of terms. Brando conferred with Elizabeth
Taylor, and she said, "Why don't you ask for a million dollars?
That's what I'm getting." He asked for it and got it.

Ray Stark's partners in Seven Arts had worried about Brando's
work habits. Their worries proved groundless. Brando knew his
lines, did not quarrel with the script and was on time. Miss Taylor
was not. But when she did appear, she was prepared, and Huston
soon made up for the lost time.

Filming began in New York locations, then the bulk of the movie was shot in Rome. Huston marveled at Brando's perfectionism. Brando had a lengthy speech on leadership to deliver to a class of soldiers. Huston considered Brando's first rendition ideal and said, "Print it." Brando asked, "May I do it again?" Huston agreed, and to his astonishment Brando delivered the speech in a completely different but totally effective manner. He asked to do the scene once more, and again it was a new interpretation. In editing *Reflections in a Golden Eye,* Huston was in a quandary about which of the three versions to select.

The filming of *Reflections in a Golden Eye* was uneventful except for one offstage happening. Tarita came to visit Marlon in Rome, bringing their son, Tehotu. *Paparazzi* camped outside Brando's rented house on the island of Tiberia, hoping for a photograph which could bring a high price from European magazines and newspapers. Two photographers saw their chance when Brando emerged from the house holding a four-year-old boy in his arms, and they started taking pictures. Marlon put the boy down, raced outside and slugged one of the photographers. He began pummeling the other until the man broke free and ran. Brando returned to the house and emerged with a broken bottle in his hand. But by this time the *paparazzi* had fled.

John Huston considered *Reflections in a Golden Eye* as near-perfect a film as he had ever made. The critics did not agree. The picture opened to good business in the big cities, then attendance fell off after the first week. This may have been partly due to the timidity of the releasing company, Warner Bros.; its executives feared the raciness of the film and kept the advertising campaign in a low key. Another factor may have been the public's unwillingness to accept Marlon Brando in the role of Elizabeth Taylor's homosexual husband. It was an expensive failure that subtracted from the box-office allure of both Taylor and Brando.

The Night of the Following Day continued Brando's unhappy relationship with MCA-Universal. It was a kidnapping tale set in France, with Brando playing a chauffeur (curiously, with his boyhood name of Bud) and Richard Boone as a sadist named Leer. The producer, director and co-author of the script was Hubert Cornfield, an American who had made a few minor films. As was his custom with a new director, Marlon tested Cornfield by making out-

With Rita Moreno, The Night of the
Following Day, *1969*

Universal Pictures

landish suggestions for script revisions. The director was too much
in awe of the great Brando to argue. That ended any chance for a
creative relationship.

Brando treated Cornfield with a mixture of derision and contempt. He insisted on calling the director "Herbert," although he
knew Cornfield's name was Hubert. "All right, Herbert, tell me
what you want me to do," Marlon would say challengingly. Cornfield became tongue-tied.

The Night of the Following Day was made tolerable for Brando by the presence of an old friend from the Actors Studio days, Richard Boone. A lusty, combative man, Boone stimulated Brando on and off the movie stage. During a beach location Cornfield gave an instruction to Boone for his scene with Brando. "Okay, Hubert, I'll do it," Boone responded. "But it makes about as much sense to me as a rat fucking a grapefruit." Brando collapsed in laughter. Every time he looked at Boone during their scene together, he began laughing uncontrollably. Cornfield had to cancel shooting before noon.

Two weeks before the end of *The Night of the Following Day,* Brando informed one of the two executive producers, Elliott Kastner, that he could no longer work with Cornfield. Kastner saw the futility of trying to argue with Brando. "Who do you want to finish the picture?" the producer asked. Brando pointed at Richard Boone.

Brando's performance had been lackadaisical throughout the film, so much so that the French film workers asked, "Is this the great Brando? He is nothing!" After Boone assumed direction, Brando continued in the same vein until Boone remarked, "Hey, asshole, it's me. Don't pull that shit on me. Quit phoning in your lines." Now, for the first time, the French film workers saw the creative Brando. But the new sense of reality came too late to rescue *The Night of the Following Day.*

Charles Champlin wrote in the Los Angeles *Times:* ". . . Marlon Brando giving still another parody of the Marlon Brando who used to be is more like tragic." Other reviews followed the same vein and *The Night of the Following Day* swept in and out of release faster than any of Brando's twenty-two films.

Candy was a bad dirty joke to which Marlon Brando lent his presence as a courtesy to his dear friend Christian Marquand. The Frenchman was directing the American-French-Italian co-production, based on the novel by Terry Southern and Mason Hoffenberg. The Brando name helped finance the film and lure other guest stars: Walter Matthau, Richard Burton, John Huston, James Coburn and Ringo Starr.

Brando was to play Grindl, an Indian guru whom the nymphet Candy accompanied on a cross-country search for the Great

With Ewa Aulin, *Candy, 1968*   Cinerama

Buddha. Brando, of course, wanted his portion of the script rewritten.

The screen writer was Buck Henry, a gifted young comedy stylist
who had written *The Graduate* for the screen. Brando went to visit
Henry at the Plaza Athenée Hotel in Paris, accompanied by the
French moneyman for *Candy,* Peter Zoref, a conspiratorial-looking
man who wore dark glasses indoors and out. The two visitors found
Henry suffering from food poisoning. Henry tried to defer the con-

ference, but Brando insisted on continuing, even while the writer made trips to the bathroom. While Henry retched, Brando shouted comments about how the comedy elements of his sequence could be heightened.

There was a brief silence from within, and Brando opened the bathroom door to find Henry nearly unconscious as he hunched over the toilet. Brando lifted the slender writer into his arms, carried him into the bedroom and laid him out on the bed. Brando sat down beside him and continued reading from the script and making suggestions to increase the hilarity. Zoref remained stolid behind his dark glasses, taking an occasional puff on a cigar.

A knock came at the door and a waiter entered to remove the dinner tray. He stopped and surveyed the scene with open mouth: an American gangster sitting in a chair like a stuffed figure; a thin corpse stretched out on the bed; a famous movie star sitting on the bed and guffawing over pages he was reading. The waiter slowly turned and walked out the door, closing it quietly behind him. It was a better scene than any that appeared in *Candy*.

Their number was dwindling, but some of the long-time Brando admirers clung to the belief that he would return to greatness in a single, awing performance. They viewed each new Brando film for evidence of such a renaissance. Some found hints of the old magic; Brando was incapable of a valueless performance. But there was no reappearance of a Stanley Kowalski or a Terry Malloy.

There seemed to be hope in 1968 when Elia Kazan announced that Marlon Brando would star in *The Arrangement*. At last Brando would be working again with the director he respected most, who had elicited his greatest performances. Of course, *The Arrangement* was not the social document that *On the Waterfront* was. But Kazan's novel had been an immense success, assuring a presold audience for the film version. Marlon made another move that held promise for his career and reputation. He agreed to co-star with Paul Newman in an original acreenplay, *Butch Cassidy and the Sundance Kid*, to be directed by George Roy Hill for Twentieth Century-Fox.

On April 4, 1968, a rifle shot crashed through the neck and jaw of Martin Luther King, Jr., at a Memphis motel. All Americans were shocked by the murder of the civil rights leader. Marlon Brando was devastated.

He had met Dr. King at a fund-raising gathering for the Southern Christian Leadership Conference at Burt Lancaster's house in 1963. Brando immediately donated $5,000 and his services for whatever the S.C.L.C. wanted him to do. He traveled around the country to raise funds and help in protest marches, and he led the delegation of film people to the March on Washington. Six weeks before the assassination he had met with Dr. King and reiterated his intention to serve the S.C.L.C.

Brando dropped out of sight after King's death. A week later he turned up at the funeral of Bobby Hutton, a seventeen-year-old member of the Black Panthers who had been shot by Oakland police in a gun battle. Bobby Seale, chairman of the Oakland Black Panthers, claimed that Hutton had been told by police to run to a patrol car, then was shot ten times; police said he ignored orders to halt. Two policemen and another Black Panther were wounded in the fight.

After inspecting the bullet-riddled house where Hutton had been killed, Brando attended the funeral and a rally of two thousand black and white people near the county courthouse where another Black Panther, Huey Newton, was jailed for the alleged killing of a policeman. Marlon addressed the gathering from the flatbed of a truck: "I have just come from the funeral of Bobby Hutton. . . . That could have been my son lying there. The preacher said that the white man can't cool it because he never dug it. That is why I am here."

His mind was too full with the cataclysmic events of early 1968 to consider playing a guilt-ridden advertising man in *The Arrangement* or a gun-happy vagabond of the Old West in *Butch Cassidy and the Sundance Kid.* He announced his withdrawal from both films, and his intention to devote full time to the struggle for human rights.

"I believe with the late Martin Luther King that we are either going to learn to live together as brothers in this country or die separately as fools," he explained. "It is either nonviolence or nonexistence. . . . I have three children, and I would not like to think that they will grow up in a world filled with strife. I want to offer my kids the best world possible; not one filled with hatred, suspicion, fear and superficial claptrap values that have nothing to do with reality."

Elia Kazan was greatly disappointed with Brando's withdrawal from *The Arrangement.* Yet Kazan, himself a one-time activist who had risked—and almost lost—his career by joining the Communist party, could not fault Marlon's decision. "I thought that his reasons ran deeper," Kazan remarked later, "that there were other reasons he didn't know or couldn't express. But I couldn't feel any acrimony toward him. He had done so much for me—helped me in three important parts—that I could feel nothing but gratitude and affection for him. You don't expect an artist to act in a normal way."

Brando didn't retire. He continued scrutinizing the film offers that came to him, searching more than ever before for messages of social import. He found a film that attacked the colonialism he detested—*Quemada,* based on a slave uprising in the Caribbean. The film maker was Gillo Pontecorvo, whose *The Battle of Algiers* Marlon had greatly admired.

Pontecorvo was a headstrong young Italian who typified a new generation of *auteur* directors of Europe, stylists who considered their own reactions of greater import than those of his actors. Many another director had failed to understand the unique creative needs of Marlon Brando. Pontecorvo didn't try.

Quemada began filming near Cartagena, Colombia, in late 1968. Conditions were miserable: incessant heat, bad food and lodging, insects and disease. Pontecorvo continued pushing his technicians and actors. Under a searing sun, the director required Brando to perform the same scenes forty times, and there seemed to be little difference between each take.

Month after month the filming continued. Half of the company required hospitalization and many quit. Brando, his hatred for Pontecorvo growing, was incensed to learn that the director was paying black extras at a lower rate than the whites; that was quickly remedied. Brando protested when horses were worked in the intense heat until they fell in exhaustion. His greatest indignation came when Pontecorvo continued working a boy actor who had become ill with a worm infection.

After seven months of production, Brando issued an ultimatum: he would work no more in Colombia; the company would have to be relocated in some other part of the world. The Italian producer, Alberto Grimaldi, argued that only ten days of filming remained, that a move would add $250,000 to the budget. Brando was adamant.

Grimaldi transported the *Quemada* company to Marrakesh in Morocco. The hostility between Brando and Pontecorvo grew more bitter, and Brando went for days without speaking to the director. "I've spent ten years on the couch," Marlon commented to a visitor, "and I still don't know what to do with the urge to kill. Right now I want to kill Gillo. I really want to kill him."

He was asked why.

"Because he has no fucking feeling for people," Marlon replied.

Pontecorvo's response: "Brando is a great artist. A great artist. He can give more than it is possible for an actor to give. But—I never saw an actor before who was so afraid of the camera. And I do not think any artist should be so difficult. I think of Bach and all those kids, still getting his work done. . . . Brando is also, I think, a little—how you say?—paranoiac. He thinks when I make forty takes it's because I want to break him. Why should I want to break him?"

Quemada was finally completed amid a flurry of recriminations, including a lawsuit against Brando for $700,000 in production losses. The film was released by United Artists under the title of *Burn!* and it displayed patchwork caused by the chaotic conditions under which it was filmed. It also exhibited in many scenes a mature Brando capable of the depth of feeling and shading of character that he had shown in the 1950s. But *Burn!* went unattended, and it soon vanished from American theaters.

A young English film maker, Michael Winner, was surprised to learn in 1970 that Marlon Brando was interested in appearing in Winner's new version of *The Turn of the Screw,* to be called *The Nightcomers.* Winner had submitted the script to a partner of Jay Kanter, who showed it to Brando.

Winner was overjoyed by Brando's interest in *The Nightcomers* and surprised that the actor would agree to the stringent terms: no salary, a percentage of the profits. The director flew to California for a day-long talk with Brando, and they reached agreement on the film.

Brando took a house in Cambridge and asked Winner to find him some Irish workingmen whose accents he could study. The director located five, and Brando spent an evening in a pub with them, listening to them as they talked and drank beer and he drank gin. Afterward Brando sent each a personal letter and a bottle of whiskey.

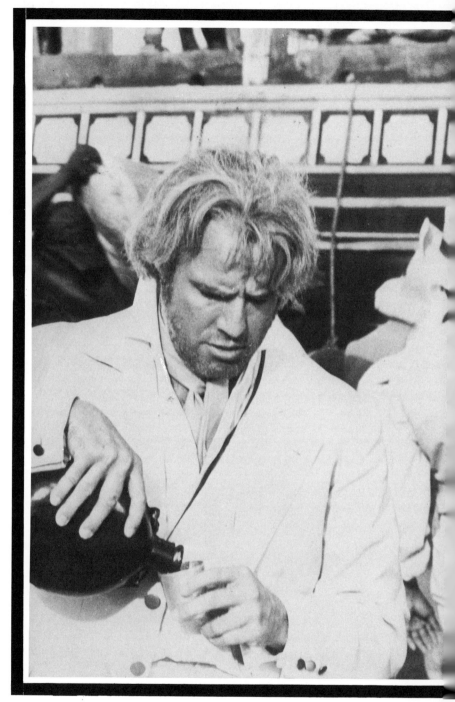

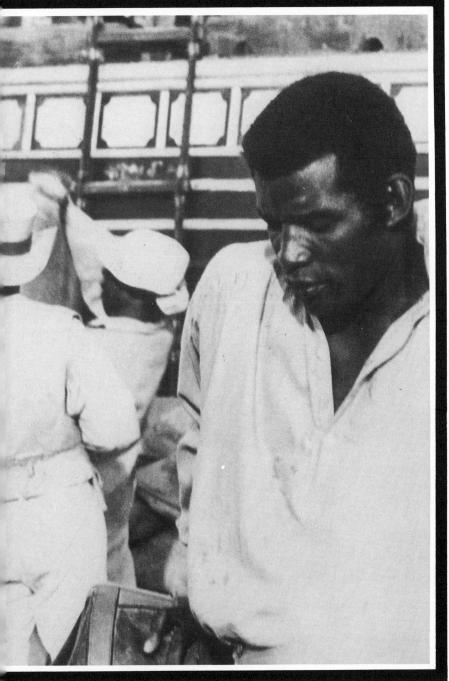

Burn! *1970*

With Stephanie Beacham, The Nightcomers, *1971*

Avco-Embassy

The filming went smoothly, and Winner remained firm but respectful—he always addressed Brando as "sir." Once he asked Brando to perform a scene a second time in a different way and was surprised when the actor repeated it in the same manner. Winner again asked for a different approach, and Brando slapped the side of his head. An ear plug fell out, and he explained that he shut out extraneous noises that way. Brando then performed the scene according to the director's instructions.

The Nightcomers finished on schedule and with a feeling of amity, and Brando flew back to California. When the film was released late in 1971, some critics remarked on the effective portrayal by Brando as the mysterious gardener, Quint. Many others simply did not review *The Nightcomers*. A Brando movie was no longer an event.

Brando did not lose money on *The Nightcomers*. MCA, seeing no advantage in future Brando films, agreed to pay him cash for a remaining film commitment and assumed his percentage of the proceeds from *The Nightcomers*.

19

Don Corleone

*"Some parts are closer to you than others,
but they're all hard work.
Sometimes you feel like being devoted to your job,
and other times you feel the antithesis.
You aren't always walking
with your head up into the sunlight, you know,
feeling as if you have reached absolute clarity
and elucidation of man's fate."*

IN HOLLYWOOD'S VIEW, MARLON BRANDO'S MOVIE CAREER WAS OVER. To be sure, he could go on appearing in films abroad, working with some foreign director who might tolerate his temperament. But the men who now ran the motion-picture business would not hire him. They were strong-minded businessmen—former salesmen, accountants, agents who knew the value of a dollar and were determined to place the studios on a sound financial basis. No more the profligacy of the past. Movies would be made on strict budgets, and those who wasted money would be fired. Marlon Brando was the epitome of the wasteful, headstrong star. Hadn't he nearly sent MGM into bankruptcy with *Mutiny on the Bounty?* To hire him in the 1970s would be suicidal.

Marlon seemed not to care. He had rejected Hollywood, not vice versa. The stupidity of the executive mind, both the new breed and the old, appalled him. His opinion of the general run of American films had not changed since his Broadway days, when he accused them of being vapid and superficial. If he had to work, it would be with European film makers, who were willing to deal with vital human issues in imaginative and fearless ways.

He couldn't quit yet. His financial demands required fresh additions of income, and if the Hollywood companies would not supply it, foreign producers would. They prized American stars to sell their projects, and there remained a degree of allure in the world market for the name of Marlon Brando.

Marlon had adopted a phantom life. He retained the house on Mulholland Drive, but stayed there only when his presence was required in California for business matters. Marlon came and went in utter secrecy; he had perfected the knack of traveling incognito. His circle of friends grew smaller; mostly they were associated from his early days in New York and Hollywood: Sam Gilman, Phil Rhodes, George Englund, Jay Kanter.

Tahiti had become his home. During his ten-year acquaintance with Tahiti, he had become convinced that it was the place where his life was happiest. But he was increasingly concerned about what civilization was doing to the islands.

"This is a snowflake civilization," he told a visitor to Tahiti in 1970; "as soon as it hits the ground, it will melt. . . . The Tahitians are being sold on an acquisitive society. They buy refrigerators and television sets, not because they need them, but because such things give them status. . . . When I first came here in 1960, everyone was riding motorscooters. Now they all want to drive cars, and the roads are jammed every morning and night when people go to and from work. The cars cause a cover of smog over Papeete. . . . Tahiti will never become another Waikiki, thank God. There isn't enough land space away from the coast, and there is no labor force to support a tourist industry. . . . Tahitians are not workers. When things start to bug them, they pull out. Just disappear. We had that happen on *Mutiny*. One of the Tahitian girls played a principal role, a beautiful girl. She said she was leaving Tahiti to join her boyfriend, who was fighting in Algiers. 'But you can't do that,' she was told. 'We'll sue you.' She said, 'All right. I have four pigs. Take them.' And she went. We had to shoot all her scenes over again with another girl."

Marlon said he wanted to do something to help the Tahitians. He had bought an island thirty miles northeast of Papeete called Tetiaroa. It was 450 acres of rich vegetation, with a dozen small atolls surrounding it and with a reef outside. Ordinarily foreigners could not buy land in French Polynesia; because Marlon's children were Tahitian—Tarita had given him a daughter, also named Tarita, in February 1970—he was able to acquire Tetiaroa. He planned to develop part of it as a resort, but the primary design of the island would be as a laboratory to help Tahiti to survive the onslaught of civilization. He wanted to find means to convert waste products into energy, to make use of solar energy, to develop native-grown products as food, to protect the big crabs and turtles from extinction. He hoped scientists could develop plankton as a human food to help the hungry of the world.

He spoke humorously, but with a note of affection, about the foibles of the Tahitians: "The way they fear their tiki gods is beyond belief. They won't even go near them at night for fear of being hexed. One day I was telling some of them what nonsense this was. I said I would prove it by sleeping all night at the foot of the big tiki out at the Gauguin Museum. They said I was a crazy man, and they feared for my life. I did it. I spent the whole night sleeping at the foot of that statue. Shortly afterward I came down with a serious kidney infection. And the Tahitians said, 'See!'"

He might have continued making a film every year or two for some foreign entrepreneur trading on the Brando name. But it didn't turn out that way. The reason was *The Godfather*.

It began because Mario Puzo, like many authors, was tired of being broke. He had a large family and a compelling urge to gamble, and the rewards from his creditable novels were not enough to support both, nor was his job editing stories for a group of adventure magazines. Finding himself $20,000 in debt, he decided "it was really time to grow up and sell out, as Lenny Bruce once advised." He undertook a novel about the Mafia.

His own publisher, Atheneum, rejected the proposal. Putnam's accepted it on the basis of a ten-page outline, with $5,000 as an advance payment against royalties. He started to write the novel in 1965, drawing from research and secondhand stories from gamblers he knew ("I never met an honest-to-God gangster"). Nor had he ever been to Hollywood. For research on the movie-world sequences in his book, he consulted a biography of the founder of Columbia Pictures, Harry Cohn.

After Puzo had written a hundred pages, he was again afflicted with the need for cash. Paramount offered $12,500 for an option on the novel, with a total payment of $50,000 if the option was exercised. His agents advised against taking the offer. Puzo overruled them.

He finished writing *The Godfather* in July 1968. Fawcett offered $410,000 for the paperback rights. The hardcover quickly landed on the best-seller list of the *New York Times* and remained there for sixty-seven weeks.

Despite the overwhelming success of *The Godfather* as a book,

Paramount executives were not enthusiastic about the film version. They had recently released a movie about the Mafia, *The Brotherhood,* starring Kirk Douglas, and it had flopped. But as the book sales of *The Godfather* mounted, it appeared that a film version might be risked, provided it could be produced at a reasonable figure. Robert Evans, a former clothing manufacturer and film actor who had become Paramount's production chief, and Stanley Jaffe, a second-generation film executive who was president of the company, tried to devise a production setup that would assure a reasonable cost. One of the possibilities was allowing the Italian producer Dino De Laurentiis to co-finance and produce *The Godfather* with Charles Bronson as star.

No combination seemed to work. Peter Bart, a former *New York Times* reporter who was Evans' assistant, suggested entrusting *The Godfather* to Albert Ruddy. It made no more sense than the other proposals; Ruddy was producer of a television series, *Hogan's Heroes,* and of *Little Fauss and Big Halsey,* a money loser for Paramount. But Ruddy was given the assignment.

Ruddy wanted Puzo to adapt his own novel as a movie script, a notion that hadn't occurred to the Paramount executives. Producer and author conferred at the Plaza Hotel in New York and discussed approaches to the screenplay. When the conversation turned to casting, Puzo remarked "There is only one actor who can play the godfather, and that is Marlon Brando."

Puzo had made contact with Brando through a mutual friend and had sent him galley proofs of the book. Brando had later telephoned, admitting that he had not read the novel; at any rate, he doubted that Paramount would hire him.

Puzo began fashioning a script, his screen writing earning him double what he had received for the film rights. Meanwhile Peter Bart made a suggestion for director: Francis Ford Coppola. As with Ruddy, the choice was unpromising. Coppola had come out of UCLA to direct a feature, *You're a Big Boy Now,* which also qualified as his master's thesis. His next films, *The Rain People* and *Finian's Rainbow,* failed, as did his plan to establish a colony of young film makers in San Francisco. In Coppola's favor were the facts that he was Italian and had a good script sense — he had co-written *Patton.*

A curious set of coincidences had happened a year before. Peter Bart and Al Ruddy were visiting Coppola in San Francisco while *Little Fauss and Big Halsey* was filming there. Bart mentioned that

Paramount owned the rights to a new book called *The Godfather* and that Coppola might be interested in it. Coppola replied that he had seen an advertisement for the book in the *New York Times* that day and had clipped the ad as a reminder to buy it; he had the impression that it was an esoteric book by an Italian intellectual. During the conversation Marlon Brando telephoned. It was the first time Coppola talked with Brando, to whom he had sent a script for a prospective movie; Brando considered the script "a little thin," but thanked Coppola for sending it.

Coppola read *The Godfather* until he reached the Hollywood sequences, then put it down. He didn't consider it as a film until Peter Bart called him with the renewed suggestion that he undertake it. Now Coppola was open to persuasion. His attempt to establish a moviemaking enterprise in San Francisco had left him $300,000 in debt to Warner Bros. He agreed to take on the writing and directing of *The Godfather* on two conditions: it would be filmed in actual locales; it would be cast with authentic types.

Terms were agreed upon, and Coppola took over construction of *The Godfather* script. During the writing period Coppola was testing actors for the title role, and several mature Hollywood actors of Italian extraction were included. Coppola and Ruddy came to a conclusion: the figure of the godfather occupied only 40 percent of the story, but he so dominated the entire action that an actor of enormous presence was needed. Their thinking narrowed down to Laurence Olivier and Marlon Brando.

Ruddy offered Coppola a $200 bet that Brando would never be accepted by the Paramount brass. Ruddy's reasoning: Brando's previous ten films had failed; he had a record of ruinous relationships with directors; to cast Brando as Don Corleone would mean a renouncement of Coppola's intention to fill the roles with authentic Italians.

Ruddy and Coppola approached Brando. He was not encouraging. He had not read *The Godfather,* and friends had told him it was the Harold Robbins–Irving Wallace kind of book that capitalized on actual happenings faintly disguised. "I don't want to play an Italian gangster," Brando remarked. But he agreed to read the book before making his final decision. Both Coppola and Ruddy were convinced there was little chance in persuading Brando to play the role.

To their surprise he told them three days later that he had read

The Godfather, and that, to him, it contained social commentary — a fact that eluded most readers. He reasoned that organized crime was allowed to flourish in the United States as in no other country. Why? Because it was business. A peculiar kind of business, but still it was a variety of private enterprise, and hence acceptable to the vast majority of Americans.

Now came the task of selling Brando to Paramount.

A summit meeting of Paramount executives gathered in the company's offices on Cañon Drive in Beverly Hills. Coppola mentioned that his choices for the godfather were either Marlon Brando or Laurence Olivier. Olivier was ill, so that left Brando.

"Francis, I'm really disappointed in you," said Robert Evans.

"I can assure you that as president of Paramount Pictures," said Stanley Jaffe, "I will not authorize the casting of Marlon Brando in *The Godfather.*"

Coppola was allowed to plead his case. He did so in almost mock heroic style, arguing like Jimmy Stewart in *Mr. Smith Goes to Washington* and even collapsing on the floor at the end. In his ten-minute oration, Coppola contended that Brando had an almost mystic relationship with other actors, and his presence would elevate the entire cast to greater endeavor. The director was unconcerned that Brando was not an Italian; he argued that the Mafia spoke less in the manner of the old-world Italian than in the kind of street language that Brando had used in *On the Waterfront.*

The Coppola performance was convincing. The Paramount executives said they would consider Brando on three conditions: if he would agree to make the film for no salary, accepting a percentage of the profits instead; if he would put up a bond to offset excess charges in case he misbehaved during filming; if he would test for the role.

Ruddy and Coppola left the meeting in a state of depression. They pondered: How to you ask Marlon Brando to test for a film role? He had tested only once; that was when he made a voice test to prove he could play Mark Antony.

Coppola found a solution. Marlon had remarked that he had been toying with make-ups for the role of Don Corleone. Coppola suggested that he come up to Brando's house and use a tape machine to discover how the make-ups would photograph. Marlon agreed.

The director arrived at Brando's Mulholland Drive house one morning at ten. He brought a tape camera and also a 16mm film camera, because of studio union jurisdiction that might have precluded the showing of tape. Three technicians accompanied Coppola.

Coppola had prepared for the encounter. Through inquiries with Brando's co-workers, he had learned that the actor disliked extraneous noise and disturbance while he was working, that he responded to impromptu happenings as he performed. Coppola brought along in his car an actor named Salvatore Corsitto, who had already been cast to play Bonasero in *The Godfather.* The director instructed Corsitto to remain outside until he was summoned.

Brando was asleep when Coppola arrived. The director and the technicians waited until Brando appeared in a robe and began talking about approaches to the character of Don Corleone. Coppola suggested a thin mustache such as his Uncle Louis used to wear. Brando penciled on the mustache and began blackening his blond hair. He added some dark make-up under the eyes, and stuffed facial tissue in his cheeks for a jowly look.

Gradually he began to take on the aspect of Don Corleone. Coppola produced a plate of apples and cheese that he had brought, a demitasse of espresso. Marlon put on a frayed shirt, a well-worn tie, a faded jacket. He spent two or three minutes adjusting the shirt collar so that it extended outside the jacket. He lighted a bent Italian cigar. The transmogrification continued without a word being spoken. The Brando shoulders began to sag, the belly extended. The face seemed to take on a waxen appearance. He breathed more measuredly, the exhalations coming as enormous sighs.

The telephone rang. Don Corleone lifted the instrument and placed it slowly to his ear. He listened, nodded slowly and patiently, then replaced the telephone without a word. The caller heard nothing but the heavy breathing of an aged man.

He changed moods. He scowled, became angry, smiled, grew indifferent. Coppola decided to chance the surprise. He summoned the actor from outside and introduced him as Bonasero. Brando was momentarily startled, but he reacted entirely in the character of Don Corleone, and the two actors played an impromptu scene together.

Marlon studied the playback of the tape on a monitor. "That's what it is," he muttered to himself. "The face of a bulldog. Mean-looking, but warm underneath."

Coppola was immensely pleased with the test, and so was Ruddy. Now they faced the task of winning over the Paramount executives. Marlon himself helped. He paid a visit to Bob Evans' Beverly Hills office and spoke frankly about his desire to play the godfather: "You may have heard a lot of crap about how I misbehaved on pictures. Some of it is true, some of it is not true. But I'll tell you this: I want to play this role. I'll work for it, work hard. It's going to be something special for me."

Evans was converted when he saw the test of Marlon as the old man. Stanley Jaffe, the Paramount president, was also won over. All that remained was to convince Charles Bludhorn, the Austrian-born enterpreneur whose Gulf and Western Corporation had swallowed Paramount, along with dozens of other companies.

Bludhorn was invited to a meeting with Paramount executives in the board room of the New York headquarters. A tape machine had been set up on the board table. "We've got something to show you," Bludhorn was told.

When Brando's face appeared on the screen, Bludhorn perceived the plot. "Oh, no!" he exclaimed and started to leave the room. Then the image of Brando began to transform into a benign old Italian. Bludhorn sat down slowly, his attention fixed on the word-less performance on the small screen. When it was over, Bludhorn admitted, "That's terrific."

Brando was hired. He was not made to suffer the humiliation of posting a bond to guarantee losses in production that he might in-cur. But the other two requirements were enforced: he had tested for the role; he would play it for no salary. The initial payment would barely cover his expenses; his share of the profits guaranteed a minimum of $150,000 and a maximum of $1.5 million. The terms were highly favorable to Paramount, which would not have to pay Brando a large amount of money unless its own profits became im-mense.

Casting of the other roles began to fall in line, the actors being eager to appear with Brando. The major problem was Michael, the Corleone son who inherited the family empire. Coppola argued for Al Pacino, a slim young New York actor who had received awards for performances off-Broadway and on. The Paramount brass did not agree with the director's choice; Pacino seemed too immature, too unimposing to assume control of a Mafia family. Discouraged, Pacino accepted a role in a Mafia comedy film, *The Gang That Couldn't Shoot Straight.*

Coppola was ordered to make tests of other candidates for Michael, and he photographed as many as ten a day. All seemed unqualified, and the Paramount executives experienced stirrings of doubt about the wisdom of their choice of director. After witnessing a procession of tests for Michael, Bludhorn figured that "All of the actors' performances are bad, and there is only one director. That must mean that it's not the actors who are terrible; it's the *director* who is terrible."

Coppola continued campaigning for Pacino as Michael and James Caan as the sexually athletic Sonny Corleone. Paramount wanted better-known actors. With the casting issue unresolved, Coppola went off to England to confer with Brando, who was completing *The Nightcomers.* After a week Coppola received a message from his office advising his return; Paramount was planning to negotiate with Warren Beatty to play Michael Corleone.

The director flew back to New York, and on his arrival he received an ominous message: "Francis Coppola — Don't quit, let them fire you." It was from his secretary, who reasoned that Paramount would not have to pay him if he quit.

Coppola had no intention of resigning. He refused to alter his view that Al Pacino was the ideal candidate for Michael. In the end it was Marlon Brando who swayed the decision. During a discussion with Evans he had remarked, "Bob, the person who plays Michael should be a man who broods. He shouldn't be the usual kind of leading man. He should be a brooder." Evans remembered the Brando comment when the time came for a final decision on casting. Evans saw Pacino in a minor film, *Panic in Needle Park,* and agreed that he might prove suitable for Michael. The other Paramount executives consented to Pacino and to Caan. The start of production was nearing, and the decisions could no longer be postponed.

With *The Godfather* about to begin production, Francis Ford Coppola found himself on unsteady ground. Time after time he had challenged the authority of the Paramount bosses, and they had conceded to him on most of the major points. He had the cast he wanted, but if any of the actors failed — particularly the star, who was notorious for his behavior on films—Coppola would be held responsible. He himself had written the final script; its success was also his responsibility. At thirty-one, with no record of a hit movie behind him, Coppola approached the filming with unease. Yet as director he would need to maintain a strong presence, to command a large and unfamiliar crew, a cast of divergent actors, and a highly complex production. All this while maintaining the overall concept of the film and protecting his rear from the Paramount bosses. It seemed like a task for a Henry Hathaway or any of the hard-bitten old-line directors, not the bearded young intellectual Coppola.

The week with Brando in England had helped him.

During the day Coppola wrote *The Godfather* script while Marlon worked in *The Nightcomers*. At night they discussed Don Corleone and how he should be played. Coppola had learned that Brando enjoyed being fed things that might give him character insight, so he had assembled material on Mafia leaders, including tape recordings of the voice of Frank Costello at hearings of the Kefauver investigation of organized crime. Brando was intrigued with the high-pitched Costello voice, and he used it as a pattern for Don Corleone. "I think the godfather could be played as a little, sweet old man," Coppola observed. "His voice should be soft and gentle at all times; powerful people don't need to shout." Brando agreed.

Marlon, recognizing that Coppola was scared, was gentle and accommodating; he even brought dinner on a tray to Coppola's room. The week at Cambridge was helpful for the director in understanding Marlon. Coppola noted that the people surrounding Brando were not the usual sycophantic entourage of a movie star. They obviously admired Marlon, but they were honest with him, too. Coppola decided that was the way Marlon wanted to be treated: in an honest, down-to-earth way.

As the beginning of production approached in early 1971, nerves grew thin. The internal troubles were enough to stagger any movie project; now there was tension from without. The Mafia was applying pressure on Paramount through the Italian-American Civil Rights League, as well as through bomb threats and other intimidation. Producer Ruddy acquiesced by promising not to mention the Mafia or Cosa Nostra in the film and by hiring persons recommended by the League to work in the production.

Coppola realized that he needed to create an air of intimacy within his cast, establishing in a brief time and for the duration of the filming a literal "family." He assembled the players for a dinner at an authentically Italian restaurant, Patsy's, in East Harlem. He reserved an upstairs room and ordered a dinner with all the customary Italian delicacies.

It proved to be a Da Vincian supper. The players assembled and engaged in the small talk of actors embarking on an uncertain assignment. All betrayed a certain nervousness, realizing the pressures under which *The Godfather* was beginning. All anticipated the arrival of Brando. For every actor in the room, Marlon Brando was a deistic figure. Most of them were in their twenties and thirties, and in their youths they had viewed the Brando of *Streetcar* and *On the Waterfront* as the ultimate American actor. To be performing in the same company with Brando was awesome.

Brando arrived, and the younger actors treated him in the manner of parish priests in the presence of the pope. Brando shattered their awe with casual comments expressed in four-letter words. Their admiration grew.

During the dinner the actors began to assume the roles they would play. The central figure was Brando, his penetrating intelligence and aura of achievement dominating everything. Al Pacino remained aloof, husbanding his reserves of power, brooding, contemplating his role in the overall scheme. James Caan played the clown, the joke-making extrovert uncertain of his position but seeking to bulldoze his way to acceptance. Robert Duvall, who was to portray the *consigliere,* moved in and out of conversations, contributing a Machiavellian presence.

The filming started—and all of Paramount's fears seemed confirmed.

Coppola began with the meeting of the Corleone family in the olive-oil company office. The scene wasn't working well, and Brando suggested more rehearsal time. Coppola declined; he knew that he was being carefully watched and felt that he had to start shooting. When he saw the footage afterward, he realized his mistake, and asked permission to reshoot the sequence. This seemed to confirm the growing suspicion among Paramount executives that Coppola was too young and inexperienced to handle such an important assignment.

The Godfather, *1972*   *Paramount*

Not only was Coppola in jeopardy from those who had hired him; he also faced sedition from the crew. Members of the company, including the cinematographer, seemed to be at cross-purposes with what Coppola intended; some of his orders were ignored or ridiculed.

After three weeks of filming, Coppola realized that he was still on trial. He heard of Paramount's negotiations to replace him with Elia Kazan or Aram Avakian. Each day's shooting seemed tentative, as if the footage might be scrapped with the advent of a new director. But Coppola hung on. He resisted the temptation to submit his resignation and escape the tension that was all around him. He was supported by Brando. "If they fire you, I'll quit," Marlon vowed.

Paramount finally decided to retain Coppola. The decision was entirely economic. To fire Coppola and assign a new director would risk an eight-month delay for *The Godfather*. Paramount had a release schedule to meet, and it would lose more money by postponing *The Godfather* than it would by allowing Coppola to continue. Now the director took command. He fired those who had questioned his authority and coerced others into accepting his will. After the three-week trial, there could be no doubt that Coppola was in charge.

One of his great concerns was Marlon's memorizing of his dialogue. It was nil. Marlon simply would not—or could not—remember his lines. Was it a total loss of memory? Marlon claimed it was not. "Look," he told Coppola, "you said you like me in *Waterfront*—right? Well, I'm doing the same now that I did then. Real people don't know what they're going to say. Their words often come as a surprise to them. That's the way it should be in a movie."

No amount of persuasion could change his mind or alter his habits. Each day he reported for work, apparently without having attempted to memorize his lines. His cues were distributed throughout the set—notes under a grapefruit, inside a drawer, on a desk blotter, cue cards written in bold words behind the camera, as on a television show. His habits led to some pranks by his fellow cast members after they had lost their awe of him. James Caan was usually the ringleader. He induced Lenny Montana, who was playing the Mafia gunman Luca Brasi, to take part in a stunt. The stolid Brasi was to pay his respects to the godfather at the Corleone wedding. After Montana recited his speech to Brando, he stuck out his tongue, on which was a tape with the words "Fuck you, Marlon." Brando was convulsed with laughter. When he performed his own closeup of the Don's thanks, he said solemnly, "Luca, my most honored friend," and stuck out his tongue with a tape on it saying "Fuck you, too." During the early stages of filming, a familiar problem developed: Marlon's mumbling. A degree of slurred dialogue seemed to fit the character of Don Corleone, but now there were fears that Brando wouldn't be understood at all. No one knew how to broach the matter to him. Finally Al Ruddy dropped in at Brando's dressing room during a lunch break. After some small talk, Ruddy remarked, "You know, Marlon, there are moments when I'm behind the camera and I can't understand you."

Brando's answer was immediate: "Hey—why didn't you tell me? It's no problem. Just tell me, and I'll speak more clearly."

His fellow actors marveled at how totally Brando assumed the role. Each morning he arrived on the set as the forty-six-year-old Brando, vital, still muscular, cracking jokes with crew members. He disappeared inside his dressing room and sat before a mirror while a make-up man applied rubber cement to his face. In an hour Brando emerged as a man of sixty-five, paunchy in an ill-fitting suit, his steps measured, his reactions slow. He plodded to the movie set, and those who had joked with him that morning stepped aside, almost in deference to his age.

During the previous decade, he had rarely enjoyed himself on a movie set. Now he did. He took a boyish delight in the gangster dramatics, especially in the scene which showed him being cut down by bullets on a New York street. The location for the shooting scene was Mott Street, a Mafia stronghold. Real-life dons gazed out of doorways at the film company, and one of them commented to Al Ruddy about Brando's wardrobe: "Why do you dress him in rags? Make him look classy!"

Hundreds of local residents watched the scene from the street and from windows above. After the gunmen had emptied their guns and Brando had fallen across the hood of a car, the crowd cheered. Brando rose and made a grand bow, like an opera singer accepting plaudits at the Met. He was so relaxed later in the day that he fell asleep while lying in the street.

As the filming progressed, Coppola learned more of Brando's work habits and how to cope with them. The director discovered that Brando was not always on time. Monday was a particular hazard for him; he sometimes flew to California over the weekend to visit his sons. Each time he was late in arriving on the set, his comment to Coppola was not about his tardiness, but something concerning the script.

The director observed that if Brando was a half-hour late, he said, "This line bothers me . . ." If he arrived an hour after starting time, he said, "I don't understand this scene . . ." For a half day's absence: "I don't like this scene at all . . ."

Coppola noted this recurring habit, and one day he brought it up. "Every time you're late, you manage to put me on the defensive," he said to Brando. "I'm afraid if you miss a day, you'll quit the picture!" Brando was amused. And he continued to be late.

Despite his tardiness, *The Godfather* continued to move along on schedule, and it appeared that Brando's scenes would be completed within the six-week span specified in his contract. But during the fifth week, heavy rains fell in New York, flooding the Staten Island estate which was being used for the Corleone compound. Al Ruddy presented his problem to Brando: "Look, I know I'm out of line, but there's something I've got to ask you. We can't shoot the outdoor scenes on Staten Island until it dries out. That means you'll have to sit around for a week without working. Under the contract, you should get fifty thousand if we go over the six weeks. But I'm responsible for the money on this picture, and I'd like to avoid that. I'm asking you if you'd do this production a favor: go back to California for a week. Remember, if you do, it'll cost you fifty thousand."

"Go back to California for a week . . ." Marlon pondered. Then he said, "Okay."

When Brando returned to the production, he was in good spirits. He had established an affectionate rapport with the other actors, to whom he occupied a position not unlike the godfather in the script. He was their spiritual leader, yet his earthiness belied any exalted position. He continued his boyish pranks. During a scene when the wounded Don Corleone was being carried on a stretcher up the stairs of his home, the actors playing ambulance attendants had difficulty lifting Brando. Two of the huskier crew members volunteered for the task, and they donned the costumes of the actors. Coppola ordered the scene to begin, and the two crewmen started to lift the stretcher and Brando up the stairway. They began to sweat and struggle, and finally they were forced to lower their burden. They discovered why: Brando had filled the stretcher with the heavy lead weights used to counterbalance the camera boom.

Brando's most frequent foils were James Caan and Robert Duvall, who had introduced him to the practice of mooning. One day after filming had concluded, Duvall, his wife and children, and Caan were being driven in a studio limousine on Second Avenue in Manhattan. Duvall gazed to the side and saw another limousine that was transporting Brando and his secretary, Alice Marchak, back to his hotel. "Moon him!" Duvall insisted to Caan.

"But the kids!" Caan protested.

Duvall ordered his children into the front seat, and at the next intersection, Brando and his secretary looked at the limousine next to them and caught the sight of James Caan's bare ass in the window. Brando collapsed in laughter on the floor. His secretary was startled and perplexed. A few days later she told Duvall, "I don't know what you fellows taught Marlon, but the other night I answered the door of my room at the Waldorf. There was Marlon in the hall, stark naked and leaning over with his back to me. He giggled and then ran down the hall to his room."

After Brando had performed his own mooning before the crowd at the wedding feast, Caan and Duvall presented him with a silver belt buckle on which was emblazoned: Mighty Moon Champion.

As with other films on which Brando worked, the other actors of *The Godfather* remained on the set to observe him work even when they were not required for the scenes. They were amazed at the inventiveness he employed to enrich the character of Don Corleone. During early scenes in the Corleone home, photographed at the Filmways Studio on 127th Street in New York, Brando made friends with a ragged old gray cat that lived at the studio. He devised the idea of keeping the cat on his lap during the scenes in which he wielded his malignant power. It was an inspired juxtaposition of gentleness and terror. The only drawback was that the cat purred so loudly that Brando's lines had to be dubbed.

Again, Brando brought shading to the character when giving orders to Duvall, the *consigliere*. His line read: "After all, we're not murderers, in spite of what the undertaker says." Between the two phrases, Brando paused to inhale the fragrance of a rose. It was a brilliant touch.

Brando's final scene was approaching—in which he was to die a natural death in a sun-filled garden—and Coppola recognized that the scene had not been fully realized in the script. With no time to devote to writing, Coppola sent for Robert Towne, a young screen writer in Hollywood with whom he had worked under producer Roger Corman. Towne contributed to scenes between Michael Corleone and his fiancée and to the scene of the killing of a Mafia leader and police detective in an Italian café. The major problem was Don Corleone's death scene, especially the preceding sequence between the old man and his heir, Michael.

"What we need," Coppola explained to Towne, "is something in which father and son can come close together and can indicate that they love each other, even though they are unable to say so. There was no such scene in the book, but we need it in the picture."

Towne constructed a brief scene, but Brando rejected it. He argued that it made the godfather too manipulative of Michael. On the evening before Brando's last day of work under his contract, Coppola, Towne and Pacino met in Brando's dressing room. All contributed to the scene of the following day, but Brando offered the key: "Just once, I would like to see this man *not* inarticulate. I would like to see him express himself well."

Towne went back to his hotel and wrote until four in the morning. Coppola picked him up at seven and they drove in silence to the Staten Island location. Finally the director asked, "Any luck?" Towne replied, "Yeah," and handed him the pages. Coppola said he liked the scene and instructed Towne to read the dialogue to Marlon.

Brando was pleased. The scene depicted the succession of power, with the elder Corleone reminding his son of duties that needed to be performed. When Michael reported that he had already done the necessary things, his father asked about his grandchildren. Michael remarked that his young son was already reading the funnies.

"I think I'd like to repeat that line: 'He reads the funnies!'" Marlon said. Again, a Brando touch that added immeasurably to the scene, underlining both a grandfather's pride and the old man's decline.

Brando performed the scene with Pacino, reading the lines from blackboards placed behind the camera. Then came the final scene of the godfather's death. He was to collapse of a heart attack in the garden after playing with his grandson.

The scene wasn't going well. The actor cast as the grandson failed

The Godfather

Paramount

to respond, and Coppola asked for help from Brando. Brando suggested a stunt he had employed on his own children: putting orange peels under his lip to make himself look like a movie monster. It worked. The boy actor reacted to the scary look of Brando with the orange peel in his mouth. And then Don Corleone, the gentle old man who in his real life had indeed been a monster, fell over dead in the garden.

Producer Ruddy had expected the Brando portions of the filming to be the most difficult; the rest, he figured, would be easy. The reverse proved to be true. After the stimulus of Brando's presence was gone, the actors and the crew felt a letdown, and the remainder of *The Godfather* became hard work. But morale was improved by the expressions of confidence by the Paramount executives. No longer were there misgivings about Coppola's performance as a director. The early footage demonstrated not only the extraordinary power of Brando's portrayal, but also Coppola's sure, clean grasp of the dramatics as well as the hazy, romantic appearance of the picture.

Paramount allowed Ruddy to exceed the $5 million budget by $300,000. The sequence of Sonny Corleone's assassination at a highway bridge tollbooth had been budgeted at $25,000. Instead of using an existing location, a new set was constructed at Floyd Bennett Airfield, and the sequence was filmed at a cost of $110,000.

Brando vanished abroad after his filming of *The Godfather.* When he returned to California six months later, he asked to see the rough cut of the film. This was unusual for him, because he rarely viewed his own movies. His reasoning: "You don't learn to be effective from film, but from life. Actors who watch themselves tend to become mannered. The less you think about how effective you are, the more effective you are."

Somehow he was drawn to see *The Godfather,* perhaps to reassure himself that it was not merely a gangster flick, that it indeed contained social commentary. He was content that it did.

"I consider this one of the most powerful statements ever made about America," he remarked after viewing *The Godfather.* He felt that it affirmed his belief that the Mafia had been able to flourish in the United States because it conformed to the system of free enterprise. He read significance into Michael's comment when his girl friend Kay expressed horror at the Mafia's tactics. He compared such activities to politics, and she countered that "senators don't have people killed." His reply: "Don't be naïve."

Paramount executives had expressed concern about the inaudibility of Brando's dialogue. It was especially noticeable in the latter part of his role, when he spoke in higher tones. (This was to indicate that he had been shot in the throat during his near-assassination; Coppola admitted afterward that he had erred in neglecting to establish the fact.)

Marlon agreed to rerecord all of his dialogue, and he did so in two days, finishing on Christmas Eve of 1971. Again he demonstrated his uncanny powers of mimicry. Usually he required only one take to match the lip movements of dialogue he had delivered on film eight months before.

It turned out that the "looping" wasn't needed. A private preview with a select audience, mostly persons outside the movie business, indicated there was little difficulty in hearing Brando's lines. And the Paramount executives agreed that the "live" sound of actual recording had better texture than the more audible dialogue delivered in a sound studio.

So enthusiastic was Marlon about *The Godfather* that he granted Paramount an unusual concession: he would submit to interviews to help launch the film. For most movie stars, particularly those who owned a percentage of the profits, the publicity routine of launching a film would be automatic. But Marlon's attitudes had changed in the years since he had barnstormed the country for *The Ugly American.* The Dark Years had increased his bitterness toward critics and interviewers. His own keen ear recorded what he said in interviews; in print his remarks seem distorted, misinterpreted. He detested the way the sensationalist press had fed upon his legal disputes with Anna Kashfi and Movita, particularly when his children were involved. Also, the years had brought further radicalizing of Marlon's political viewpoints, and he saw the establishment press as ally to the government in oppression of the Indians, the blacks and other poor, in continuing the brainless war in Vietnam.

Marlon knew enough about the mechanics of publicity to realize that coverage of *The Godfather* by the news magazines would greatly enhance its launching. He agreed to interviews with *Newsweek* and *Life*—but not *Time*. His dislike of *Time* dated back to its first cover story in which he was designated The Slob; it carried down through the years of snide reporting of his personal and political activities, punny criticisms of his performances. Also, he considered

Time a proponent of the American adventure in Vietnam.

Brando talked at length in his Paris apartment to a *Newsweek* reporter, Steve Saler. Brando's analysis of *The Godfather*:

"I don't think the film is about the Mafia at all. I think it is about the corporate mind. In a way, the Mafia is the best example of capitalists we have. Don Corleone is just any ordinary American business magnate who is trying to do the best he can for the group he represents and for his family. . . . I think the tactics the Don used aren't much different from those General Motors used against Ralph Nader. Unlike some corporate heads, Corleone has an unwavering loyalty for the people who have given support to him and his causes, and he takes care of his own. He is a man of deep principle and the natural question arises as to how such a man can countenance the killing of people. But the American government does the same thing for reasons that are not much different from those of the Mafia, and big business kills us all the time—with cars and cigarettes and pollution—and they do it knowingly."

Marlon agreed to be interviewed for *Life* if the story was done by Shana Alexander, whom he knew and trusted. It didn't matter that she had left *Life* and was editor of *McCall's*. He insisted on Shana Alexander. She agreed to take on the assignment for her former employer.

"For reasons that are not completely known to me consciously, I cannot reconcile myself to sitting and blabbering to you for public benefit, and money," Marlon told her. But he did so, with the provision that nothing personal would be asked.

Again he interpreted *The Godfather* as "a useful commentary on the corporate thinking in this country. I mean, if Cosa Nostra had been black or socialist, Corleone would have been dead or in jail. But because the Mafia patterned itself so closely on the corporation, and dealt in a hard-nosed way with money, and with politics, it prospered. The Mafia is so . . . *American.* To me, a key phrase in the story is that whenever they wanted to kill somebody it was always a matter of policy. Just before pulling the trigger, they told him: 'Just business. Nothing personal.' When I read that, McNamara, Johnson and Rusk flashed before my eyes."

20

Tango

*"The only thing
an actor owes his public
is not to bore them."*

THE FILM TO FOLLOW *The Godfather* HAPPENED BY CHANCE. A LONG-TIME friend of Marlon's, a Chinese woman, told him of a foreign film she had seen. It was *The Conformist*, directed by a young Italian, Bernardo Bertolucci, and she had found it so compelling that she had seen it seven times.

When Brando went to Paris in the summer of 1971, a friend arranged a meeting with Bertolucci. Brando knew nothing about the director and may have been surprised to find him so youthful. Bertolucci had been born in Parma thirty years before, the son of a film critic and poet. Bernardo himself turned to poetry and produced a prize-winning volume when he was twenty-one. But he did not want to follow his father, and he turned his poetic insight to film, apprenticing with Pasolini and adopting (later rejecting) Godard as his spiritual mentor. With his fifth film, *The Conformist*, Bertolucci achieved maturity.

Although a generation apart, Brando and Bertolucci had much in common. Both were political radicals and idealists. Both had undergone intensive psychoanalysis. Both were uncompromising artists. Language was a problem, since they could not converse in their native tongues. Their only recourse was French.

"I felt right away that there was only one way of communicating with him," the director recalled later, "and that was through the instincts. I think to understand that is to know the secret of how we were able to collaborate with each other. Since we had to speak in an alien tongue for both of us, we had to look at each other more intently. That gave us deeper understanding."

For a few months Bertolucci had been working on a screenplay with Jean-Louis Trintignant in mind, but the French actor had other commitments. Now Bertolucci was taking an extremely long chance in pitching it to Marlon Brando. The basic plot: a middle-aged man, grieving over his wife's suicide, meets a feckless young girl for a series of sexual encounters without revealing their identities. Bertolucci explained the nature of the theme: "It is like an edifice constructed over a cavern. The cavern is this great question mark: Can a man and a woman still live together today without destroying each other?"

If Brando was overwhelmed by the project, he gave little indication. He seemed more curious about the complex young poet who was addressing him. To Bertolucci it appeared that Brando was prepared "to accept or reject me like a man who meets a new arrival on a desert island."

Brando expressed some encouragement about the film, but his energies had been depleted by a jet flight from America. He agreed to a showing of *The Conformist* on the following day. It was a near-disaster. Marlon was suffering from influenza, and during the last five minutes of the showing he became violently sick. Bertolucci was disturbed, but he shrugged and said, "At least he's not indifferent toward my work."

Marlon was far from indifferent. He was impressed by the truthfulness of the Italian, both on the screen and in conversation. Bertolucci expressed his theory of film making in a way Marlon thoroughly approved: "I treat all actors the same: they are my co-authors. My method of work is to make a documentary about people. I'm interested in people, and fiction is my way to create the kind of atmosphere within which you can perform a deep kind of probing. This gives a dynamic power to film. Contradictions are created between the script and the actual truth, and the personal contributions by the actors make it true."

This was the way Marlon had always envisioned film making: as a collaboration, in a very deep sense, between actor and director. It had rarely worked that way during his previous twenty-six films. With Kazan, perhaps; Gadge and Marlon were so much alike—in their rebelliousness, in their intensity of feeling, in attitudes toward their art—that they could become almost as one in a collaborative effort. Few other directors could achieve that. They had been hard-nosed and jealous of their directorial function, and

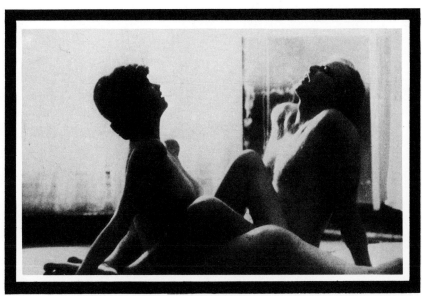

With Maria Schneider, Last Tango
in Paris, *1973*

the relationship proved combative and destructive. Or they had been weak-willed, awed by Brando the superstar, with the result that he viewed them and their projects with contempt.

Bernardo Bertolucci completed the script with another Italian, Franco Arcalli, and sent it to Brando. He agreed to undertake it, and the contracts were drawn up. In September 1971 Bertolucci flew to Los Angeles for two weeks of talks with Brando. It was more a period of growing acquainted than a film consultation; they talked of a myriad of things but rarely their mutual project, which was called *Last Tango in Paris.*

"Who is going to produce it?" Brando asked.

"Alberto Grimaldi," said Bertolucci.

"Grimaldi!" Marlon exclaimed. "He's crazy. How could he do business with me after what I did to him on *Burn!?*" It was true that the Italian producer had sued Marlon over his errant behavior on *Burn!,* but Grimaldi was willing to try again.

Brando and Bertolucci discussed the erotic aspects of *Last Tango in Paris.* Both agreed that sex had to be treated explicitly in the film if they were to remain true to the characters and the theme. The sexual depictions disturbed the executives of Paramount, where *Last Tango in Paris* was offered for financing and distribution. So did Brando's insistence on $200,000 and 10 percent of the gross receipts. Paramount declined the package, even though the company officials realized that Brando's career would be revived by the then-unreleased *Godfather.* United Artists quickly agreed to take over the project and ensure the $1.1 million production cost.

Another major decision concerned Brando's co-star. Bertolucci had originally designed *Last Tango in Paris* for Dominique Sanda, his heroine of *The Conformist.* But she was pregnant. So was Catherine Deneuve, his second choice. He finally decided on Maria Schneider, nineteen, uninhibited daughter of a French actor, as the best of a hundred other actresses he considered.

The collaboration of Bernardo Bertolucci and Marlon Brando began in Paris in January 1972 and continued for ten weeks of filming. Each required adjustments to the other's creative habits.

When Marlon arrived on the set for the first day's shooting, he wore his usual make-up, which Bertolucci described as three centimeters thick. His Italian cameraman, Vittorio Storaro, studied Marlon's face, took a handkerchief and wiped away most of the make-up. The director explained that while Marlon may have needed such make-up for brightly lighted films of the past, *Last Tango in Paris* would be filmed with only a minimum of lighting. Marlon wiped away the remaining traces with his hands. "That okay?" he asked. Director and cameraman agreed.

Bertolucci also learned to accommodate. He was accustomed to working the normal Italian filming hours from nine in the morning until evening. It became obvious that such a starting time did not agree with Marlon, and the film was made on the "French timetable"—beginning at noon and filming without a meal break until seven in the evening.

Also, Brando would not agree to the European custom of working on Saturdays. Hence the company worked five days with Brando, then filmed the scenes involving the girl's film maker–fiancé, Jean-Pierre Léaud; he became known as "our Saturday actor."

Bertolucci asked Marlon to do something he had never attempted: to superimpose himself over the written character. Before, he had been able to cloak himself as Kowalski or Zapata or Malloy or Corleone, borrowing from the storehouse he had accumulated from his ceaseless study of human behavior. Now he had no putty nose, no rubber-cement scars, no make-up at all. Nor could he affect a punch-drunk slur, a Broadway-Runyon accent, the clipped tones of an English gentleman. It was his own broken-nose face, his own Midwestern mumble, his own troubled psyche.

"I asked him to do quite different things," Bertolucci said afterward. "I had at my disposal two alternatives: one was the great actor, with all the technical experience that any director would require; the second was a mysterious man who was there waiting to be discovered in all his richness of material. It was like leaving for an adventurous journey with two or three spare tires in the trunk of your car. If one of my tires blew out, I always had a spare. But I never used it."

Marlon seemed willing, even eager to contribute to the character Paul from his own deepest feelings. At times it was almost painful to watch as Marlon pulled from his own experiences variations on the theme of his life. The most revealing soliloquy came when Paul began to disclose his real identity to Jeanne. The scene was ad-libbed by Marlon and was photographed in one take.

He began by describing his past; he had been a boxer, an actor, a bongo player, a revolutionary, a journalist, a resident of Tahiti. All the things that Marlon had been, or had wanted to be. He talked

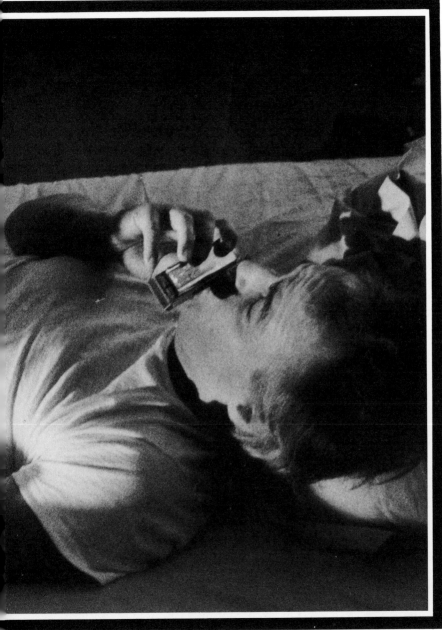

Last Tango in Paris

United Artists

about his childhood:

"My father was a drunk, a screwed-up bar fighter. My mother was also a drunk. My memories as a kid are of her being arrested. We lived in a small town, a farming community. I used to have to milk a cow every morning and every night, and I liked that. But I remember one time I was all dressed up to take this girl to a basketball game. My father said, 'You have to milk the cow,' and I said, 'Would you please milk it for me?' He said, 'No, get your ass out there.' I was in a hurry, and I didn't have time to change my shoes, and I had cowshit all over my shoes. Later on, it smelled in the car. I can't remember many good things."

Fantasy? Marlon's father was never a bar fighter, but he was a stern, unyielding man who might have insisted that the youthful Marlon milk the cow before taking his girl to the Libertyville basketball game. And his mother did drink.

Marlon proved to be magnificently creative in the scenes where he could invent his own dialogue; it was his greatest skill—bringing moments of unexplainable truths from within. But Bertolucci was experienced enough to know that a string of improvisations did not make a movie. There were scenes with Brando that had to be delivered as written, in order to maintain the progression of the story. Those were the scenes that proved difficult.

Marlon could not remember. He required the usual notes hidden among the props, cue cards behind the camera. Bertolucci struggled with Brando's lack of memory, yet he found it useful: "It is marvelous how he transfers the insecurity of memorization into probing looks." The director also came to the conclusion that Brando's lack of memorizing was deliberate, that he used the sense of danger in forgetting dialogue as a means of heightening his dramatic powers.

The most difficult scenes were those in which Marlon was required to deliver lengthy dialogue from the script. One such challenge was the infamous "butter scene," in which Paul conducted anal copulation with Jeanne. During the scene Brando was required to recite a litany which Bertolucci had borrowed from the writings of August Strindberg ("Holy Family . . . Tabernacle of all virtues . . . where innocent children are tortured until they tell their first lie . . . where the will is broken by authoritarianism and repression . . . where conscience is assassinated by blind egoism . . . Family, you are the seat of all social vices . . .").

The Last Tango   *United Artists*

Bertolucci insisted that this was one speech which Brando had to memorize. "Is it all right if I write my lines on her ass?" the actor joked. He managed to get through the scene without visual aids.

The sexual scenes proved more embarrassing to Bertolucci than to Brando. In both the dramatic and the sexual scenes, Brando found in Maria Schneider a compliant partner. She considered him immensely stimulating as an actor, less so as a lover ("He's almost fifty, you know"). Marlon's attitude toward her was unfailingly paternal, regardless of their simulated couplings. It was best exemplified in the bathtub scene, in which he soaped her with the gentleness of a father bathing his five-year-old.

The filming of *Last Tango in Paris* proved an immensely stimulating, yet a punishing ten weeks for Marlon. He was forced to draw from within himself not only painful memories, but long dormant emotions as well. The scenes in which his grief welled up were no actor's inventions; they came from his own intimate experience. Before those scenes, Bertolucci waited patiently while Marlon commanded memories of his past. His face grew clouded with sorrow, then he nodded to the director that he was ready to begin.

When filming was finally over, Marlon said to Bertolucci, "Never again will I make a film like this one. For the first time, I have felt a violation of my innermost self. It should be the last time."

21

Return of the Rebel

"Everything passes.
Love, hate, fear—
all the emotions.
Nothing lasts
for more than a little while.
You can love a girl so much
you could cut your stomach open.
A year later,
you never want to see her again.
If you have learned that,
it makes life easier.
I suppose."

AS *The Godfather* APPROACHED RELEASE IN MARCH 1972, COVER STORIES
in *Newsweek, Time* and *Life* heralded the news: Marlon Brando,
after a career filled with hyperbole, had made the most complete
and unchallengeable comeback in the history of film. Suddenly
the ten lamentable years that preceded *The Godfather* were almost
forgotten. Producers who had treated Marlon Brando as a kind of
tragic joke now sent him scripts with imploring letters. To most
of them, Marlon did not even reply.

He was understandably pleased with the renewal of his esteem.
He even agreed to attend the premiere of *The Godfather* in New
York, after eliciting from Paramount a promise to invite twenty
friends of his—Indian chiefs from Eastern tribes. The chiefs made
it to the premiere; Marlon didn't. As had happened before in his
life, tragedy impinged on triumph.

A Mexico City newspaper published a story that Marlon Brando's
son, Christian, had been kidnapped in northern Mexico. Christian's mother, Anna Kashfi, had taken him out of his school at
Ojai, sixty miles north of Los Angeles, and had driven in a truck
with him and two men to a remote fishing village in Baja California. She entrusted him to a man she knew only as Barry and

departed for the border town of Calexico. She boarded a bus to Los Angeles, but en route the driver stopped and handed her and a woman companion over to local authorities for being disorderly. Booked in the Calexico jail, Anna told her jailers that she feared for her son's safety. That was the basis for the Mexico City report.

Marlon was told the news in Paris, and he issued a statement that "there is nothing at all to be alarmed about." But he was alarmed enough to fly home to California and hire an El Paso private investigator and Interpol agent to find his son.

The agent used a helicopter to locate Christian, now thirteen, in a hippie campsite in Baja California. The boy was hiding under a pile of clothing and wore only slacks; he appeared to be suffering from bronchitis. One of the eight adults told the agent that Anna Kashfi had promised them $30,000 for hiding Christian. The boy was returned to California, and all eight of the colony were deported as undesirables.

Christian appeared in court with his father, and Brando was permitted to take the boy with him to Paris. En route, he could have stopped in New York for *The Godfather* premiere, but he refused. Bob Evans was on the telephone with him until four o'clock in the morning before his departure, but Marlon wouldn't relent. He would not expose his son to the inevitable sensation that would be caused by their stopover in New York.

Even without the presence of Brando, the premiere of *The Godfather* on March 14, 1972, was an event for the news columns. It received almost unanimous approval from reviewers; the same critics who had danced on the grave of Marlon Brando's career proclaimed him anew as the once and present king. Within a few months Paramount announced that *The Godfather* would make more money than any film in history. Marlon was gratified, but he hadn't forgotten the humiliating conditions under which he had been granted the role in *The Godfather.* When Robert Evans later sought Marlon to play Jay Gatsby opposite Evans' wife, Ali MacGraw, in *The Great Gatsby,* Marlon shunted his agent aside and conducted the negotiations himself. His demands proved so high that Evans gave up his quest for Brando.

To the unmatched success of *The Godfather* was now added the sensation of *Last Tango in Paris.*

Little was known about the Bertolucci film until it appeared for one performance at the close of the New York Film Festival on

October 14, 1972. From that showing came a review by Pauline Kael in *The New Yorker* that compensated a thousandfold for the vitriol she had directed at Marlon Brando during the Dark Years. Kael began by saying that the Film Festival date should become a landmark in film history, as had the date of the debut of "Le Sacre du Printemps" in music history. She added:

> There was no riot, and no one threw anything at the screen, but I think it's fair to say that the audience was in a state of shock, because *Last Tango in Paris* has the same kind of hypnotic excitement as the "Sacre," the same primitive force, and the same thrusting, jabbing eroticism. The movie breakthrough has finally come. Exploitation films have been supplying mechanized sex—sex as physical stimulant but without any passion and emotional violence. The sex in *Last Tango in Paris* expresses the characters' drives. Marlon Brando, as Paul, is working out his aggression on Jeanne (Maria Schneider) and the physical menace of sexuality that is emotionally charged is such a departure from everything we've come to expect at the movies that there was something almost like fear in the atmosphere of the party in the lobby that followed the screening. Carried along by the sustained excitement of the movie, the audience had given Bertolucci an ovation, but afterward, as individuals, they were quiet. This must be the most powerfully erotic movie ever made, and it may turn out to be the most liberating movie ever made, and so it's probably only natural that an audience, anticipating a voluptuous feast from the man who made *The Conformist,* and confronted with this unexpected sexuality and the new realism it requires of the actors, should go into shock. Bertolucci and Brando have altered the face of an art form. Who was prepared for that?

Certainly no one was prepared for such a film review. It astounded United Artists, which thereupon reprinted Kael's critique into a two-page advertisement in the *New York Times.*

Italian moralists also helped the United Artist cause. Obscenity charges were filed in Bologna against Bertolucci, Brando, Schneider, Grimaldi and the United Artists distributor on an allegation of "obscene content offensive to public decency, characterized by an exasperating pansexualism for its own end, presented with possessive self-indulgence, catering to the lowest instincts of the libido, dominated by the idea of stirring unchecked appetites for sexual pleasure, permeated by scurrilous language—with crude, repulsive, naturalistic and even unnatural representation of carnal union with continued and complacent scenes, descriptions and exhibitions of masturbation, libidinous acts and lewd nudity—accompanied offscreen by sounds, sighs and shrieks of climax pleasure." Not even a turncoat priest in the employ of United Artists could have written a more enticing encomium for the film.

Defendant Brando was far away, but Bertolucci appeared in the Bologna court to defend his work: "I can confirm that neither the performers nor myself ever contemplated for a moment commercial benefits or entertainment devices. We were interested in the question of possession of a component of a relationship, a self-destructive one prevalent in today's society."

The director's lawyer argued: "Marlon Brando personifies the fall of man. It is he himself who falls into the bottomless pit. And this is the message: every man risks the same end. The beast which we find inside Marlon may be in us, too, but we are cowards, and we try desperately to suffocate it."

The three Italian judges hearing the case agreed with the defense, and the film makers were acquitted. *Last Tango in Paris* was released for showings in Italy, and the notoriety of the case helped its box-office appeal everywhere. By the time the film opened in New York on February 1, 1973, it had already attracted more than $100,000 in advance sales. The Kael overkill, plus cover stories in both *Newsweek* and *Time,* prompted a negative reaction from other critics, some of whom denounced *Last Tango in Paris* as prurient and pretentious trash. Meanwhile *Last Tango in Paris,* despite its X rating, was on its way to becoming the biggest moneymaker in the history of United Artists.

Again, triumph for Marlon Brando. Again, tragedy.

On February 16, 1973, the message was radioed to Marlon on his Tetiaroa Island: Wally Cox had died in Hollywood of a heart attack.

Marlon flew back to California. He arrived in time to attend the wake held by long-time companions and working associates of the gentle comedian, although Marlon remained in a back room of the Cox home and didn't mingle with the others. He comforted the widow and offered his services for Cox's final request. Cox had wanted his ashes to be spread on a favorite mountain stream where he had spent long hours amid nature. That was against California health laws, so the press was informed that Marlon and another friend of Cox's had disposed of the ashes over the Pacific Ocean. But they had in reality fulfilled Wally's wish.

As the season approached for movie awards, it became apparent that Hollywood would necessarily recognize the return of Marlon Brando as the standard of acting excellence. There was a feeling of nervousness in the film community about how Brando would respond. The first hint came when the Hollywood Foreign Press Association elected him the best dramatic actor for his performance in *The Godfather*. He neither attended nor accepted the award. Instead, he dispatched a political statement:

> There is a singular lack of honors in this country today what with the government's change of its citizens into objects of use, its imperialism and warlike intrusion into foreign countries and the killing not only of their inhabitants but also indirectly of our own people, its treatment of the Indians and the blacks, the assault on the press and the rape of the ideals which were the foundation of this country. I respectfully ask you to understand that to accept an honor, however well-intended, is to subtract from the meager amount of honor left. Therefore, to simplify things, I hereby decline any nomination and deny anyone representing me.

Now the wonder grew: What would Brando do if he won the Academy Award for best actor?

Two of his former partners foresaw what he would do. When Marlon was nominated for a best-actor Oscar in 1957 for *Sayonara*, he told Walter Seltzer and George Glass that if he won, he would refuse it in protest of the government's policies toward Negroes, Indians and other minorities. He had composed a letter of explanation which he planned to publish as an advertisement in the Hollywood trade papers. Seltzer and Glass told him they would resign if he did such a thing. The issue never came to a head. Marlon didn't win that year.

Nor was he nominated for an Oscar for the next fifteen years. But he was nominated for *The Godfather*, and his victory seemed certain.

Marlon remained invisible. He responded neither to the Academy's invitation to the awards ceremonies nor to a personal letter from the president, Daniel Taradash. Marlon seemed to be playing the suspense in a Hitchcock manner, and on March 27, the day of the awards, his secretary, Alice Marchak, asked for tickets for Mr. Brando. But he didn't use them. Instead he sent Miss Marchak and a young actress, an Apache militant who called herself Sasheen

Littlefeather. When Marlon Brando's name was announced as best actor, Miss Littlefeather went onto the stage of the Los Angeles Music Center Pavilion to announce that Brando was declining the Oscar as a protest of the film and television treatment of the Indian. The announcement was greeted with boos, the first in forty-five years of Academy history.

Miss Littlefeather told the audience that she had paraphrased Brando's words, since the statement he had given her to read was too long for the Academy program. This is what he had written:

Good evening.

What is said here on my behalf by Miss Littlefeather is not in any way designed to demean or embarrass those who believe in the worthiness of this custom and make this evening possible. It is not my wish to offend or diminish the importance of those who are participating tonight.

I would hope that those who are listening would not look upon this as a rude intrusion but an honest effort to focus attention on an issue that might very well determine whether or not this country has the right to a say from this point forward in the inalienable rights of all people to remain free and independent on lands that have supported their life beyond living memory. For 200 years we have said to the Indian people who are fighting for their land, their life, their families and their right to be free, "Lay down your arms, my friends, and then we will remain together. Only if you lay down your arms, my friends, can we then talk of peace and come to an agreement which will be good for you." When they laid down their arms, we murdered them. We lied to them, we cheated them out of their lands.

We starved them into signing fraudulent agreements that we call treaties that we never kept. We turned them into beggars on a continent that gave them life for as long as life can remember. And by my interpretation of history, however twisted, we did not do right.

We were not lawful, nor were we just in what we did. For them we do not have to restore these people, we do not have to live up to some agreements because it is given to us by virtue of our power to attack the rights of others, to take their property, to take their lives when they are trying to defend their land and liberty, and to make their virtues a crime, and our own vices a virtue.

But there is one thing which is beyond the reach of this perversity and that is the tremendous verdict of history. And history will surely judge us. But do we care?

What kind of moral schizophrenia is it that allows us to shout at the top of our national voice for all the world to hear that we live up to our commitments when every page of history and when all the thirsty humiliating days and nights of the last 100 years in the lives of the American Indians contradict that voice?

It would seem that the respect for principle and the love of one's neighbor has become dysfunctional in this country of ours and that all we have, all we have succeeded in accomplishing with our power is simply annihilating the hopes of the newborn countries in this world as well as convincing friends and enemies alike that we are not humane and that we do not live up to our agreements.

Perhaps at this moment you are saying to yourselves what the hell does all this have to do with the Academy Awards? Why is this woman standing up here ruining our evening, invading our lives with things that don't concern us and that we don't care about. Wasting our time and money and intruding in our homes. I think the answer to those unspoken questions is that the motion picture community has been as responsible as any for degrading the Indian and making a mockery of his character.

Describing him as hostage, savage and evil. It's hard enough for children to grow up in this world when Indian children watch television and they watch films and when they see their race depicted as they are in films, their minds become injured in ways we can never know. Recently there have been a few faltering steps to correct the situation, but too faltering and too few so I as a member of this profession do not feel that I can as a citizen of the United States accept an award here tonight. I think awards in this country at this time are inappropriate to be received or given until the condition of the American Indian is drastically altered. If we are not our brother's keeper, at least let us not be his executioner.

I would have been here tonight to speak to you directly, but I thought that perhaps I could have been of better use if I went to Wounded Knee to forestall in whatever way I can the establishment of a peace which would be dishonorable as long as the rivers shall run and the grass shall grow.

Thank you for your kindness and your courtesy to Miss Littlefeather.

Thank you and good night.

The boos of the Oscar night were followed by cries of indignation from the film establishment. Daniel Taradash: "He said he didn't wish to seem rude, but he was." Gregory Peck: "It shows that it doesn't take intelligence to be a good actor." Charlton

Heston: "Childish! The American Indian needs better friends than that." *Daily Variety:* "Rudeness has never advanced any cause." *Hollywood Reporter:* "He deeply offended the public and the industry whose sympathy and help he is seeking."

Anna Kashfi seized on the incident to renew her attempt to regain custody of her son. She filed a petition in Superior Court claiming that Christian had been humiliated and embarrassed by his father's "blatant disregard for conventional social decorum" before millions of television viewers. She also claimed that her son had been ridiculed and embarrassed because of his father's portrayal in *Last Tango in Paris* of a "sexually maladjusted and perverted person" who utters "obscene, foul, shocking, distasteful profanities."

Marlon never made it to Wounded Knee. A sheriff reported that someone had requested protection for Brando to enter the historic North Dakota town that had been occupied by Indian militants. But Marlon didn't appear. He remained out of sight. Four weeks after the Oscar furor, he departed for an Easter vacation in Tahiti, taking along his two American sons.

The moralists and the keepers of public dignity continued to rage at the rebel artist after he had vanished into Polynesia with his progeny. He had removed his public presence, and he might never emerge in full view again.

But for his own generation and others in the future, he had placed on film an indelible view of himself and of American life in the third quarter of the century. The most revealing of the films was *Last Tango in Paris,* the only autobiographical work that he undertook.

It is all there. Marlon and the bongo drums. Marlon in a T-shirt. Marlon at his most scatalogical, using the language in outrageously incisive ways (no Italian could have written *that* dialogue). Marlon adoring and hating women, simultaneously. Marlon obsessed by sex, in all its aspects.

The sequences seem wrenched from life. The soliloquy of Paul's past, so reminiscent of Marlon's youth. The mannerisms, the prestidigitation, the shuffle of the song-and-dance man in the tango parlor, the imitations of Cagney and Colman and other charmers — these came from Brando, not out of an actor's bag of shticks. Above all, the undercurrent of violence — Paul's battering of his fists

Marlon on the Dick Cavett Show, 1973   Wide World Photos

against the wall, his beating of the whore's errant customer, his view of sex as violence.

Last Tango in Paris will occupy the critics for decades. But it is possible that the greatest profundity came toward the end of the film when Paul's antic dance infuriates the contestants and judges of the tango contest. As he is chased off the dance floor by a lady official, he pauses long enough to lower his pants and underwear and display his naked ass.

Marlon mooning again.

Index

About the Author

BOB THOMAS was born in San Diego and reared in Los Angeles, where he attended public schools and UCLA. He joined the Associated Press in Los Angeles and in 1944 became Hollywood correspondent, a position he continues to hold. He also edits the Directors Guild magazine, *Action*. The books he has written include biographies of Harry Cohn, Irving Thalberg, David O. Selznick, Walter Winchell and Howard Hughes, and the novels *The Flesh Merchants* and *Weekend 33*. He is married and has three daughters and lives in Encino.